Super Freak

The Life of
Rick James

Peter Benjaminson

CHICAGO
REVIEW
PRESS

An A Cappella Book

Copyright © 2017 by Peter Benjaminson
All rights reserved
Published by Chicago Review Press Incorporated
814 North Franklin Street
Chicago, Illinois 60610
ISBN 978-1-61374-957-9

Library of Congress Cataloging-in-Publication Data

Names: Benjaminson, Peter, 1945- author.
Title: Super freak : the life of Rick James / Peter Benjaminson.
Description: Chicago : Chicago Review Press, 2017. | Includes bibliographical
   references.
Identifiers: LCCN 2016050314 (print) | LCCN 2016050669 (ebook) | ISBN
   9781613749579 | ISBN 9781613749586 | ISBN 9781613749609 | ISBN
   9781613749593
Subjects: LCSH: James, Rick, 1948-2004. | Funk musicians--United
   States--Biography. | African American rock musicians--Biography.
Classification: LCC ML420.J233 B36 2017 (print) | LCC ML420.J233 (ebook) |
   DDC 781.644092 [B] --dc23
LC record available at https://lccn.loc.gov/2016050314

Interior design: Jonathan Hahn

Typesetting: Nord Compo

Printed in the United States of America
5 4 3 2 1

To James Ambrose Johnson Jr., 1948–2004
Vocalist, lyricist, musician, composer, performer, and record producer
US Naval Reserve, 1964–1967
and
Albert Benjaminson, 1918–2013
Engineer, sailor, rancher, boat builder, and home builder
US Naval Reserve, 1943–1946
and
Susan Harrigan, 1945–
Scholar, journalist, girlfriend, wife, and mother

Contents

Acknowledgments

My wife, **Susan Harrigan**, has played all her life-altering roles with great love and kindness. In her role of editor, Susan brought her considerable skills to bear on my first book about the Motown Record Corporation, *The Story of Motown*, and my third, *Mary Wells: The Tumultuous Life of Motown's First Superstar*. She also did the initial edit of this book. In doing so, she helped raise the level of my writing from near incompetence to, dare I say it, competence-plus, a level I otherwise could not have achieved. Thank you, Susan, for everything.

Additional special thanks are due to:

Our daughter, Annie, for suggesting Rick James as a subject for a book and for giving birth to our first granddaughter in 2015, and to her husband, Greg Naarden, for helping to make that birth possible.

Our grandchildren, Leo Alexander Naarden and Abigail Susan Naarden, for filling out the family in fine form.

My sister, Wendy Benjaminson, who has helped me greatly on this and previous projects, and to my brother, retired United States ambassador Eric Benjaminson, a fellow author and consultant, who keeps me laughing.

Yuval Taylor, a fellow author and an editor who with great skill has edited both this book and my two previous Chicago Review Press books about Motown musicians, Cynthia Sherry, publisher of Chicago Review Press, who has been working tirelessly with me to bring movie versions of those books to fruition, and Michelle Williams, who line edited both this book and my biography of Mary Wells.

LeRoi Johnson, Rick's brother and a very informative interviewee, who made it possible for me to interview many of Rick's other family members and many of Rick's former employees and associates.

Nick Warburton, a prolific author who very generously gave me full access to his research and writing on Rick's early career and recommended me to his sources. Nick is now working on a documentary covering Rick's rise to fame and the musicians who helped him make his big breakthrough.

Stan Endersby, a great interviewee and one of Nick's sources, who convinced many of Nick's other sources to meet me over a two-day period in a Toronto hotel, and in his own apartment, so I could interview them in person.

The other members of Rick's family who graciously shared their memories of Rick: Camille Hudson, Lori Stokes, Chuck Stokes, Louis Stokes, and Shelley Stokes-Hammond.

My other sources and interviewees, who, although not related to Rick, gave generously of their time and knowledge, either in person, over the telephone, or via e-mail, to make this book as accurate and complete as possible: Rick Abel, Nick Balkou, John Bracken, Dan R. Bruggeman, David Colin Burt, Jim Bush, Michael Carr, Bob Doughty, William G. Downey, Joanne McDuffie Funderburg, William Gersten, Richard Grand, Les Greenbaum, Joe Jackson, Andre Jardine, Peter Kelly, Daniel LeMelle, Pat Little, Rick Mason, Peter McGraw, Neil Merryweather, Kelly Misener, Syville Morgan, Tony Nolasco, Sade Oyinade, Dick Romer, Ed Roth, Levi Ruffin, Mike Rummans, Chris Sarns, George Semkiw, Robert Sheahen, Malcolm Tomlinson, Artie Wayne, Harry Weinger, Stanley Weisman, and Richard Wesley.

Margaret Acquista, judicial assistant to United States District Judge Robert W. Sweet, who aided me greatly in my quest to locate and fully examine the records of *Motown Record Corporation v. Mary Jane Girls*, a federal case in which Rick was a major player as well as a major target; Jennie Thomas, head archivist of the Rock and Roll Hall of Fame and Museum Library and Archives in Cleveland, her fellow archivist Anastasia Karel, and their fellow staffers, who helped me immensely with my research in the library's LeRoi C. Johnson Collection on Rick James; the equally cooperative staffs of the New York Public Library's Schomburg Center for Research in Black Culture, Library for the Performing Arts,

Mid-Manhattan Library, and Stephen A. Schwarzman main branch, and the staff of Columbia University's Nicholas Murray Butler Library.

Dr. Richard "Duke" Hagerty and Dr. Robert Shalhoub, who helped me sort out the causes of Rick's death; Barbara Hagerty, who urged me to write an article about my attempt to make my *Lost Supreme* book into a movie; Roger Allen, a former high school classmate of mine, now an attorney, who helped me understand the legalese of various legal allegations; Greil Marcus, another former high school classmate of mine and America's major rock 'n' roll critic, who read the manuscripts for my last two books and helped me place an article in *Rolling Stone* about my efforts to make one of them into a movie; and my assiduous Los Angeles researcher, Lynne Bronstein.

The cooperative, hardworking, and efficient officers and staff members of the US Navy Judge Advocate General's Corps, who provided me with the records of Rick's court-martials and agreed to my requests that I be allowed to see previously censored material within those records: Capt. Robert J. Crow, Lt. G. T. Farris, Lt. Denise L. Romeo, Thomas Gauzer, G. E. Lattin, and Tomiko Thompson.

Mario Echemendia of www.GoDaddy.com, who helped me obtain the domains www.imrickjamesbitchbook.com and www.superfreakbook.com, which will allow me to keep in touch electronically with the readers of this book and berate and hector any who don't buy it and read it.

Michelle Bega, who was able to plumb actor Danny Glover's knowledge on my behalf.

My longtime friends who have supported me on numerous previous projects over the years and have continued to support me on this project: the late Al Abrams, Paul Berardino, Rick Bueche, Stephanie Campbell, Liam Castro, Calhoun Cornwell, Sheila Anne Feeney, Ron Ishoy, Elaine Jesmer, Sara Jordan-Heintz, David Kirby, Dorothy Klein, Kurt Krug, M. L. Liebler, John Oppedahl, Sade Oyinade, Roger Pearson, Gerald Posner, Tim Sheard, John Smyntek, Bill Staiger, and Marc Taylor.

Introduction

God took a little extra time to make Rick James. He said,
"I've got to make him interesting. I've got to make him intriguing."

—Actor Jamie Foxx, speaking at one of Rick's funerals

In **February 2004** Dave Chappelle iconically portrayed Rick James as an obnoxious, coked-up lunatic on *Chappelle's Show* on Comedy Central, giving a boost to James's legendary status. Rick's out-of-control drug use and crimes against women in the 1990s had received widespread publicity, informing Chappelle's characterization.

But years earlier Rick had blazed a musical trail that led to him becoming one of the Motown Record Corporation's final superstars. He was a talented composer, a riveting performer, and a gifted producer who made hits in the 1970s and '80s not only for himself but for his protégés, including Teena Marie, the Mary Jane Girls, and the Stone City Band, with whom he signed a contract with Motown's Gordy Records in 1977.

His popularity was truly immense and long-lasting. He recorded nine albums during his ten years with Motown's Gordy label, five of which hit the pop Top 20. Those albums, and the four others he recorded after leaving Motown, showcased eighteen Top 20 R&B singles and two Top 20 pop singles.

Rick was born into a divided family. On one side were members distinguished by their unrelenting drive to reach the top and their success in doing so. He inherited this drive—which made that side of his family very successful. But he also fought for most of his life against the tendencies toward interpersonal violence that plagued the other side. These tendencies might have remained unrealized in Rick were it not for his lifelong drug use, starting with marijuana and ending with crack cocaine.

Rick James's musical legacy is marked by creativity, originality, and a singular style that can still be heard blasting from speakers to this day—both in the form of his own albums and those by musicians paying him the ultimate compliment: emulation. But the music is just the most well-known facet of Rick James's life, the most public of his adventures, which also included desertion from the military, drug dealing, fighting against MTV's entrenched racist policies, and sundry other notable events.

His death in 2004 was a loss to the gods of music and the lords of persistence. This is his story.

1

Birth of a Super Freak

Rick James's staying power and superstardom is not limited
to the often unpredictable music business.
It is based on his solid family allegiance.

—Congressman Louis Stokes (D–Ohio), Rick's second cousin and former
chairman of the United States House Select Committee
on Assassinations, addressing his fellow United States
representatives from the floor of the House in 1981

It's tempting to think of Rick as the black sheep of his family.
But considering his fourteen years of creative struggle to make it to the
top and his relentless efforts to stay there, it makes more sense to think
of him as an active and intelligent family member who just happened
to work in the music business instead of politics, journalism, or law, as
others in his family did.

Through his mother, Rick had formidable second cousins. A US
congressman for thirty-one years, Louis Stokes investigated the mur-
ders of President John F. Kennedy and Rev. Dr. Martin Luther King
Jr. as chairman of the House Select Committee on Assassinations. His
brother Carl Stokes was mayor of Cleveland from 1967 to 1971—the
first black mayor of a major American city. Rick also was the cousin
of Lori Stokes, presently coanchor of *Eyewitness News This Morning* on
New York City's WABC-TV, and Chuck Stokes, editorial/public affairs

director for WXYZ-TV in Detroit and producer and moderator of *Spot-light on the News*, that city's oldest weekly public affairs and news show. As Chuck Stokes put it, "This is a family with the drive to be productive and successful and to make it."

Rick also has been said to be the nephew of Melvin Franklin of the Temptations. But Rick's brother LeRoi Johnson, a prominent Buffalo, New York, attorney and artist, says flatly that Franklin, who died in 1995, "is not related to us." Johnson did say that Franklin might be connected to the late Alberta Franklin, who was Rick's aunt through marriage.

Finally, Rick also was a distant cousin of singer James Brown and actor Danny Glover. According to Johnson, during the slavery era Brown's great-great grandfather and Rick's great-great grandfather were brothers enslaved on the same plantation in Wrens, Georgia, a small town thirty miles south of Augusta. One of their sisters was Glover's great-great grandmother. These three siblings had been enslaved on a plantation in another state but were eventually brought to Georgia and sold to separate but nearby plantations in the Wrens area. Rick's ancestors worked on the Stone Plantation, and Glover's and Brown's on the Dove Brown Plantation. Johnson says an employee of Glover's has confirmed this account and Glover confirmed through his spokeswoman that he, Rick, and Brown are distant relatives.

Rick James was born James Ambrose Johnson Jr. in Buffalo, New York, on February 1, 1948. The family eventually grew to four boys and four girls, presided over most of the time by a single mother. That mother was former nightclub dancer Mabel Sims, who eventually became known as Mabel "Betty" Gladden. Mabel was a petite woman, 5 feet, 5 inches, who spent most of her career working for two prominent black numbers runners in Buffalo who reported to Buffalo Mob boss Stefano Magaddino.

Born in Cleveland, Ohio, Sims, the granddaughter of a slave, may have danced in a traveling troupe before moving to Buffalo during World War II, according to family members. There, she appeared at the Moonglo club. LeRoi Johnson, Rick's brother, describes his mother's dancing as seductive, à la Josephine Baker. A barely distinguishable family photo shows her performing on what looks like a low table covered with a tablecloth. She is barefoot, wearing a somewhat modest halter top with a bare midriff and a long skirt slit high on the sides. She stopped dancing at age sixteen when she gave birth to her first child, Carmen Sims, a boy, in Cleveland.

She then had a second child, Camille, with a man named Homer Robinson before marrying James Ambrose Johnson Sr. in 1946. James Ambrose Johnson Jr. was Sims's first child with Johnson, and LeRoi Johnson, born eleven months after Rick, was her second. The couple had three more children—Sheryl, Alberta, and William—before divorcing in 1959. The former Mrs. Johnson then married Elliott Gladden and gave birth to her final child, Alicia Penelope Gladden—known as Penny—in 1961.

Although Sims had given up her career as a dancer by the time Rick was born, once she saw Rick's nascent talent as an entertainer, she passed her own ambitions on to him. In 1998 Rick's brother Carmen told *Behind the Music* that their mother's frustrated show business career was the major force driving Rick. "He was the favorite," Carmen said. "[My mother] saw talent in him, and with her unfulfilled talent, she wanted to live it through him." Rick felt this pressure throughout his life.

Rick's mother had an intense interest in music, and strove to cultivate this in her children as well. She constantly played albums by Dinah Washington, Billie Holiday, Billy Eckstine, John Coltrane, and Sarah Vaughan at home. Rick later called these albums "the musical textbooks of my youth." Rick's mother also visited clubs in Buffalo to hear these and other rhythm and blues and jazz musicians, sometimes taking one or more of her children with her. One of Rick's goals in life was to unite these two forms of music, a goal he later achieved in some of his hit songs.

———

The family lived in the Willert Park Courts housing project on Buffalo's east side, which had been built exclusively for African Americans in 1939. In 1956 they migrated across the Swan Street Bridge into the previously majority-white Perry Projects. According to LeRoi Johnson, "The white kids were fine with us until the parents would say something to the kids and the kids would come out and say something like, 'My mother told me you're just a nigger.'" Rick, LeRoi, and their siblings often punched it out with the white kids.

Rick became a skilled fighter, as did LeRoi, and both were known to throw punches later in life. When the harassment became intense, LeRoi Johnson said, their father and their older brother Carmen "beat the hell" out of their harassers.

After their mother married Gladden in 1960, the family moved to a two-family house on Ferry Street in Buffalo's Cold Spring neighborhood. Gladden's parents lived upstairs and the rest of the family lived downstairs.

Although Rick's mother officially worked as a house cleaner, as Rick sang in his 1981 song "Below the Funk (Pass the J)," "Mama raised me on the numbers racket." Gladden indeed made most of her money by running numbers and administering a numbers racket office. An illegal precursor to today's widespread and legal state lottery games, the numbers racket allowed its players to bet money on three numbers they'd pick in the hope of matching the three numbers that would be announced the next day. Runners like Rick's mother would carry the bet money and the numbers chosen (written on betting slips) from each bettor to the "numbers bank," or headquarters.

Rick's mother "worked her ass off," Rick told author Davin Seay, who interviewed Rick for his e-book *Super Freak: The Last Days of Rick James.* "Every day she'd be out in her snow boots, house to house, under mats, in mail boxes and behind the garbage cans where people would leave their [betting] slips." She often took Rick and LeRoi with her. As Rick said, "We'd carry a shopping bag with all the money and books, so we could run with it in case the cops stopped her."

The money from the numbers operation helped Gladden support her eight children well. Both LeRoi and Rick remembered good meals; a two-level, three-bedroom apartment; and sufficient clothes for everyone, even when no father was around. LeRoi also remembered that their mother employed her own housekeeper and kept two new cars for family use, although she parked them blocks away from the projects. As Rick sang in his 1997 release "Mama's Eyes," "She took it to the streets on her feet and she fed us well."

Johnson said their mother's numbers earnings also financed Rick's musical career until 1973. That year, however, the massive steel mills that had made Buffalo an industrial powerhouse and a magnet for wage earners shut down, and the family's good times were over. Gladden told Johnson that although Buffalo residents still played the numbers, they were betting pennies, not dollars.

———

Rick's father, James Ambrose Johnson Sr., was born in Nashville, Tennessee, and lived in Canton, Ohio, before moving to Buffalo. He worked in a Chevrolet assembly plant, then at Republic Steel's South Park Avenue plant, and later in construction. He served in the navy during the Korean War. James Sr. retired from Laborers' Union Local 210 around 1988, and Rick remembered him dressing up in a Shriner's hat and escorting Mabel to an Elks Lodge ball.

Later in life, Rick told a California court psychologist that Johnson Sr., also known as Hitchy-Boy—for reasons no one can remember—was "an abusive alcoholic." Rick also told California criminologist Sheila Balkan that his father was "very sadistic" to his mother and beat her often. "Once in a while I would try to help her, but my father told me I'd get it if I didn't stay out of it." He told another interviewer that when he heard his father beating his mother, he'd wish he was grown up "so I could kill him."

Levi Ruffin, a childhood friend of Rick's and later a member of Rick's Stone City Band, describes Rick's father as a hustler. "He hit Mom every now and then. Came home when he felt like it. Screamed 'cause his meals weren't cold or hot enough, whatever, that kind of dude."

Johnson Sr. left the family when Rick was seven, and eventually divorced Rick's mother. "I woke up one morning and he was gone,"

Rick told *Behind the Music*. Rick also said his father was "never really into family life." Rick's brother LeRoi defended their father, however, noting that after breaking up with Rick's mother, Johnson Sr. partnered with a woman with whom he spent the rest of his life.

Although Rick described his mother as "an incredible, incredible woman," she passed the abuse she'd received from her husband on to Rick. "My father would beat my mother on a daily basis, and my mother would take it in turn and beat on me," Rick told author Pamela Des Barres in *Rock Bottom*. After his arrests in the 1990s he told California authorities that his mother would beat him with a knotted electrical cord for little or no reason, "letting out her frustrations."

Social service workers visited the family's home several times, but Rick said the children refused to leave because "we were all a team." And as he grew older, his relationship with his mother improved. She became supportive of his musical career and later became his "best friend." Nevertheless, his father's abuse, neglect, and eventual absence severely damaged Rick's understanding of how to be a husband and father.

———

The Buffalo ghetto, where Rick was born in the pre–civil rights era, also damaged him, as it did others who lived there, even though it provided the themes for his best songs.

"I always thought there was something mentally wrong with me," Rick said in 1979, attributing his perceived problem in large part to "being black and born in the ghetto and not thinking that you can get out." He described the place as dominated by poverty, drugs, pimps, gangsters, prostitutes, and guns. "Most black people born in the United States today have a psychological defect. We're born into something that's not what we perceive life to be. Black people are mental patients in the hospital of fucking life . . . and to get well, we have to say we are somebody, we are relevant to life, we can get out of here."

Rick devoted much of his life to accumulating enough wealth to avoid ever sinking back into the ghetto. He returned to Buffalo after becoming a music business success in the 1980s but lived in splendor in one of its suburbs, Orchard Park, rather than in the inner city, and later moved permanently to Los Angeles.

———

Rick began rebelling against his family at an early age, much to his mother's chagrin. Rick's sister Camille, now Camille Hudson, describes their mother as "a devout Catholic who went to church all the time" and insisted that her children do the same. Camille says both LeRoi and Rick were even altar boys "until Rick was kicked out 'cause he was a little too hyper for them." Rick was "bad . . . real hard to handle . . . a real handful." It's possible Rick's rebellious behavior was a typical response to being raised in a strict environment. But Camille provides a different possible cause of Rick's behavior pattern: both Rick and his Mom were "hyper," neither of them could sit down and be still. "If you tried to put him in front of the TV, you had to chase him around, because he couldn't sit down."

His mother thought there was something wrong. "My other children were always so calm, but Rick had so much get-up!" she once said. She was so alarmed at what might now be diagnosed as attention-deficit/hyperactivity disorder (ADHD) that she took him to a psychiatrist early in the 1950s. "The doctor couldn't explain it, but he didn't think it was a mental problem."

Rick, speaking with California psychologist Raymond E. Anderson after his arrests in the 1990s, said that he would run away often to get attention. Sometimes he would walk ten to fifteen miles, absorbed in thought. LeRoi said Rick began running away from home at age five and that Rick dragged him along on this first attempt to escape. Because of their age, and the fact that they were dressed like cowboys, their attempt ended at the local police station.

When his mother would draft Rick and LeRoi to carry her numbers books in big shopping bags while she went door to door on her rounds, the two boys would often cry and wail in protest. Rick told one interviewer, "I hated it. It was so fucking cold." Finally, Johnson remembers, during a snowstorm when the buses weren't running, their mother wanted them to accompany her as she crossed Buffalo's Hamburg Street bridge on foot even though the blowing snow had cut their visibility to zero. Rick took a stand and threatened to call the cops if she forced him to go. That was the last time she took Rick with her.

———

Rick was often in trouble with the law. As a teenager, he was sent to two juvenile homes for stealing vehicles—including a bus, which he stole, he later said, because "it was big and there were keys in it."

He didn't restrict himself to vehicles. According to LeRoi, Rick was arrested as a teenager for stealing some leathers from the C&B Men's Shop in Buffalo. "He stayed in it after it closed, then broke out." It was hardly an intelligent theft; the police tracked Rick home by following his footprints in the snow. Rick committed a very similar robbery, and made very similar mistakes, just a few years later. Perhaps his love for clothes warped his judgment in both instances.

Rick also was a youthful drug user and dealer. He started smoking marijuana at fourteen. According to court records, he experimented with cocaine and heroin in his teens as well. In April 1978, at age twenty, he was arrested in Buffalo for possessing more than two ounces of what the Buffalo Police Department quaintly spelled "Marihuana." Camille was hardly surprised. "They could have caught him any day with marijuana," she said. LeRoi contributed the mug shot and police report from that 1978 arrest to the Rock and Roll Hall of Fame and Museum Library and Archives in Cleveland, where they are preserved.

———

Rick became sexually active at an early age as well. According to LeRoi Johnson, Rick started having sex at the age of nine, with a girl of the same age. "Rick was always ahead of his time with women," Johnson said. At fifteen, Rick had an affair with an African dancer in her twenties who was renting a room in his mother's house.

Later on, Rick favored prostitutes, "both as people and as an inspiration for music," Johnson says, adding, "In our life, hookers were just people. We didn't demean them because of what they were doing to earn a living." As Johnson sees it, sex workers "were a part of life, black life. The girls we knew were attracted to pimps, and a lot of them became hookers." He also notes that the sex workers Rick was around were "gorgeous, high-end beauties."

Drugs and precocious sex weren't Rick's only problems: he tried to avoid school entirely. Levi Ruffin, his childhood friend, says "Rick got kicked out of almost every school he went to. He wouldn't go to class. So they'd put him in another school, and he wouldn't go to class there either. He didn't like it, and to hell with it."

When Rick and his brother were at Catholic school together, LeRoi Johnson says, one of the nuns tried to discipline Rick by rapping him on the knuckles with a ruler, but Rick took the ruler from her and broke it in half. Rick soon started attending public schools. After being expelled from Buffalo's Bennett High School, he attended Grover Cleveland High School and East High School, but he had dropped out of school entirely by 1964, when he was fifteen years old. Ruffin says the reason Rick saw school as a waste of time was that he wanted to become a musician and get out of the ghetto.

A poor or absent student with an early arrest record, young Rick was beginning what could have been an anonymous life of crime, incarceration, and drug use, followed by an early and mostly unnoticed death. His interest in music saved him. "He liked sounds," Camille Hudson says. "Very, very early he knew he wanted to be a musician." At home, Rick "would be in the cupboards taking stuff out and beating things." Or, as a later press release about Rick put it, "at the age of three, he first started creating rhythms on tin cans and bottles."

While a student at East High School, Rick had taken advantage of extracurricular musical offerings by serving as a solo snare drummer and playing conga drums and bongos with the Brown Cadet Corps, an all-black marching band. He also studied the trombone and the bass guitar at school, and sang on street corners with a group of friends he called the Duprees.

After dropping out of East High School, Rick spent a lot of time at the African American Cultural Center in Buffalo playing conga drums, learning Swahili, chanting, and hanging around other young people interested in music. His participation in the center's programs resulted in one of his first solo performances as a singer: Malcolm Erni, the head of the center, was so impressed by Rick's ability to perform African chants that he took Rick to Chicago to perform them there.

As Rick's interest in music increased, he adopted a pattern that did not vary for the rest of his life. Rather than become a specialist on any one instrument, he learned just enough about several to be competent on them. "He wasn't a great bass player, but he could play what he played as good as most people," LeRoi Johnson notes. "Then he learned a little bit about singing" and went on from there.

Although Rick would occasionally boast about being a great instrumentalist, no musician who heard him play any instrument for more than a couple minutes ever believed him. "People talked about Rick's ability to play instruments, but Rick couldn't play worth shit," Levi Ruffin says. "Percussion, yes, and he could work out a song on a guitar, and he could mess around on the bass and . . . figure it out . . . but he could never really finish it. He could sit there and figure it out, but as far as him playing, oh my God, oh hell no, I wouldn't hire him to play nothing, man."

Rick wrote in his 2007 autobiography, *The Confessions of Rick James: Memoirs of a Super Freak*, that he "never had confidence in [his] own playing" and that he didn't want to be constricted as a performer by being tied to an instrument. LeRoi Johnson says that what Rick was trying to do "was put together just enough of what was needed to be a star."

The varied musical knowledge Rick obtained by dabbling with different instruments enabled him to pick out good musicians and direct and produce them knowledgeably in the groups he would form and direct during his career. Many of these groups backed him onstage or on records and then went on to perform on their own, with him as their producer.

Ruffin notes, however, that Rick did work hard on developing his voice, and for a reason. "Rick realized when we were all young that the guys that get most of the broads were the singers," he says. He also characterizes Rick's voice as "rough and powerful." "It had that dirt on it, that edge to it," he says. "To this day I don't know how Rick could sing like that."

Rick's early musical talent, his attempt to learn all the parts of a song, both vocal and instrumental, his work on his own voice, and his flexible ethics came together one day in 1961 when Rick and LeRoi, then in their early teens, heard of an upcoming talent show at the Carpenters' Hall in Buffalo. Although the contestants had already been chosen, LeRoi says, Rick lied to the organizers, insisting his name had been on the list and he had been eliminated by mistake.

When Rick went onstage, he performed a then-popular song but, showing either his naïveté or his versatility and understanding of different musical roles, sang both the background and the lead parts himself. Johnson saw this performance as a joke and was laughing under his breath, but the judges were so impressed they awarded Rick second place in the competition. This was one of several local talent shows in which he did well.

Possibly referring to this talent show, Rick told *Rolling Stone* years later that "the feeling of the crowd singing, the people dancing in the aisles, cast a magic spell on me. . . . I made a pact with myself from that day on—music was my life."

A short time after that talent show, Johnson said, Rick wrote a song called "Dorinda," a tribute to his real high school girlfriend of that name. Under the name "Malinda," it would be recorded and released by the Motown group Bobby Taylor & the Vancouvers in 1968. Rick's professional musical career was on its way.

2

Out to Sea

Blue, navy blue,
I'm as blue as I can be
'Cause my steady boy said "Ship ahoy"
And joined the Nay-eh-ay-vee.

—"Navy Blue," sung by Diane Renay, written by Bob Crewe,
Eddie Rambeau, and Bud Rehak (1963)

No one who knew Rick James as a hyperactive kid with an early arrest record would have thought of him as great material for the US military. "I was a juvenile delinquent," Rick told one TV interviewer years later about his life as a kid in Buffalo. "I was crying out for attention." Unfortunately for Rick, by dropping out of high school, not going to college, not marrying, and not producing any dependents, he became a prime candidate for the US military draft, which had begun in 1940 and would last until 1973.

It was Malcolm Erni, the head of Buffalo's African American Cultural Center, who suggested Rick join the US Navy to avoid being drafted into the US Army, the fate of many young men of that era. If Rick joined the navy, Erni told him, he could fulfill his military obligation merely by attending two weekend drills a month at a site near his house, and he would never have to become a full-time sailor. He'd also get paid and be able to return to high school if he wished. Rick also might have been influenced by the fact that his father had served in the navy; he was certainly influenced by a neighbor named Jerry Long, who wanted to be in the navy and who signed up at the same time as Rick.

Rick might have done well in the navy and avoided combat service if he'd actually attended most of the drills and obeyed an order or two, but anyone who examined his school record could have predicted the chances of his doing that were less than zero.

His sister Camille Hudson says she was surprised when Rick joined up "because I didn't see him following anybody's instructions for more than five minutes." She was "amazed" that "he even lasted a couple of months" in the military. "You could tell him to go upstairs and he'd go downstairs," just to disobey.

Nevertheless, Rick joined the US Naval Reserve on February 18, 1964, for a six-year stint. He was sixteen years old. The navy allowed volunteers to join at seventeen with parental permission, but no one younger was allowed to join. Rick and his mother lied about his age to get him into the service, and Rick backed it up by borrowing a birth certificate from a man named James Johnson who was older than he was.

Rick's mother knew what her child was like, of course, but as LeRoi Johnson said in 2013, "She would sign any paper to get him out of the house. My mother had a thing that if you were fifteen years old, you were grown, which would never be what any of us [as parents] would do right now."

Naval lieutenant Dan Bruggeman, who was involved in one of Rick's court-martials, put this in a slightly different way: "These were ghetto kids," he says. "Nobody wanted them around. They wanted to try being in the military, and the parents said, 'Fine, get out of here.'"

Rick soon began skipping his required twice-monthly weekend drills. After about six months of such behavior, Rick was ordered to spend forty-five continuous training days at Naval Station Great Lakes near Chicago, the navy's only boot camp. He managed to survive his time there, but once released, he began missing drills once again.

Exasperated navy superiors ordered Rick to report for full-time duty as a crew member on the USS *Enterprise*, a nuclear-powered aircraft carrier that was on its way to the waters off Vietnam. Only in the military would such a poor performer be ordered to continue his poor performance aboard a nuclear aircraft carrier. Rick left Buffalo to report to the *Enterprise*, but changed his mind in Rochester, New York, and instead climbed aboard a bus for Toronto, Canada. He had become a US Navy deserter.

3

Toronto Was Cold but Its Music Was Hot

A weekend in Canada, a change of scene,
Was the most I had bargained for.

—"Canadian Sunset," music by Eddie Heywood
and lyrics by Norman Gimbel (1956)

Rick may have felt lonely staring out the window of the Grey-hound bus that carried him north from Rochester toward Toronto, but he wasn't alone. By the spring of 1964, hundreds of American draft dodgers and military deserters had already fled to Canada, and hundreds more would follow.

More important to Rick—and to the super freak he would become—thousands of musicians from all over Canada and many from the United States also had left their hometowns and were heading to precisely the Toronto neighborhood Rick was aiming for: four or five blocks of mid-town Toronto called Yorkville.

Canadian folksingers such as Gordon Lightfoot, Joni Mitchell, and Buffy Sainte-Marie, and American vocalists including Tom Rush, Kris Kristofferson, and Simon & Garfunkel, had either moved to Yorkville in recent years or made a habit of performing there. R&B and rock 'n' roll artists played in the neighborhood's clubs, as well as in Toronto venues outside the area. By 1966, according to assiduous researchers, fourteen hundred musical acts were playing in the city. Most were gathered into two competing camps: the folksingers on one side, and the R&B singers and the rockers on the other.

As soon as Rick got off the bus and wandered into Yorkville, he stood out like a sore thumb. He was still wearing his navy blue uniform, the only clothing he had brought with him. Four drunks with Buffalo accents immediately accosted him, accusing him of being "an AWOL nigger." A fight was about to start, which Rick was not sure he could win, when he was rescued by three men—Pat McGraw, Garth Hudson, and Levon Helm—who punched out the assailants. Hudson and Helm were members of rockabilly singer Ronnie Hawkins's backup band, the Hawks, who would later become Bob Dylan's backing band when he decided to go electric, and eventually morphed into the Band.

Hudson and Helm left to rehearse shortly after the dust-up on the street, but Rick and Pat McGraw repaired to a Yorkville club called Café El Patio, where they smoked some pot in the back room. A band called the Epics, led by Nick St. Nicholas—later of Steppenwolf—began performing. St. Nicholas, a bassist doubling as a vocalist, was not a very impressive singer, and McGraw urged Rick to try out his vocal talents on the spot. St. Nicholas was willing, and Rick's performance was, comparatively at least, very impressive. He had become a Canadian musician.

Musician Chris Sarns, who later played in several bands with Rick, says it was apparent Rick "was not a very good singer." But "he was a great entertainer, and being an entertainer is better than being a great singer. He was energy and movement onstage, and he was live, loud, energetic, enthusiastic, and fun to watch."

Many of the musicians who saw Rick that night, and after, were flexing their musical muscles in Toronto while hoping to break through to the big time. And some of them realized immediately that Rick's talent offered them what appeared to be a heaven-sent opportunity.

Recording opportunities in Canada were very limited then. Canadian record companies were small. According to musician Stan Endersby, who played in the band Heaven and Earth with Rick in 1971, Toronto "had a tremendous number of great bands, terrible managers, and two-track recording studios, but nobody who could produce records," and there was no real outlet for those records except in the United States and Europe.

In the words of Rick Abel, a red-haired Texan who later became Rick James's road manager, what some of these musicians feared most was spending their lives "riding the velvet rut." Toronto boasted numerous nightclubs featuring live music, and musicians in the city knew they could spend their entire professional lives playing the local circuit. They would earn a good living, but they would rarely become nationally or internationally famous, and rarely make bestselling recordings. For fame junkies, this was a prescription for life in hell, and there were plenty of fame junkies in Toronto.

Breaking through to popularity primarily meant breaking through to America and its major recording companies. Many musically inclined Canadians were plagued with dreams of performing for huge, adoring crowds in New York and Los Angeles and selling records around the world. But unless their own skills were outstanding, their ambitions were condemned to wait for someone like Rick: an obvious up-and-comer who could carry them to stardom. Many immediately saw Rick's talent and determination as the magic carpet that would lift them out of local obscurity and loft them into the big time.

As guitarist Nick Balkou puts it, "Did we really want to stay here in Toronto and end up, as I have, working at a bar on the Danforth [a road in Toronto]? I mean, really. We had to get out of Dodge and go down to L.A. That was really where it was happening."

Rick's potential for rising to the top was blazingly obvious. Horn player Bob Doughty, who later played with Rick, told author Nick Warburton that when he first spotted Rick on stage he saw a "non-stop, fast-moving, harmonica-playing wailing fool the likes of which no one had ever seen before." Chris Sarns soon realized Rick was not only "a very talented, highly energetic go-getter" but also a person "with an insatiable drive, and drive is more important than talent."

One way various Toronto musicians were made aware of Rick's drive was from Rick himself. Drummer Richard Grand remembers Rick constantly saying, "I'm bigger than . . . I'm better than . . . I'm more than" other musicians. Grand calls him "the Muhammad Ali of musicians" and a "flamboyant braggart" but adds he didn't mind any of it because "hey—those were his aspirations."

To remain in Rick's orbit and to enjoy the promise of success that he radiated, these and many other musicians—all of them male and most of them white—would tolerate almost anything from him. His flaws, which soon became obvious to most of them, included taking over any band he joined, "borrowing" money, autos, and other valuable objects that he never returned, destroying other people's property, repeatedly deserting bands he was leading (sometimes mid-tour), signing contracts behind the backs of his fellow band members that benefited him and hurt them, and pocketing monetary advances meant for them. It all meant little to them. All they cared about was what the philosopher William James (no relation to Rick) had called "the bitch-goddess Success."

For Rick, Toronto, a hotbed of skilled and ambitious musicians that was out of reach of US law enforcement, was the perfect incubator for his incipient superstar career. While based there, he bounced back and forth between the United States and Canada, founding new bands, touring with many, then leaving old bands and forming successor bands. He was skilled at crossing the border even while wanted by US authorities, but it wasn't as big a trick as it is today, because a passport was not required, and most of the time the border guards did not even request identification. Since Rick did not perform as James A. Johnson Jr., the name of the naval deserter on the federal wanted list, he believed, correctly, there was little chance he'd be arrested.

Yorkville would also become Rick's base for making four separate attempts to be signed on as a vocalist at the Motown Record Corporation, both while Motown remained in Detroit, where it had been founded in 1959, and after it moved to Los Angeles in 1972.

Rick's Toronto-based struggle to reach the big time through some major record company consumed the next fourteen years of his life, along with the lives of those Toronto musicians who had harnessed their ambitions to his monumental effort. His struggle was an eventful one: he was arrested several times, deported to the United States, served several terms in military and civilian jails, had two children with one woman, and married another. For some that's a whole lifetime, but for Rick, it was only the beginning.

4

A Defiant Rick Forms the Sailor Boys and Becomes Rick Jagger

Jagger rose unsteadily from his seat at a table strewn with bottles
of Cristal and Jack Daniel's. He was totally drunk. "Rick James!"
slurred the legendary front man of the Rolling Stones.
"Oh man! Super Freak! I just *had* to meet you!"

—From *Scary Monsters and Super Freaks*, by Mike Sager

A **fter Rick's first performance** on his first night in Toronto,
Pat McGraw invited him home to his apartment, which he occupied with his girlfriend, vocalist Shirley Matthews. (Shortly before Rick
met her, Matthews had recorded her first and last hit record, the major
Canadian hit "Big Town Boy.") After hearing about the fight over Rick's
AWOL status that introduced the two men, Shirley suggested Rick—
who was using his real name, James Ambrose Johnson Jr.—start calling himself Ricky James Matthews, the name of her dead cousin. Rick
started using the alias immediately.

The next day, Rick went over to Nick St. Nicholas's apartment, where
he was practicing his hobby of painting. A nude white girl was acting as his
model, which impressed Rick. St. Nicholas invited Rick to join his band.

Soon thereafter, the band had a new name. Though Rick was using
his new name to hide from the military, he was unable to resist the urge

to flip the bird at the navy by convincing the other members to call the band the Sailor Boys. He even continued to wear his uniform while playing with the group. (In any case, he had nothing else to wear and very little money.) Soon the other members bought uniforms and accessories to echo Rick's outfit, and a short time after that, fans of the band began wearing their own US Navy gear.

Toronto was in such a fever of band destruction and replacement that the other Sailor Boys were not surprised when St. Nicholas—whom Rick was starting to edge out of the bandleader spot anyway—left for another band, along with keyboard player Goldy McJohn. New musicians signed on, including Jimmy Livingston, who often shared the vocals with Rick. The lineup continued to evolve as the band—later changing its name to the Mynah Birds—continued to play for the next two and a half years.

(St. Nicholas and McJohn soon joined another Toronto group with a bird-themed name: Jack London and the Sparrows. This group didn't seem to be going anywhere for a while, but with a slightly altered membership it later became the ultra-famous Steppenwolf.)

Rick, meanwhile, continued to attract attention. Author Nick Warburton described Rick's stage personality as "charismatic and dynamic." Rick certainly fit that description, but his act wasn't nearly as original and creative as it would become. Strutting around the stage, Rick riled up the crowds with imitations of such Rolling Stones classics as "Time Is on My Side," "Under My Thumb," "Get Off of My Cloud" and "(I Can't Get No) Satisfaction." He was so hooked on the Stones that he was often called Rick Jagger.

It may be disconcerting to some that Rick, a black American, spent much of the first half of his career imitating a white English vocalist who imitated black soul singers. Nevertheless, as late as 1983, a reviewer for the *Toronto Globe and Mail* said that some of the tunes on Rick's then-latest album, *Cold Blooded*, confirmed his standing as "something like the black Mick Jagger." And Rick's fans saw the talent beneath the performance. One of the reasons Rick imitated Jagger as opposed to, say, Gordon Lightfoot, was that he was absolutely determined to become a rock star, not a folksinger. Rick was also very skilled at tailoring his performances to the audience he needed to impress. Neil Merryweather, a bass player and singer who would later play in the Mynah Birds with Rick, noted one evening that Rick was without lodging. So Merryweather asked his mother-in-law if Rick could sleep on her couch. The mother-in-law agreed, but when Rick got there, she asked him to sing. Rick probably would have loved to perform "(I Can't Get No) Satisfaction" or "Get Off of My Cloud," but realizing he was singing for a middle-aged white woman, he sang the 1945 Perry Como song "Till the End of Time," in what Merryweather calls "a big, schmaltzy voice." The mother-in-law was so thrilled by Rick's performance that Rick got his place to stay.

5

Rick James, Thief

In June 1971 I went to a party, and this woman told me,
"There's a terrific artist you should meet who
needs a lawyer . . . he's in jail."

—Stan Weisman

Music was not the only thing Rick got up to in Toronto;
he persisted with some of the bad behaviors from his youth. Stan
Weisman, the Toronto attorney who defended Rick, negotiated his contracts, and financed him for years, first met Rick when Rick was in a
Toronto jail in the mid-1960s.

Rick's record in the criminal division of the provincial court, the lowest level of the Ontario criminal court, reveals quite a few run-ins with
the law in 1965 and 1966. On April 7, 1965, he was convicted of guitar
theft and received a suspended sentence and twelve months on probation. Later that year, he was convicted of possession of stolen articles. On
September 12, 1966, a judge ordered him deported to the United States
because of his Canadian criminal record after a hearing held in Toronto's
Don Jail. It's not clear if he was deported and then returned to Canada or
whether he appealed his original deportation order and stayed.

He was again ordered deported on July 7, 1967, and eventually left
the country. Because crossing the border was easy in those days, he later

returned to Canada. He was ordered deported again on June 4, 1971, but was released on $500 bail pending appeal. In October 1971, he was convicted of marijuana possession and fined $200.

Legal problems aside, Rick's penchant for theft often made it difficult for people to continue liking him. As Canadian musician Tony Nolasco puts it, "He borrowed money from everybody and never paid it back."

During Rick's early days in Toronto, Weisman was always slipping him money to get by on, and Rick would take it without offering anything in return. On one occasion, though, apparently under attack by his conscience, Rick told Weisman, "I feel bad taking money from you. I have a reel-to-reel tape recorder [the ne plus ultra of the era's technology]. Give me one hundred dollars and you can have the recorder."

Weisman gave him the hundred dollars and took the recorder. But "two days later he phoned me saying, 'I need the tape recorder. I've got tunes in my head I've got to record! This is my career!'" Weisman says. "So I gave it back to him." When Rick finally returned the recorder to Weisman, it was useless: the reels were wobbling, most likely from overuse.

It's unlikely Rick sabotaged the tape recorder, but he definitely sabotaged other items that weren't his. For instance, Danny Marks, a guitarist in one of Rick's later bands, incurred Rick's anger by quitting over Rick's objections. Marks had lent the band a concert amplifier, which he now wanted back, but fearing a confrontation and perhaps physical retribution from Rick, he asked a fellow musician to retrieve it. Marks told Nick Warburton that the other band member brought it back and it looked OK. Then he plugged it in and turned it on "and poof, a big pall of smoke comes up." Marks turned it around and looked in the back of the cabinet, and each of the four vintage speakers had a hole poked through its paper core.

In the mid-1960s Weisman lent the carless Rick his five-year-old Oldsmobile and, as he noted in 2013, "I have yet to find that car. I never saw it again." This was not an unusual move for Rick. People grew so aware of his "borrowing," in fact, that one of the songs later recorded (but not released) by one of his Canadian bands was a funk instrumental called "Rip Off 1500" about Rick's alleged "borrowing" of that dollar amount.

"Whenever he'd visit my house, I'd get an eighty-dollar bill the next month for a long-distance call he'd made on my phone," musician Stan Endersby says. Most of Rick's associates were not terribly angered by Rick's borrowing because they assumed he was using the money to rise in the music business and would take them with him. Rick also occasionally took the trouble to buck up friends who were in trouble. When Peter McGraw was going through a difficult divorce, he remembered fifty years later, Rick was the only person who came up to him and said, "You know, Peter, she doesn't know what she's throwing away."

But Rick Abel, who worked for Rick for years, remembers the time he was sharing a house with a couple in the Los Angeles area. "[Rick] came over to our house, we had nothing, we were barely scraping by, but Rick was the kind of guy, he'd walk into your house, and he would be like a raccoon. . . . His eyes would be immediately drawn to whatever he saw that looked like it might have some sort of value. He was like a kleptomaniac . . . it's like he felt that, 'It's there, and I want it, so I can take it.'

"He had gone into the bathroom that was right next to [the couple's] bedroom where [the woman who lived there] kept a little silver pillbox. He just took it and walked out. Right after he left, she says, 'Hey, he stole my pillbox.'"

It was when Rick "borrowed" from those who weren't in his orbit that he got in trouble. On one occasion early in his stay in Toronto, for instance, Rick crossed Jack Long, part-owner of a popular Toronto music store called Long & McQuade. The store was very musician friendly and had a reputation for benevolence. "If you were late on a payment, they'd be OK," Endersby says of Long & McQuade. "And they gave people credit that shouldn't get credit." But credit was not an option for Rick. He visited the store one day and stole three microphones he needed for his band's performance at a club that night.

As it happened, Endersby was in the audience that evening while Rick was performing "Hitch Hike," the Marvin Gaye tune later performed

by the Rolling Stones. "Rick was singing 'Hitchhike! Hitchhike, baby!'
when suddenly Jack Long walked in," Endersby says. "Then there was
a *click* as Jack grabbed the first microphone. Then Rick goes to the next
mic and [sings], 'I'm gonna find that girl if I have to hitchhike 'round
the world,' and Jack took that mic too. Then Jack went for the third mic,
and Rick said, 'C'mon, leave me that mic. I need one to sing.' But Jack
took it, and the show was over."

Although he was never arrested during this period for a crime of
violence, Rick was certainly capable of such behavior. According to
Weisman, during a regular basketball game in Toronto in January 1973,
Rick and one of Weisman's private investigators, whom Weisman calls
"a mild-mannered guy," jumped up for a rebound simultaneously. "Rick
claimed he got elbowed in the face," Weisman says, "and as he came
down he hit the other guy in the face, splitting his lip open almost down
to his chin. The guy passed out and Rick ran away." Others in the group
carried the injured man to a nearby hospital.

"That's an extreme example," Weisman admits but adds, "Rick
would lose patience easily. He was a lovable guy but had things from
childhood, I suspect, that made him angry and frustrated. . . . He knew
he had a lot of talent but was dealing with small-time people."

Asked if he ever considered pulling the plug on Rick, particularly
because of his nonstop "borrowing," Weisman responds by talking about
Rick's "genuine charm" and said, "Rick knew he was going to succeed,
he knew he was going to pay me back . . ."

6

Rick Joins a Flock of Mynah Birds

Mynah Byrd, O Mynah Bird, I was lonely as can be.

—"The Mynah Bird Song," by Colin Kerr & Rajah (1965)

Rick thrived on imitation during his early years in Canada, so it should hardly have been a surprise when the owner of a shop near Yorkville that sold mynah birds, among nature's greatest imitators, offered to sponsor the musician and his band the Sailor Boys.

Colin Kerr, an oddball Toronto entrepreneur, had been telling people for years that when he had been playing golf in India during the 1950s, he had sought help for his under-par performance from a local mynah bird named Rajah who was said to grant good luck to all who sought it out. (Its nine-year-old owner supposedly managed its affairs.) Kerr became so infatuated with the bird's ability to attract luck, he said, that he purchased it after the boy died of leukemia, brought it back to Canada, and opened a store devoted to selling its cousins to what he hoped would be grateful Canadians.

Unsurprisingly, Kerr's condition for financing the Sailor Boys was that they change their name to the Mynah Birds. Eventually, he asked them to imitate their black-and-yellow namesake by dressing in black Beatle boots with yellow heels, black pants, black leather jackets, and yellow turtlenecks, all of which Kerr gave them.

Kerr further extended his brand, opening a three-story club in Yorkville and calling it the Mynah Bird Club, where the band soon began performing. Shortly thereafter, Kerr required the band to imitate the Beatles—whose name, of course, imitated the name of one of the Mynah Birds' favorite foods—and insisted that all the band members sport Beatles-type haircuts.

Fully aware of the tendency of Beatles fans, mostly young women, to scream out "The Beatles!" and chase that band whenever they saw them, Kerr took the Mynah Birds to Eaton's, Toronto's largest department store, and paid a mob of girls to meet them there. On cue, the girls shouted out "the Mynah Birds!" and chased them out of the store and into the band's waiting limousine, preventing it from moving until the police dispersed them. Kerr repeated this trick several more times until it began happening naturally.

Kerr's methods may seem comical, but they gave the Mynah Birds a boost. The publicity resulting from the girl riots enabled Kerr to negotiate a record contract for the band with Columbia Records of Canada. After weeks of rehearsing, the group cut two tunes for its debut 45 single. A fanatic brander if there ever was one, Kerr insisted one of the tunes be named "The Mynah Bird Hop," an R&B belter on which Rick shared vocals with Livingston. The B-side was the tune "The Mynah Bird Song," a soulful, calypso-flavored ballad. Both songs' lyrics glamorized mynah birds, with "The Mynah Bird Song" containing such lines as "Mynah Byrd, O Mynah Bird, I was lonely as can be," delivered with great emotion.

Very few copies of the record were sold, it never hit the charts, and nobody reviewed it. But to support it when it was released in early 1965, the band appeared on several Canadian TV shows, including *Hi Time* and *Mickie a Go-Go*. On *Hi Time*, Rick sang "The Mynah Bird Song" to a blind mynah bird perched on his hand while it defecated on his palm and dug in its claws. He told other interviewers that the bird defecated on his shoulder on another occasion. Laughing about this shortly before his death, Rick said, "I used to sing to this blind mynah bird that would shit on me onstage. It was a kind of sick situation."

As part of Kerr's campaign to support the record, the Mynah Birds also performed in four sold-out shows at the Colonnade Theatre in downtown Toronto. A few more gigs followed, but by then Kerr was becoming discouraged with what he saw as the band's unprofessionalism (they often tried to shuck their Mynah Birds outfits or "forgot" to take the real mynah birds on the road). To show them the kind of comportment he favored, Kerr sent them to Montreal's Esquire Show Bar for three weeks. There, they were the supporting band for a group that one former Mynah Bird, musician Richard Grand, describes as "well-rehearsed, well-dressed young ladies who delivered a perfect Motown sound."

Once away from Toronto and Kerr's supervision, Rick led the band away from Mynah Birds tunes toward the music he favored: rock 'n' roll. According to Grand, the audience was shocked when the young ladies took a break and the audience was suddenly confronted by Rick and the Mynah Birds' full-throated Rolling Stones imitation. But many women in the audience found Rick attractive. According to musician Nick Balkou, "When [Rick] smiled, it was very charismatic. He just lit up the room. It was very endearing, especially for the ladies."

At this stage of his career, however, by most accounts, Rick ignored the few groupies the band attracted. Musician Chris Sarns, who shared a room with Rick on another Mynah Birds tour shortly thereafter, says Rick didn't have any sex that Sarns was aware of during the entire time they were on the road. "I had a girl one night and Rick [in the next bed over] had to pretend he was asleep," Sarns says. "But he himself never had a girl during the whole tour."

Meanwhile, it was becoming obvious to Rick and his fellow band members that they were not exactly taking off as Mynah Birds. They finally dropped Kerr as their manager in late 1965 when he told them to increase their resemblance to real mynah birds. To do so, he suggested they cut a V in the hair on the sides of their heads to more closely resemble the natural "hairstyles" of their avian models.

Undeterred, Kerr went on to expand the Mynah Bird Club from a musical venue to a pornography palace, first by hiring young women to dance topless in his club and silhouetting them in the club's window. Later he added body painting, X-rated films, and a chef who cooked in the nude.

7

Rick James, International Drug Smuggler

*It's not unusual for Rick to be doing something new. He did it as a
teenager in Buffalo and he did it as a black musician
in the white world of Canadian Rock 'n' Roll.*

—Motown Press Release, 1985

Many musicians in the 1960s floated from one venue to
another on marijuana fumes, and the Mynah Birds were no exception. Most of them smoked pot, consumed hash, and inhaled amyl
nitrites, or poppers. However, various Mynah Birds members described
Rick as using no more drugs than anyone else. Mynah Birds drummer
Rickman Mason recalls Rick as only "dabbling" in marijuana use. Chris
Sarns says he and Rick "smoked pot but not excessively, usually in cele-
bration of something."

A band member who asked not to be identified says he did remember Rick buying seven bottles of Romilar cough syrup for immediate
consumption because he was scheduled to go onstage in four hours and
"needed to be prepared." Rick wasn't trying to stave off a cold: Romilar contained a high concentration of dextromethorphan, the chemical
in many cough suppressants that turns them from medicine into recre-
ational drugs at larger-than-prescribed doses. Rick was slowly moving
toward the drug addiction that would later cripple him.

Some thought Rick and his pals were doing more than dabbling. When LeRoi Johnson would visit Rick in Toronto, "Everybody would be high on primo hashish and primo weed," he says. "I didn't smoke or anything like that, and once I had contact with this stuff, I got so high I had to stay away."

Rick's trips across the border sometimes involved buying drugs for himself, for his bandmates, or to sell. These trips caused panic among those of his associates who weren't accustomed to crossing international borders while "holding." Johnson accompanied Rick on a trip to Colombia on one occasion and says Rick put some drugs in Johnson's bag that he didn't even know about. "But that was the kind of guy Rick was. He'd let his own brother be a fall guy and not tell you until you got back." Johnson says this with amusement rather than bitterness, although he admits he yelled at Rick when he realized he'd been turned into an unwitting drug mule.

Levi Ruffin says Rick once went to Cartagena—a Colombian drug trafficking center—and then to India, and came back "with all kinds of product. Matter of fact, the first time I ever sniffed cocaine was when he came back from there." Rick also smuggled in drugs from Turkey and various European countries. Johnson remembers Rick returning from Turkey with hash in the form of a black candy bar.

Ruffin was certainly impressed with Rick's daring as a drug dealer. He was aware of the danger involved in buying dope from Cartagena's drug cartels and smuggling it into the United States. According to Ruffin, Rick smuggled the drugs back in a leather men's bag with zippers on it, and let Ruffin hold the bag after Rick got back. "You could feel the weight of the cocaine in it. Can you imagine all the customs he had to go through with all that product? You could get a lifetime in jail if they caught you. My God!"

But, Ruffin says, "Rick had to do what he had to do. It cost $150 to $175 an hour to record in those days." Ruffin also notes that he and Rick sampled the drugs they sold. "That was back in the sixties, when you tried liquor, drugs, everything."

Ruffin's claims about Rick's illicit income clashes with LeRoi Johnson's assertion that their mother financed Rick's career until at least 1973. But Ruffin said that with eight children, the help she could provide "was not nearly enough to record an album or anything like that. You needed big money and you needed it quick. Studios didn't take credit cards, not from no brothers, so you had to bring that cash in."

On one occasion Weisman, Rick's very straight attorney, was with him on a crossing from Canada into the United States. When the customs inspector looked into the front seat, he saw a white businessman and a young Rick, wearing a Spanish-style hat reminiscent of those worn by male flamenco dancers, which he sometimes wore onstage. "Pull over to that shed," the inspector said.

On the way to the shed, where searches were performed, Rick asked Weisman, "What do I do about my dope?"

Weisman, who hadn't realized that Rick was carrying drugs, panicked. "Rick, you can't do this to me," he whispered. Rick surreptitiously dropped the bag of dope out the window before the car reached the shed. The search uncovered nothing, but the inspector asked Weisman why he was traveling with Rick. Weisman stuttered for a while, because, in his words, "I couldn't say I was his lawyer. That would get him in trouble, because they'd want to know why, what trouble he was in, and they'd arrest us."

Rick and Weisman managed not to incriminate themselves and were released. As Weisman drove away from the shed, Rick jumped out of the car and retrieved his dope, and the two sped off toward America, the land of opportunity.

On another occasion Weisman and his wife were driving down St. Nicholas Lane in Toronto one balmy day when they saw Rick standing in the street. Mrs. Weisman and Rick had met and liked each other, so Weisman stopped the car and the three of them chatted. Suddenly, Rick said, "Oh, shit, the cops are coming," and threw a bag of marijuana into the backseat of the Weismans' car. Weisman pulled away as the cops arrived and began interrogating Rick. Mrs. Weisman began shrieking, "No! No! What is that?" so Weisman threw the bag in a garbage can around the corner, saving both Rick and Mrs. Weisman any further trauma.

In addition to the profit involved, LeRoi Johnson thought Rick also enjoyed the thrill of smuggling and selling drugs. "Rick liked doing things on the edge. That was part of his character." Rick would prove that to be true again and again throughout his life.

8

Rick James and the Birth of Buffalo Springfield

There was a band playing in my head and I felt like getting high.

—"After the Gold Rush," by Neil Young (1970)

The first task the band had taken on when quitting Colin Kerr was to rid themselves completely of their mynah bird costumes, as well as the birds themselves, and to dress instead like Rick's idols, the Rolling Stones. The only thing they kept was the band's feathered name.

Then, already aware from their previous forays into Eaton's that its well-heeled owner, John Craig Eaton, was interested in musical groups, they solicited and received his financial backing and used it to buy more and better equipment. Entrepreneur Eaton loved owning the Mynah Birds and gave them Knute Rockne–like pep talks from time to time. He also didn't seem to mind when band members would barge into his office and ask him for more money—in fact, he often gave it to them. Occasionally, he even let the group crash at his mansion, in Toronto's upper-class Bridle Path neighborhood. But Eaton didn't really want to dirty his hands by getting too deeply involved in the music business, and asked a neighbor of his, Morley Shelman, to actually manage the band.

The Mynah Birds' final accomplishment was to lure more and better musicians into their lineup. In February 1965 Bruce Palmer, a bass player who later found fame with Buffalo Springfield, joined the group. Shortly thereafter, Rick noticed folksinger Neil Young performing in a Toronto coffeehouse. Rick was impressed that Young had composed his own songs, and that he was accompanying himself with an acoustic guitar and a harmonica, à la Bob Dylan. Rick had been thinking that the band needed a folksinger to add to its versatility, so he asked Young to join. Soon Rick and Young became roommates in a Toronto apartment where, according to Jimmy McDonough's book *Shakey: Neil Young's Biography*, Young and Rick lived on baked goods that Rick would pilfer from delivery trucks in the wee hours of the morning.

Palmer and Young worked well with Rick, and Young used Eaton's largesse to buy himself a Rickenbacker six-string electric guitar to replace his old folk-style twelve-string semi-acoustic model. Rick claimed later that he had convinced Young to make this switch, telling him, "Come on, man, forget this acoustic guitar and let's plug in." Young was torn between two camps: the rockers, who used electric guitars, and the folkies, who stuck with their acoustic models.

But Rick provided Young with something to help him forget the tensions he was suffering from: poppers. As Young told another of his biographers, John Einarson, he and Rick "used to pop amyl nitrates [*sic*] before going on stage and walk on just killing ourselves laughing and rolling around from these things."

On at least one occasion, this habit interfered with Young's ability to play. At a high school gig, Young jumped off the stage, inadvertently pulling his guitar plug out in the middle of a song. The audience was surprised to see Young play the rest of the song on his silent guitar, apparently still hearing the music playing at full volume via the drugs circulating through his system. Young gave up poppers a short time later.

But most of the duo's appearances together were terrific. McDonough quotes Comrie Smith, a friend of Young's, who said she watched what Smith called a "show-stopping" performance by Young and Rick on the song "Hide Away." She said, "Neil would stop playing lead, do a harp solo, throw the harmonica way up in the air, and Ricky would catch it and continue the solo."

Levi Ruffin was one of many people in later years who heard Rick's stories about playing with Neil Young and associating with superstars like Joni Mitchell and Crosby, Stills, Nash, and Young but never quite believed what he heard. "Rick used to tell us a pack of lies," Ruffin notes. One day, however, he and Rick were having lunch "and we were sitting there and here comes Neil Young and he kept calling him Ricky. And they were huggin' . . . and Rick says, 'This is Levi Ruffin, and this is fuckin' Neil Young.'"

9

From Yorkville to Motown

> The biggest thing I ever wanted when I was a kid
> was to be with Motown.
>
> —Rick James to *Rolling Stone*, 1981

Both Palmer and Young were still in the band's lineup when, in 1965, they accompanied Rick to Detroit on his first attempt to start his Motown career.

Morley Shelman had met the actor and vocalist Sal Mineo while Mineo was in Toronto to film *The Gene Krupa Story*. Shelman sensed a future for a white band fronted by a talented black vocalist and asked Mineo if he could help get the group an audition at Motown Record Corporation headquarters in Detroit.

In 1965 Motown was near its all-time peak and was besieged by struggling artists and groups, but Mineo was a big name in movies. To add to his clout, his 1957 tune "Start Movin' (In My Direction)"—one of two he had recorded that year—had risen to number 9 on the *Billboard* pop chart, earning him a gold record. Given his fame, he had no trouble reaching Motown executives. Those execs asked for a tape of the Mynah Birds, then invited them to visit Detroit for an audition.

This was a major milestone in Rick's life. From his earliest days, he had thought about being a Motown artist—few black artists in America or Canada hadn't—and now a band he led had been invited to audition for the legendary Detroit company, the largest and most successful black-owned record company ever established in America.

The Mynah Birds performed for vocalist Smokey Robinson and Motown president Berry Gordy and passed their audition, becoming only the fourth white (well . . . mostly white) band ever signed by Motown Records (the previous three all-white groups—the Rustix, the Dalton Boys, and the Underdogs—did not score any hits while with the company).

Mynah Bird Neil Merryweather thought one reason Motown was willing to sign Rick's group was that everyone at Motown was going crazy over Vanilla Fudge's new version of the Supremes song "You Keep Me Hangin' On." Vanilla Fudge, as the name implies, was an all-white group, and their version of the song had reached number 6 on the pop chart. But it was released by the Atlantic Recording Corporation, not by Motown.

Soon Motown would sign a fifth white group, Rare Earth, who would score several hits for the company. Motown created a new subsidiary label named Rare Earth that began releasing other white groups. "They [Motown] were experimenting with all kinds of things," Rick said later. "I guess they could associate with our band more easily because of me being black and in the group."

After their initial visit, the Mynah Birds went back to Canada. They returned to Detroit in January 1966 to begin work on an album and stayed there about a week. Motown immediately put the Mynah Birds to work. "We were in a Motown studio all the time we were in Detroit," band member Rickman Mason complains. "We were driven to compose and record. 'Get it done'—that's what Motown wanted."

Although the company put them under what Mason calls an "overseer" while they slaved away, he gives Motown points for assigning white Canadian R. Dean Taylor to the job, matching the ethnicity and nationality of all the band members except Rick. (Taylor, then working as a Motown vocalist, songwriter, and producer, later became well known when his song "Indiana Wants Me"—released on Motown's Rare Earth label—reached number 5 on the US *Billboard* pop chart and number 1 on the Canadian pop chart in 1970.)

Mason claims he and the others worked so hard he's not even sure how many records they made. He says he remembers creating four tunes but adds, "We may have made an album. I don't know."

Billboard magazine reported the group recorded four tracks in January and planned to return to Detroit the next month for more. But Mason's confusion is understandable, because the band members mostly worked on instrumental tracks, which Motown producers later put together with vocals recorded by others. This was a Motown specialty. In other words, the band members all played on the Mynah Birds cuts but then individual members of the band worked independently on instrumental tracks that were to be used for other bands.

In keeping with this separation ethos, Motown never offered the Mynah Birds a contract as a group. Instead the label offered each member of the band a separate six-month contract, which each gladly signed. Neil Young groused years later that the contracts gave Motown 100 percent of each artist's publishing rights, standard Motown practice during that period. But neither he nor anyone else complained at the time. Instead, they swiftly signed the contracts and went right to work. Mason says it was "great fun" working at Hitsville, the name emblazoned on a huge sign on one of the several former residences that comprised Motown headquarters on Detroit's West Grand Boulevard.

During their time off, Rick, who had been progressing in his drug use, turned Merryweather on to acid, but he did not do so blithely. "He watched me like a hawk after I'd dropped the acid," Merryweather says. "He was a very caring guy." Rick told author David Ritz that around this time he also fell in love with doing speed.

While Rick's drug use grew, his interest in women—which would become almost compulsive and all-consuming later in his life—remained relatively undeveloped. Merryweather says that when he and Rick were about to leave their hotel room one evening, two young women knocked on their door and indicated they wished to visit with the two musicians. Merryweather says he expressed enthusiasm, but "Rick threw them some drugs and told me, 'They'll be here when we get back.' He was into his career, his image, and being a rock guy."

While the band members labored to write and record at Hitsville, numerous Motown greats walked in and out of the studio, listening, giving advice, singing on some of the tracks, and finishing some that the band members had left unfinished. Among them were the songwriting trio Holland-Dozier-Holland (brothers Brian and Eddie Holland and Lamont Dozier), Smokey Robinson, vocalists Tammi Terrell and Junior Walker, the Four Tops, the Temptations, and Berry Gordy himself.

Neil Young told author Nelson George in *Where Did Our Love Go?* "If we needed something, or if they thought we weren't strong enough, a couple of Motown singers would just *walk* right in and they'd *Motown* us. If somebody wasn't confident or didn't have it, they didn't say, 'Well, let's work on this.' Some guy would just come in who had it, and do it."

In his autobiography, *Waging Heavy Peace*, Young said Motown even fitted the Mynah Birds for non-birdlike costumes and sent them for training at the company's famed choreography school, then run by Cholly Atkins, an accomplished dancer and choreographer. Morley Shelman told *Billboard* the group would return to Detroit in April 1966 for more sessions, "with an album in sight and talk of a US tour upcoming."

The band members definitely improved their musical skills during their stay in Detroit. Mason notes, for instance, that when the band left Toronto, he himself was "just a mediocre drummer. But after I spent [that week] at Motown, people kept asking me, 'Did you take lessons?'"

Unfortunately, however, much of what the band actually produced in Detroit was never released and may be lost forever. None of the tunes the band recorded there were released until 2006, when Universal Motown, Motown's successor company, released a five-CD package containing 127 tracks made by Motown artists in 1966. The package was part of the company's *Complete Motown Singles* series.

Among the forty-year-old songs in the package were the Mynah Birds' "It's My Time" and "Go On and Cry"—both featuring Rick's vocals—which originally had been scheduled for release as the A and B sides of a single on Motown's V.I.P label in the spring of 1966. The single was withdrawn just before its scheduled release due to legal issues with Rick (more on that momentarily). In 2012 the tunes saw their intended release as the A- and B-side of a limited edition 45 rpm record on Universal bearing original-style Motown V.I.P labels.

Singing "It's My Time," Rick's voice is harsh, and rhythmic drumming dominates the tune. It's a poor attempt at a Stones imitation. Rick called the record "the Four Tops meet the Lovin' Spoonful, a combination of soul and folk/rock." Although Neil Young has claimed coauthorship of the song with Rick, in 2012 Motown identified the writers of the tune as Rick, under the name Ricky James Matthews, plus Motown staffers R. Dean Taylor and Michael Valvano.

"Go On and Cry" is a very effective soft ballad backed with Spanish-type guitar licks. Rick's vocal is sensitive and empathetic. Motown credited the song to Rick, the band's rhythm guitarist John Taylor, Valvano, and R. Dean Taylor.

Harry Weinger, Universal Motown's artist and repertoire chief, says that the company still holds only two other unreleased songs containing Rick's vocals—"I Got You (In My Soul)" and "I'll Wait Forever"—the former resembling a Rolling Stones up-tempo rockin' blues composition (with harmonica) on which Rick imitates Mick Jagger; the latter is also very Stones-ish.

John Taylor's widow, Carolyn, has been said to have separate songwriting contracts signed by Rick and her late husband, all dated January 18, 1966, for three still-unreleased songs not mentioned by Weinger: "We Gotta Go," "Don't Change Your Mind," and "Pretty Words."

After the Mynah Birds had finished their first week of work at Motown in January and returned to Toronto, Rick became annoyed, as he later told David Ritz, that Morley Shelman had never given him his share of the Motown advance money and kept stalling Rick when he asked for it. The two men began a vociferous argument that ended with Rick punching out Shelman. Shelman had his revenge when he informed Motown that Rick was a fugitive from American naval justice and that federal warrants had been issued for his arrest.

This made Motown nervous. Gordy had seen the feds go after record companies for the illegal payments they were making to disc jockeys in the 1950s and early '60s, in what became known as the payola scandal, and had become sensitive about his relations with the government. Whenever his accountants would approach him with a tax-avoidance scheme that might or might not be approved by the IRS, for instance, he always told them to forget it and pay as much as necessary to keep the IRS off his back.

Influenced by this philosophy, Motown executives told Rick that after he'd cleared up his legal problems, they'd be happy to have him and his band back at Motown, but that none of the tunes the band had recorded so far would be released. Motown didn't want to turn the federal government against them by releasing a tune on which the lead singer was a fleeing federal felon.

This devastated Rick and his band; they had lost what had seemed like a heaven-sent opportunity to become Motown recording artists. And for Rick personally, the situation soon got much worse.

10

Rick Is Court-Martialed . . . Twice

I was drowned, I was washed up and left for dead.

—"Jumpin' Jack Flash," Rolling Stones, by Mick Jagger
and Keith Richards (1970)

Rick returned to Canada and took out his frustration by breaking into a Yorkville boutique and stealing numerous outfits. After rationality returned, however, he knew the future he wanted lay waiting for him at Motown and other big American record companies. He would just have to take his punishment for deserting the navy to realize that potential. He returned to Buffalo in 1966, surrendered to the FBI, and soon found himself facing US military justice. He had not yet turned nineteen.

FBI agents flew with him to New York City, where he was tried before a special court-martial. Convicted of an "unauthorized absence" of 542 days, Rick was sentenced to confinement at hard labor for five months. On the same day he was court-martialed, May 19, 1966, he began serving his sentence in the Third Naval District Brig, US Naval Station, Brooklyn, New York, otherwise known as the Brooklyn Brig.

The Third Naval District was commanded at the time by Admiral John McCain Jr., son of World War II veteran Admiral John McCain Sr. and father of future Republican presidential candidate John McCain III.

But being locked in a cell in the Third District's brig was no better than being in a cell in any other district's brig.

In fact, it must have seemed even worse to Rick than living in the barracks at Naval Station Great Lakes, because at 2:55 PM on June 26, 1966, just six weeks later, he managed to escape. This was quite an achievement. A military lawyer who worked in the brig when Rick was an inmate there said in 2014 that that he didn't remember anyone else who escaped, because at that time "it wasn't easy to get out."

Apparently it wasn't easy to *be* out either, at least not with the possibility of a new court-martial hanging over one's head. Rick only lasted about six months as a second-time fugitive. He considered his position while free, and quickly regretted his escape. He asked his cousin Congressman Louis Stokes to write to the navy urging leniency, and asked his mother to contact navy lawyers on his behalf. He then turned himself in again on January 20, 1967, and was re-incarcerated in the Brooklyn Brig from January 25 until his second court-martial, for his escape, took place on March 7.

This time he had two charges against him. Not only had he been illegally absent from his naval duties again (his "duties" this time being to serve time in the brig) but he had broken out. As a result, he was charged with desertion.

Desertion was a serious charge, and Rick was provided counsel. John Bracken, a captain in the Marine Corps Reserve and a lawyer who had left active duty in February 1967, was hired in March. Bracken says he can't remember who hired him but that he was working for a firm that specialized in criminal defense cases. (Rick told an interviewer in 1978 that his mother had hired Bracken's firm.) Bracken says, however, that he remembers *why* he was hired: after working for years as a lawyer in the Court Martial Division of the Third Naval District, both for the prosecution and the defense, he knew and outranked all the key players.

Bracken says while "tons of people were being charged in those days with unauthorized absence, being charged with desertion was unusual." It looked bad for the future super freak. Penalties ran as high as five years of confinement at hard labor plus a dishonorable discharge. But

Bracken immediately began negotiations with the authorities to reduce the charge against his client from desertion to unauthorized absence, the equivalent of reducing it from a felony to a misdemeanor. In an unusual move, the navy agreed to this on the condition that Rick plead guilty to the charge.

The authorities also agreed that although this was Rick's second offense, he would be tried before a special court-martial rather than a general court-martial—that is, in a misdemeanor court rather than a felony court. Bracken says he took this affirmative response to his negotiating stance to mean "there had been a command decision to get rid of" Rick rather than subject him to further punishment.

Rick's second court-martial took place on March 7, 1967. According to the records of the trial, released by the Navy Judge Advocate General's Corps in response to requests under the federal Freedom of Information Act, no witnesses testified. Rick said almost nothing other than "Yes, sir" and "No, sir" throughout the proceedings. His only utterance came when asked if he wanted to assert his legal right to delay his trial for three days. He told the court, "Go to trial now." Also, as agreed in advance, he said "guilty" when asked how he wished to plead to the charge of unauthorized absence.

Bracken went on to present several arguments to the three navy officers who constituted the court that were aimed at reducing or eliminating any further punishment that might be imposed on Rick. First he argued that Rick's background had made him unfit for the navy, going so far as to call his client's family situation "grossly chaotic." In a 2014 interview, Bracken appropriately noted that Rick's mother perjured herself to put her sixteen-year-old child into the navy's clutches a year before he was legally allowed to volunteer. "That his mother would lie to put her son in the military says volumes about his home life." He called Rick's life at the time "unstable, with no family support." In that same interview, Bracken also referred to Rick at the time of his court-martial as "emotionally and educationally unready." He noted that Rick "did not come from an intact family and was simply not ready for the regimens of life in the military."

Second, Bracken pointed out to the court that Rick's age alone made him immature, again noting Rick had been just sixteen years old at the time of his enlistment, and was still sixteen years old at the time he began his unauthorized absence. He went on to tell the judges that according to a Dr. Meyerson, a navy psychiatrist who examined Rick while Rick was imprisoned in the brig, Rick had "an emotionally immature" personality, and "his behavior during the interview and his attitude toward the service render him an extremely poor risk for service life."

Bracken also claimed Rick "did not understand the contract he entered" with the navy. In 2014 he said he had meant it wasn't clear to Rick that the navy wasn't just a job you could leave with no legal consequences, that if you quit the navy, they would come looking for you and criminally prosecute you for leaving once they found you.

Also in a 2014 interview, navy lieutenant Dan Bruggeman, who served at the court-martial as the trial counsel (the military term for prosecutor), put it another way: Rick, he says, was "a young kid who probably never should have been in the military in the first place. We were never going to turn him into a military person, so why spend time and money on him?" Instead, Bruggeman says, "Give him a bad conduct discharge and let him spend some time in the brig. It's nothing we need . . . to make a big deal of."

According to the records of Rick's second court-martial, Bracken also blamed the navy for Rick's plight, telling the court that "what happened [with Rick] was a result of our messing around." What he meant was that under navy regulations, if navy officials had acted quickly enough they could merely have discharged him from the service for enlisting when he was underage before he had completed the sentence handed down at his first court-martial. Bracken also argued that by the time of his second court-martial Rick had already been subjected to "severe punishment" as a prisoner in the brig and that "to be confined in the brig does not do him any good. . . . Very often the result is worse than what you started out with." He pointed out that Rick and his fellow prisoners were not allowed to have mattresses in their cells during the day, and were not allowed to communicate with anyone other than the sentries guarding them. "They also weren't allowed to take part in any activities. It was something like solitary confinement." Finally, Bracken told the court that if sentencing Rick to serve additional time "can serve any purpose, I don't know what it is." At that point, prosecutor Bruggeman spoke up: "I would say that there is no need in retaining this man," he told the court. "I don't see what the government would gain by keeping this man as a guest in our brig."

Bracken also argued, "For the rest of [Rick's] life it is going to have to be on his shoulders that he was convicted." If Rick had gone into any industry other than rock 'n' roll, that might have been true.

Bracken's arguments and Bruggeman's stated agreement convinced the court to deal mercifully with Rick. Although he could have been sentenced to six months at hard labor, the judges sentenced him to a new term of only two months, plus the three months remaining on his original conviction.

Rick remained in the Brooklyn Brig for about six weeks after the court's ruling and then was transferred to the Portsmouth Naval Prison (also known as the US Naval Disciplinary Command) in Kittery, Maine. Calling the transfer a good idea, Bruggeman noted that back in the Brooklyn Brig, former escapee Rick "would have been an embarrassment" to brig officials. "He'd get nasty to them and they'd get nasty to him," Bruggeman said. "We didn't need the brig master going down there and raising hell with him, and we didn't need Rick baiting them" about his previous escape, which might lead to trouble.

Portsmouth, sometimes called the Alcatraz of the East, was built on an island whose tidal currents made escape impossible. The facility was so tough that legendary actor Humphrey Bogart got his trademark facial scar there. According to one version of the incident, Bogart, a US Navy sailor in 1920, was uncuffing a Portsmouth inmate when the inmate took the opportunity to smash the future star across the face with an open handcuff while the other cuff was still on his wrist. If Rick had any similar opportunities, he didn't take advantage of them, and served out his term without incident.

During Rick's stint in the brig, Neil Young and Bruce Palmer returned to Toronto, sold the equipment Eaton had bought them, bought a hearse they named Mort, and drove it to California, hoping to find Stephen Sills, whom Young had met in Canada. They soon found him stuck in a traffic jam in Los Angeles. After also recruiting Dewey Martin and Richie Furay, they formed Buffalo Springfield.

Former Sailor Boy/Mynah Bird Goldy McJohn joined the Sparrows, which later became Steppenwolf, and added Nick St. Nicholas to its ranks. Rick's former bandmates then rode these two now-legendary groups to the top of the pop music pyramid, where their reputations remain today.

After being released from Portsmouth in 1967, Rick languished in obscurity for another eight years. "It bothered me for a long time to see them make it," he said. But he didn't lose his drive.

11

Rick Goes a Second Round with Motown

Once you're a Motown artist, you're always a Motown artist.

—Motown artist Smokey Robinson

On his release from Portsmouth, Rick returned to Toronto and started recruiting musicians to replenish the ranks of the Mynah Birds. One was Bruce Cockburn, who later became famous as a singer-songwriter. A short time later, Rick flew to L.A. to see his old musician friends and soon returned to Toronto with a girlfriend.

One night Rick was to join Nick Balkou in watching the Tripp, featuring Neil Merryweather and Stan Endersby, perform at a nightclub, when one of Rick's previous mistakes caught up with him. When Rick entered the nightclub, Endersby says, "he had this lady with him, just drop-dead gorgeous. And she had this address book, and it was just huge, and it had 'John Lennon' and his phone number prominently displayed in it. You could see it from about four feet away." But as the Tripp was playing, the police came in, arrested Rick, and took him out of the club and off to jail. When he'd robbed a Toronto boutique after leaving Detroit, he hadn't worn gloves and had left many fingerprints at the scene. Once the police found his fingerprints, they went to his apartment and discovered that he'd hung the stolen clothes in his closet. He hadn't even removed the tags identifying them as the store's property. Endersby says the girl was crying piteously, and Rick said later he never saw her again.

Merryweather says a waitress in the club remembered the police had been searching for Rick and called them when he walked in. Rick spent nine months in jail for breaking and entering, during which he celebrated his twentieth birthday, on February 1, 1968. Upon his release, he was deported. Although he left as ordered, he continued to go back and forth across the border using phony names and IDs.

While Rick was in the Toronto lockup, he talked by phone with Merryweather, who was buoyed by financial assistance from John Eaton. The two agreed that Merryweather would begin putting together another band in anticipation of Rick's release. Because Rick remained in custody longer than anyone had planned, however, this new Mynah Birds group, which still included Cockburn, changed its name to the Flying Circus and began scoring gigs with big-time stars like Jimi Hendrix and Wilson Pickett. Later that year, when Rick was released and summoned the band to his side, their career without him had taken off, and they turned him down.

Momentarily lacking a band, or any alternative, Rick returned to Motown once again as Ricky Matthews. He worked as a producer and songwriter for several major Motown acts, including Smokey Robinson and the Miracles, the Spinners, the Marvelettes, and the Four Tops, but as he later put it to one interviewer, he spent most of his time "working with all the little people there."

Among them was the group the Originals and a new Motown group, Bobby Taylor & the Vancouvers, who recorded and released Rick's song "Dorinda"—renamed "Malinda"—in 1968. The authorship of this song has long been disputed on the Internet because it was officially credited to Al Cleveland, Terry Johnson, and Smokey Robinson. However, LeRoi Johnson says Rick wrote it in Buffalo; that he, Johnson, was with Rick in Detroit when he first played the song for Smokey Robinson; and that the only change made in the song was when Robinson changed the name of the tune from "Dorinda" to "Malinda." Back then, many record companies, including Motown, made a habit of assigning songwriting credit on numerous songs to people who hadn't actually written the songs, or to those who had only made suggestions for the alteration of those songs. Such credits could mean substantial publishing royalties for those to whom the songwriting credits were assigned.

It's appropriate, in any case, that Bobby Taylor & the Vancouvers released Rick's song because they had a Canadian background, having performed in both Calgary and Vancouver. They were also multiracial: among the group's members were whites, blacks, an Australian aborigine, and Tommy Chong, a half-white, half-Chinese Canadian. (While in Calgary this group called themselves the Calgary Shades and then, for a short time, adopted the shocking name Four Niggers and a Chink, later shortened to Four N's and a C.) Chong, with his humor only slightly tempered, later went on to become half of the comedy duo Cheech and Chong.

Via its Gordy label, Motown released "Malinda" as a track on the LP *Bobby Taylor and the Vancouvers* and as a single. (The group had altered its membership by the time this LP was released.) The album rose to number 20 on the *Billboard* R&B (black) album chart and was released for a second time as a CD in 1994, while the single rose to number 16 on the R&B chart, stayed on that chart for nine weeks, and hit number 48 on the *Billboard* popular music (white) chart. It also became one of only four singles recorded by Bobby Taylor & the Vancouvers ever to hit any chart anywhere.

The success of "Malinda" says a great deal about Rick's talent and potential: the very first song he had written to be recorded and released became a Top 20 R&B hit. Released at the height of Motown's popularity, it shows very few traces of Rick's later work and a great deal of Motown's at its height. It's dominated by a black male soprano vocalist (Bobby Taylor, who sounds something like Smokey Robinson), catchy, present-tense lyrics, a heavy background beat, and a beautifully harmonized background chorus. Its lyrics are an inside-out version of Mary Wells's "My Guy," a major hit in 1964, in that the male vocalist in "Malinda" talks about how devoted Malinda is to him.

Soon after "Malinda" was released, Taylor discovered the Jackson 5, brought them to Motown (Diana Ross has been erroneously credited with discovering them), and began producing them. This occupied so much of his time that Taylor left the Vancouvers and became a solo Motown artist.

Rick was among the Motown writers employed to write the songs for Taylor's first solo LP for Motown, *Taylor Made Soul*. Rick's contribution, "Out in the Country," was a somewhat upbeat song obviously influenced by "I Wish It Would Rain," a hit Norman Whitfield had written for the Temptations. Although "Out in the Country" was not a hit on any chart and was never released as a single, Rick—along with Ronald Matlock and Roderick Harrison—was credited as one of the song's official writers. This indicated that his stock at the company was rising.

The success of "Malinda" aside, Rick saw no future for himself at Motown. "I was no Holland-Dozier-Holland," he said. "I just could not get to work" with artists such as the Supremes, the Temptations, Marvin Gaye, or Diana Ross, or make much money. Frustrated, he headed back to Toronto in 1968 with the aim of recruiting a new group that would back him as a Motown performer.

Rick took the unusual step of breaking into former Mynah Birds member Rickman Mason's house through a back window to ask Mason, who was alarmed, surprised, and flattered all at once, to join the band Rick intended to form. Mason later said he would have gone with Rick except that he wanted to take his drums with him, and a dispute over their ownership prevented him from doing so.

One of those who agreed to accompany Rick was Neil Merryweather, the musician whose mother-in-law had been charmed by Rick's rendition of "Till the End of Time." Merryweather had recently quit his band after a dispute. Rick took advantage of that charm when he realized the keyboard player he was hiring was too young to sign a contract with Motown. In a demonstration of the power of Rick's appeal to women of all ages, he convinced Merryweather's mother-in-law to fly to Detroit, pose illegally as the keyboard player's guardian, affirm illegally that he was seventeen, and illegally cosign his contract with Motown, allowing him to work at Motown in Rick's new band.

With another Rick James band back at Motown, its first task was to record a new version of "It's My Time," since none of the band members who recorded that number were still at Motown except Rick. In June 1968 the mostly new band also cut two new songs, "Masquerade" and "Fantasy." They then resumed their role as track makers, with Motown producer R. Dean Taylor resuming his role as overseer.

Everything was running like clockwork for about a month. Then one day Rick asked one of his new recruits, guitar player Bill Ross, to play a certain riff. Ross refused, Rick insisted, and Ross responded with the n-word. Rick was hardly the type to take such an insult without reacting physically. "Rick was wearing a white dress shirt," Merryweather says, "and he actually rolled up his sleeves. I couldn't believe it. It was like a scene from an old movie. Then he grabbed Bill and pushed him into the band's drum set, causing him to fall over. Ross then got up, took his guitar, and threw it at the control room window, which was sturdy enough to bounce the guitar back into the studio."

At that point the drummer, Al Morrison, alarmed by the whole fight, sided with Ross against Rick. Both Ross and Morrison quit. The young keyboard player that Merryweather's mother-in-law had perjured herself for "just disappeared," Merryweather says.

12

Rick Quits Motown in Disgust
and Forms Salt 'n Pepper

Rick carried himself like a rock star before he was a rock star.

—Malcolm Tomlinson

Once again, Rick's rise at Motown had stalled. His Motown career was not aided by the fact that Gordy was spending most of his time in Los Angeles, and the word was that the company would soon leave Detroit and join him there.

But Rick had made friends with Motown bass player Greg Reeves, who also was discontented, mostly because he was earning only thirty-eight dollars a week as a session musician. The two men quit Motown and headed to Los Angeles in the summer of 1969 in search of opportunity. Both vaguely hoped they might hitch a lift on the rising star of their old friend Neil Young, who by then was playing in Crosby, Stills, Nash & Young.

Rick and Reeves first formed their own band, which included drummer Steve Rumph, guitarist Michael Rummans, and a keyboard player. The new recruits were impressed by Rick's skills and charisma and also by the fact that Reeves had honed his craft with legendary Motown bass man James Jamerson. Because the band included both white and black musicians, Rick named it Salt 'n Pepper.

The band started rehearsing, and around May 1969 Rick and Reeves visited a Crosby, Stills, Nash & Young rehearsal to watch their old friends Young and Palmer in action. Reeves was invited to jam with the group, and the band recognized his talent. They soon pushed Palmer out of the band so Reeves could take his place as bassist.

Although Palmer had greased his own exit chute with numerous drug arrests and a reputation for unreliability, he held a grudge against Rick for bringing Reeves around for some time after his dismissal. He studied kung fu and fantasized it would enable him to take revenge on Rick; he was wrong. According to Stan Endersby, for a few months after Palmer's firing, whenever he would see Rick "he'd start this kung fu thing with Rick, and Rick would say 'Don't fuck with me, Bruce. Stop it.' But Palmer wouldn't stop, and Rick would beat him up."

Palmer temporarily forgot about his grudge against Rick the following year, when he solicited some jazzy scat vocals from Rick for his only solo album, *The Cycle Is Complete*. The record, which one critic described as an "aural, drug-induced nervous breakdown," was a commercial failure. Years later Palmer would ask Rick for more help, after Rick had started another band, White Cane. Rick Abel, who was working as the road manager for White Cane at the time, says Palmer "was trying to get a gig . . . or wanted to get into the band, 'cause he was broke and needed money." Rick declined. "Rick got pissed off, and Rick and Bruce got into this big knock-down, drag-out [fight], swinging and punching, going at it tooth and nail."

Even with Reeves gone, Salt 'n Pepper came together as a band and began to look like the group that would carry Rick to stardom. And it almost did. In the spring of 1970, Salt 'n Pepper opened for the English prog band Renaissance at the Whisky a Go Go in West Hollywood, and for Jethro Tull, Fairport Convention, and Clouds at the Fillmore West in San Francisco.

But one member of the group just wasn't working out, and Rick got a chance to show how well he could handle personnel matters when it suited him. Chris Sarns, formerly the equipment manager for Crosby, Stills, Nash & Young, had been added to Salt 'n Pepper to replace

Reeves, but Rick had decided he had to go. "Rick told me face to face, 'I'm replacing you. I'm letting you go,'" Sarns says. "He had the balls to face me and just say it like it was. For that he gets my undying respect."

What Rick told the other band members was that Sarns "was too white and folksy" for the band. Sarns's replacement was a bass player named Ron Johnson, a black musician who wore an old floppy-rim cowboy hat over one eye and spoke in a very deep, funky voice. Johnson, who became the only black band member other than Rick, was definitely not folksy. At one point, wanting to compliment a fellow musician, he looked over at him and said, "You stink." The musician in question shot back, "Whaddya mean I stink?" and Johnson replied, "You stink of funk." Johnson talked to concert audiences the same way. He would get up onstage and ask the audience, in an even deeper, funkier voice than usual, "Are you ready to taste the jam?" The audiences were.

Another white musician said Johnson once took him to his home neighborhood in East L.A. in the 1960s, "and black guys were yelling because a 'whitey'" was present. But Johnson told them, in his trademark deep voice, "Lay off him; he's pretty funky," and they did.

With the nucleus solidified, things were going well for the band. Word soon reached them that Phil Walden of Capricorn Records in Macon, Georgia, was coming to L.A. Walden was no small-time desk jockey at the label; for one thing he was the manager of the incredibly successful Allman Brothers Band. Somehow Rick convinced Walden to visit the band at their house. When he arrived, everyone was rehearsing and smoking in the garage, which was dense with cigarette and pot smoke. Nevertheless, they played for him then and there. Walden "was just blown away," and not by the smoke.

Walden got the band an audition with Atlantic Records, a major record company that distributed Capricorn's discs. Atlantic executives liked the music and told the band to go to Miami to record at Criteria Recording Studios with legendary producer Tom Dowd, who had popularized the multitrack recording method. Famous acts, including Fleetwood Mac and Aretha Franklin, had recorded at Criteria under Dowd's tutelage.

It's difficult to overstate the importance of such an opportunity. "Here we were," said one of the band members, "signed with the Allman Brothers' manager, with Atlantic Records, and with Tom Dowd, living legend, who was supposed to produce us in the best studio in the south. . . . But we didn't have enough money to live on."

The band had been paid an advance to take care of such things, but the members said Rick had kept it for drugs. "I think it was obvious around this time that he was putting quite a bit of money into coke," one band member, who requested anonymity, says. Weisman says advances were often going up Rick's nose by this point, and the rest of the band had to make do with next to nothing.

Stuck in Miami in the summer, with the band rehearsing in a hot church basement without air-conditioning, Rick kept calling Walden in Macon, Georgia, to try to get more money out of him. He called him so many times Walden no longer responded, so Rick decided to go over Walden's head to Atlantic Records executive Jerry Wexler in New York City.

Wexler was a top Atlantic exec, who allegedly had coined the term "rhythm and blues." He had signed or produced numerous stars, including Ray Charles, Aretha Franklin, Wilson Pickett, and Bob Dylan, and was one of the most highly regarded artist and repertoire (A&R) execs in popular music. He knew Salt 'n Pepper had been given an advance, sent to a large music store to buy guitars, saxophones, and other instruments, and assigned to Walden.

Apparently Wexler told Walden to get rid of the band, and Walden wasted no time. The day before the band was to begin recording, they were scheduled to enter the recording studio for the first time to meet Dowd, their producer, and get a feel for the place. According to one of the musicians present, a music exec named Bunky Odom walked into the studio shortly after they did, and Dowd began to look uncomfortable, probably because he knew why Odom was there. "I'm from Mr. Phil's [Walden's] office," Odom said. "I understand you guys are not happy."

"We all started talking," one musician says. "'Yeah, we're not happy. We're not getting any money. We've got nothing to live on. Blah Blah Blah Blah.' So Bunky says, 'Well, I'm prepared to give you your release.' And we said, 'Yeah, give us our release. Screw it!'" (Odom did not reply to a request for an interview for this book.)

The group signed the release right there in the studio. "Nobody thought we should see a lawyer about this," the musician says. "Rick thought we could do anything," one band member says. "We felt that we were just on this shooting star, and were damned good." Dowd, who had been about to record their album, shrugged and said, "You're not with us anymore." And the next thing the band members knew, they were back in L.A. "We gave all our equipment back, and that was that," one member said.

Rick later told David Ritz the breakup with Atlantic occurred because the band never received the promised advance and the company had refused to give the band an air-conditioned house to practice in or the equipment they needed.

It wasn't quite the end for Salt 'n Pepper. They hooked up with Gabriel Mekler, producer of Three Dog Night and Steppenwolf, who said he wanted to produce the band for one of his own labels, Lizard Records. Salt 'n Pepper also met with an agent from Columbia Records—who listened to the band and said he loved their music—and with Bob Maurice, the producer of the movie *Woodstock*, who expressed an interest in them. But nothing happened. One band member speculates they'd been blackballed for their behavior at Atlantic.

Mekler, trying to start something for the band, got them a one-week gig in a soul club in Sacramento. On their first night, Rick "was straining or something and blew a blood vessel in his throat," one band member says. "It could have been coke, but we were smoking a lot and drinking a lot of Courvoisier too." This band member remembers that they were even putting Courvoisier on their pancakes in the morning after Ron Johnson introduced them to the practice.

The club owner thought he had hired a psychedelic band, which they weren't, and after Rick's throat had been disabled, all they could perform were instrumentals. Nevertheless, Salt 'n Pepper "actually jelled in Sacramento," one band member says. The band then returned to Los Angeles. While they were there, Rick recorded some jazz vocals, and he and Ron Johnson played congas and bass on a cover of Sam Cooke's song "A Change Is Gonna Come."

But no change occurred. In fact, nothing happened. Salt 'n Pepper was through. Rick wrote in his autobiography that Salt 'n Pepper had broken up "mainly because I lost interest. I just wasn't ready to make music yet."

13

Rick Has Two Children with One Woman and Marries a Second

Some girls give me jewelry, others buy me clothes,
some girls give me children I never asked them for.

—"Some Girls," Rolling Stones, by Mick Jagger and Keith Richards (1978)

While Rick later became a rampant womanizer, his initial forays into serious relationships, which took place around 1969, were much more conventional.

He met Syville Morgan, a young African American woman, at a party in Hollywood in the late 1960s. They rented a Hollywood apartment together. Syville "had the ability to cook her ass off," Rick wrote in his autobiography, *The Confessions of Rick James*. "I mean, there was never a time when I didn't wake up to a serious meal. That's how she kept me there."

"We were pretty hot and heavy," Syville says. "He was fun, funny, intriguing, had a great sense of humor, and always kept me laughing." She became pregnant soon after they moved in together. However, their relationship became rocky after a few months because Rick was snorting a lot of cocaine and smoking a lot of pot.

Late in 1969 Rick, who was doing a lot of traveling around for singing gigs, got work at a club in Toronto and met Kelly Misener, a pretty, white eighteen-year-old Canadian student at the North Toronto Collegiate Institute. They soon began an affair.

On July 13, 1970, Syville gave birth to her and Rick's daughter in Los Angeles. Tyenza Matthews, now known as Ty James, was Rick's first child. About two years later, Syville became pregnant with Rick's second child, Ricardo Matthews, now known as Rick James Jr. Soon after Syville became pregnant, Rick admitted to her that he had been having an affair with Kelly, and he and Kelly moved into a house in Toronto together.

Syville was angry. "Can you imagine Rick telling me that he was going to be with this girl in Canada when I was pregnant with his child?" she says. Rick added insult to injury by marrying Kelly a couple years later. Syville remarks, "He married Kelly and wouldn't marry me, when I had his children and I was in love with him!"

Kelly was very attractive, but Chris Sarns says Rick's motivation for breaking up with Syville was deeper than that. "Rick didn't want anything to do with parenthood," he says. After growing up without a father, Rick had no desire to be one—he had no idea how it was done. Syville began raising Rick's children alone.

Rick's attorney, Stan Weisman, says Kelly was "very beautiful. . . . I'll compare her with any girl out there, ever." He also describes her as being "very nice, probably too nice for Rick," and adds Kelly "was a wise, intelligent, and clever woman." He admits he was surprised when Kelly took up with Rick.

Rick Abel had similar recollections of Kelly. "She wasn't wild," he says. "I think she smoked pot, but it was never like she was the party girl." He also opines that Kelly "didn't seem like the type of person that would be with Rick at all."

Levi Ruffin says Kelly cultured Rick somewhat. "Remember, Rick wasn't a really educated guy," Ruffin says. "She taught him how to order wine, things like that, things that he would never have learned because he never had the opportunity. She taught him how to be a gentleman." Nevertheless, even after this training, "sometimes Rick would be an asshole 'cause he was just Rick," Ruffin says. "He couldn't help it sometimes. But we were crazy about Kelly." Kelly and Ruffin's wife, Jackie, became very close.

So why was this lovely and intelligent woman with Rick? In a statement that perhaps explains how Rick got (and got away with) most things, Kelly once told Nick Warburton that Rick "had an uncanny knack of endearing himself to people. He was quite a charming guy."

This charming guy was about to create his best band yet.

14

Rick Creates Heaven and Earth . . . and Then Destroys Both

There are more things in heaven and earth, Horatio,
than are dreamt of in your philosophy.

—*Hamlet*, William Shakespeare

Rick, never discouraged for long, was looking around for an opportunity to form another band when he stumbled across bass player Neil Merryweather once again. Merryweather had stayed with Rick's band after Rick had been arrested for deserting the navy but had left the group after it changed its name to Flying Circus. He then formed another band in Toronto, moved that band to Los Angeles in late 1968, and changed its name to Merryweather. Merryweather the band then recorded two albums for Capitol Records. But by the fall of 1969, Merryweather the person was having trouble with his fellow musicians, as well as with his girlfriend.

Rick, always on the move, was back in town and had found out where Merryweather and his band were living. As Rick was driving toward their motel, Merryweather and his girlfriend, Lynn, were arguing in a bedroom in one of the motel's suites. When Merryweather left the bedroom angrily in the middle of the argument, his guitar player, in Merryweather's words, "stepped into the argument like Mr. Macho

Man." Merryweather looked to his drummer for support, but "he didn't back me up. Which got to me emotionally, so basically I erupted." He walked out of the motel. "There was Rick, coming to see me. I was still mad and disgusted, so I said, 'Rick? You want a band? Take it, it's yours.'" Merryweather then walked away and did not return.

Merryweather says he regretted this incident partly because he gave up his band's seven-year Capitol Records contract with this one hot-headed gesture. He also hadn't been told the band had been booked to do some concerts a week later with John Mayall, a popular English blues singer, which would have been lucrative and given the band some great exposure.

Merryweather's regrets aside, Rick had now solved the problem of having no band. The one he now led included Pat Little, Ed Roth, David Burt, Coffi Hall, Denny Gerrard, and Chris Sarns. They were all good musicians, but they were very short on equipment. A lot of it had been consumed or destroyed as they rambled from one cheap motel, crowded slum, condemned apartment, or porous communal band house to another. They had very little money and spent it on renting places where they could all stay.

Rick's reaction to the problem was to go out walking with some of the band members. That was rational at the time, Roth says. It was L.A. in 1970, when, according to Roth, "Everybody was in the streets, looking for the answer." As they were walking along, Roth says, they heard some people chanting in a room just off the street, another fairly common occurrence at the time. They walked in and started chanting with the group. Roth says they couldn't understand the chants, which sounded like they were in another language, so they started chanting in plain English about how much they wanted and needed new equipment.

During breaks in the chanting, Roth started talking with another chanter named Eddie Singleton about their equipment needs. A few chants later, Singleton told Roth, "I like the way you talk. I've got a band, and all their gear's in storage. I'm going to let you use their stuff." Roth insists the chanting was what did it but also admits he had been studying the book *This Business of Music*, the classic guide to the music business, and apparently had learned enough from it to impress Singleton.

At the time, Singleton, whose band was named Von Ryan's Express (after the 1965 movie of the same name starring Frank Sinatra), was married to the former Raynoma Gordy, the ex-wife of Motown president Berry Gordy. Singleton had recently resigned as a Motown company executive and journeyed to Los Angeles while his wife remained in Detroit. After this chanting introduction, he became more and more involved with Rick and Rick's new band.

A short while later Raynoma Gordy joined her husband in Los Angeles, and she met Rick on her first day in town. In her book, *Berry, Me, and Motown*, she described Rick as "funny and warm, with tons of talent pouring out of him. At this juncture, he was a very nice, clean-cut, ordinary-looking guy with short hair. He didn't think of himself as an R&B or soul singer at all. He was a black kid who loved rock, probably idolized Jimi Hendrix, and hung out with all the rowdy white boys."

Soon afterward, some of these rowdy white boys—the members of Rick's new band, which he had renamed Heaven and Earth—moved into a band house in a Los Angeles suburb. It had previously been occupied by actress Katharine Ross when she was filming *The Graduate*. Red was her favorite color, so Ross had painted the refrigerator red, and letters in red envelopes kept arriving for her in the mail. The band members also noted with glee that the house included both a pool and a garage; although it was a one-story house, they found a way to climb out onto the roof and rehearse in the sun. Their neighbor, who also was their landlord, loved them and loved their playing, and didn't discourage them.

"We were writing music, all the time," all through 1970, Ed Roth says. "I was writing like crazy, everybody was writing, but Rick had a little bit of Motown savvy in him, and was somehow able to pull all this writing into one cohesive whole. We were starting to jell into something beyond our individual capacities and getting really strong."

They were also recognizing Rick's varied musical talents. "We'd be in the band house at night, and he'd start doing Swahili chants," says one musician. "He'd just go on forever." Rick was also a great percussionist, playing the timbales and conga drums.

Of course, he also had his limitations. "He'd pick up a guitar and start strumming it, and I'd think, 'This guy can't play guitar to save his life,'" one musician says. Handed a trumpet, he'd figure out something to play on it, but he never could finish the song. Moreover, former band members said, he had a hard time converting his ideas for the words of a song into finished lyrics.

Rick's larcenous streak also remained evident. According to one member of Heaven and Earth, "Musically, we were constantly fiddling around. I'd pick up the guitar and start strumming, and before you know it, he's singing something on top of it, and then it becomes his song. Before one record was actually released, he came around and said the record company wanted me to sign some stuff, and apparently I signed away my publishing to Rick, for two hundred dollars."

Rick was larcenous with record companies as well. Chris Sarns says Rick would sign record contracts with other companies when he already had a contract with one company, "with no intention of living up to anything" in the new contract. All Rick wanted was the cash advance he would demand for signing. Sarns says Rick would tell lie after lie to the executives involved.

This didn't upset those in Rick's circle then as much as it would now. As several of the musicians pointed out, they were all young guys just trying to get ahead in the antiestablishment 1960s, a period in which moneymaking was scorned and the word "careerist" was used as an epithet. Music and fame were their main concerns, drugs and girls were in second place, and money ranked dead last.

Touchingly, they continued to rely on Rick to help them if they got into trouble. And he was always there when those he cared about needed him. Stan Endersby says that when he was undergoing a painful convalescence from a medical procedure and couldn't work, Rick offered him $20,000 to tide him over. "I didn't need it, so I didn't take it," Endersby says, "but if I had said 'Rick, I need $20,000,' he would have given it to me."

Endersby was probably right. When Rick finally did reach the top, he'd make gestures such as taking thirty-seven band members, crew members, roadies, security people, and valets to Maui, Hawaii, for a two-week vacation at his expense, or renting a theater so the band could watch movies in it for the whole day. One year he donated $125,000 to a Buffalo charity to provide Christmas dinner for the poor. He gave $10,000 to a guy he grew up with. He gave another $10,000 to his friend Peter Kelly after he was released from jail so he could buy a car. He bought Levi Ruffin an 18-carat gold Cartier watch as a Christmas present one year. And eventually he gave out mounds of cocaine for free night after night, very often not only to his friends but to anyone who showed up.

While Salt 'n Pepper had been dissolving, Endersby had gone to England and returned to Canada and had used his contacts to help an English sound engineer land a job at a Toronto recording studio. The engineer returned the favor by offering Endersby some free studio time, which Endersby offered to Heaven and Earth.

Heaven and Earth was a potential winner. The band signed a recording deal with RCA Victor, recorded some songs, and actually saw some of them released. Rick kept the advance, as usual. But the band members didn't mind too much, because RCA was recording them.

Two of the tunes they recorded, "Together People" and "Suite to a Soldier," were never released. But four were, two on one 45 single in 1971 and two on another in 1972. On the first disc was "Big Showdown" (credited to James Johnson Jr.), with "Don't You Worry" on the flip side. The second disc carried "You Make the Magic," which Rick and band member Mike McKenna cowrote, backed with "Rip Off 1500." (Rick was identified on the label as James Johnson Jr.) According to Endersby, "Rip Off 1500," which has been described as a "funk instrumental," was a song about the time Rick borrowed $1,500 to buy coke and never paid back the Canadian tape operator who had lent him the money.

"Big Showdown," "Don't You Worry," and "You Make the Magic" were big moves forward for Rick in the sense that none of them sounded like the Stones. But all three were average bouncy rock 'n' roll songs of the era, with nothing particular to distinguish them from many others.

None of the tunes made the charts. Rick was not pleased, but he had a bigger problem. With his drug habit growing, and having already spent the whole band's advance, he needed another contract to keep the drugs flowing. Telling his lawyer, Weisman, he "didn't like RCA," he demanded Weisman "get [the band] out of the contract."

Weisman was appalled. "I was taught in law school that a contract is binding," he says. Nevertheless, bound by legal codes of conduct to follow his client's instructions, Weisman made an appointment to see Barry Keane, RCA's A&R man, who later became a drummer for Gordon Lightfoot. "I was hemming and hawing" about how Rick didn't like RCA, he said, when Keane interrupted and said, "RCA likes our artists to be happy. If he's not happy, we'll give him a release." Weisman says he took the release and immediately "went back a hero" to Rick.

Unfortunately Heaven and Earth's departure from RCA also marked the dissolution of the band.

15

Rick Breaks His New White Cane

White cane lying in a gutter in the lane if you're walking home alone . . .

—"Don't Let It Bring You Down," Neil Young (1970)

Now free of his obligations to RCA, Rick and two Heaven and Earth members, Denny Gerrard and Ed Roth, started a new band in early 1972: White Cane.

The source of the name has long been disputed by Rick's former bandmates. Because Rick liked cocaine, which is white, and *Cane* can be read to mean '*Caine*, many believe the name reflected Rick's enthusiasm for the drug. The theory that White Cane and white cocaine were linked was strengthened during the band's first rehearsal in what guitarist Nick Balkou calls the "dingy little basement" of a house Rick was renting in Toronto. The various band members, some of whom did not know each other well, were trying awkwardly to get acquainted in the house's smoke-filled, unventilated basement when, Balkou says, "Rick came downstairs in a flurry and plumped this bag on the table." It was a quarter ounce of cocaine.

Rick said, "'OK, boys, come on, line up, then we're rehearsing,'" Balkou says. He thought Rick might be kidding. "This was my first exposure to cocaine, let alone anything else, and we dove right in. Of course we all thought we were amazing after all that coke." Even decades later, Balkou seemed grateful to Rick for exposing him to a new world. "Sex, drugs, and rock 'n' roll . . . that was the essence of what Rick was all about," Balkou says.

On the *Great White Cane* album the band produced, its members were identified as Rick, singing lead vocals and playing congas, timbales, and percussion; J. Cleveland Hughes, an African Canadian, on percussion and vibraphone; Ian Kojima, an Asian Canadian, playing saxophone; Ed Roth on flute, piano, and organ; Nick Balkou (now using the name Sonny Nicholas) on lead and rhythm guitar; Norman Wellbanks on drums and percussion; Bob "Cool Breeze" Doughty on trumpet and euphonium; and Denny "Pookie" Gerrard on bass. Balkou was also listed as a songwriter and arranger, though under his given name.

Doughty says that after that initial rehearsal, the band reworked some of the songs from Milestone, Doughty's former band, as well as some Heaven and Earth songs, and recorded a sixteen-track demo tape. Shortly thereafter, the White Cane musicians moved to LA. to seek a record contract.

They started their new stay in town with a scam. According to their financial backer, Weisman, "I'm renting all this stuff for them and the van to take it down there to L.A. They call me, tell me they're renting two apartments, and send me pictures of the apartments." The band told him they needed rent money each month, so Weisman sent it for an extended period. Then he found out they were living in two condemned apartments for which they paid no rent.

With eight band members—plus Rick Abel, girlfriends, and pets— the two apartments were somewhat crowded. Abel considered himself lucky to be given the hall closet in the entranceway to one of the apartments as his sleeping area. His dog, a Great Dane, slept outside the closet door, protecting his privacy. Rick James lived elsewhere. The band members occupied the two apartments for about seven months while searching for a record deal.

In Abel's view, Rick James's modus operandi at the time, while seeking a record deal, was "to bring in musicians who were good players but nobody of repute, set them up somewhere where he would more or less provide housing for them, and more or less provide them with the common necessities." The necessities provided in this case, Abel says, were basically one meal a day and all the pot you could smoke. Whenever one of the band members would receive five or ten dollars in the mail from their parents, "we'd go down to the grocery store and buy old dented cans of SpaghettiOs or whatever," Abel says.

The apartment they were living in certainly provided them with entertainment. According to Abel, the building next door was a house of prostitution, and the windows of the apartments in which the women entertained their guests were at most ten feet away from theirs. The band members needed only to open their windows on a nice evening to be serenaded by the sounds of active sex from their hardworking neighbors. A similar operation was going on down the hall from their own digs. On one occasion the band members heard screaming in the hallway only to see one of the prostitutes bolting out of her apartment and running down the hall until she was tackled by a man, presumably her pimp, who then dragged her back into the room by her hair.

The most dramatic event, however, occurred one night when the band was sitting around one of their apartments smoking pot. Suddenly a pot smoker's worst nightmare occurred: two LAPD cops in uniform with drawn guns burst through the door. The toking band members were instantly paralyzed with fear, but then they noticed the cops had their fingers over their lips, warning them to keep quiet. The two cops crept up the apartment's internal stairway to a door leading to an upper hallway that ran behind a higher apartment, where they soon arrested some of the band's neighbors. They did not return to the band members' apartment, throwing those musicians who had seen them into a cascade of relief.

In return for this level of existence, all the musicians were required to do was rehearse, except on the rare occasions they landed a club gig somewhere. But mostly they sat around and smoked pot. When asked why he stuck around, Abel says, "It was just that I had nothing else going on. I was nineteen and dumb, and ambitious at the time but not exactly an overachiever."

Also keeping him around was his admiration for the band's skill. They had recorded a cassette tape of their musical numbers and played it for him when he joined the band's crew. "I was like, 'These guys are wow! They are actually good." He was impressed that they weren't doing cover tunes, that each and every one of the tunes they were rehearsing was an original composition, and that Rick had written most of them.

Abel says the band's music was reminiscent of the music produced by Chicago, rock music with brass and soul in it. He also says he heard the California rock of the time in the music, a sort of Mother Earth theme, because Rick "liked to get real cosmic and all that."

Abel, whose job at the time was restricted to setting up and taking down the band's equipment, says, "It wasn't like we had a lot of things to do besides practice, so Rick would regale us with his stories of playing in Toronto with the Mynah Birds and Stephen Stills and them, and how he really got a little bit of that California rock 'n' roll under his skin."

Although the White Cane's music was good and they had hopes for the future, the band members were not exactly living the American dream. So they were thrilled when they were invited through a friend of a friend to a huge barbecue party at the expansive Beverly Hills house of the Chambers Brothers, who had been very famous during the 1960s and were still hanging on in the 1970s.

"This was like Christmas, New Year's, and everything else rolled into one," Abel says. "We were going to a party!" Unfortunately his car had broken down and been towed away, and he certainly did not have the money to recover it. But a friend of his was visiting from Toronto and agreed to ferry the band members across town to the party in his Volkswagen in groups of two or three.

The party was not scheduled to start until 2:00 PM, but the hungry band members showed up at noon. "We arranged to get there at the earliest moment we thought we could arrive without being way out of line," Abel says. Although the caterers were still setting out the huge feast for the 150 or so expected guests, the band members were grudgingly allowed in. They were ecstatic to encounter large barrels filled with ribs, chicken, and shrimp and other barrels full of beer and wine, and immediately began an eating and drinking marathon. By the time various celebrities arrived, including Three Dog Night, the White Cane musicians were close to unconsciousness.

After darkness fell, Abel was sitting in the dining room talking to the other guests when, he says, "It sounded like someone was spilling a pitcher of water on the carpet," and he heard people gasping. He shouldered his way to the scene of the disturbance and found out that one of the White Cane band members, who had been snoozing in a chair in the living room "in a comatose, catatonic state" after eating and drinking heavily, had suddenly stood up, pulled out his penis, and urinated for some time on the carpet in front of all and sundry, including many who had brought their small children to this allegedly family-friendly event. Several guests frog-marched this band member, who still seemed to be asleep, out the front door and shut it behind him.

The Chambers Brothers' manager, livid and embarrassed, ruled that would be the very last party to which he would ever invite White Cane.

Perhaps inspired by the need to escape their decidedly down-market accommodations and attend more Chambers Brothers–type parties, the band performed well at several local gigs. Weisman, while admittedly not a musician, was definitely a music fan, and he liked White Cane. He called them "a horn band, a more driving band, a bigger band" than he'd been involved with before. "It was an exciting band indeed," he says. Motown later called White Cane "an eight piece jazz-rock-funk band."

Weisman particularly complimented the bass player, Denny Gerrard, calling him "phenomenal and fantastic. He had fingers. Gerrard's bass playing would come out so loud, you could hear it clearly over all those nine musicians." The band played so well it was invited to negotiate an album contract with Mike Curb, the president of MGM Records, for that company's Lion Records label.

Curb took exception to the band's name because he said it promoted the use of illegal drugs. (In 1970 Curb had dropped eighteen MGM acts he said promoted drug use through their music. Partly due to his anti-drug stance, he was elected lieutenant governor of California in 1978.) Rick attempted to overcome Curb's objections by telling him *Cane* referred to sugarcane and that the band was "sweet as sugar." Curb was not convinced. When Rick said the band would leave if Curb insisted on a name change, and promised to produce no songs promoting drugs, Curb finally backed down.

Balkou says the name of the album the band produced, *Great White Cane*, was actually meant to indicate disgust with society in general. He points out that the cartoonish cane-like figure on the cover of the album the band eventually produced had a third eye, and that third eye was blind, indicating society's alleged blindness. This interpretation is clouded by the fact that it's not clear which, if any, of the figure's three eyes is not functional, and the "eyes" are actually drawn as sunglasses.

Some saw the name and the figure as a direct reference to blind and other visually impaired people, who often carry white canes, and Rick was aware of this potential meaning. When he and Bob Doughty drove past a big banner with a white cane on it that was being displayed by the Canadian National Institute for the Blind, Rick joked about the banner being a reference to the band.

Abel supports the idea that blindness, rather than cocaine, was the origin of the name, claiming that it was lifted from a verse from the Neil Young classic "Don't Let It Bring You Down": "Blind man running through the light of the night with an answer in his hand . . . white cane lying in a gutter in the lane if you're walking home alone." Maybe Rick wanted to let his former bandmate know that Rick remembered him.

When the band members, still living in abandoned apartments, were told they'd been signed by a big record company, "Oh God, it was like nirvana," Abel says. Abel, as the band roadie, received $500 as his portion of the advance, "which seemed like a fortune at the time," he says. Each musician received approximately $1,000. This wasn't much, considering the advance was for $250,000, but Rick said at the time that the band would have to pay production costs out of that amount.

"It was nothing really much, but to us it was *owowowowowowow*," Abel says, "and we just went shit crazy. I don't think anybody ever appreciated money more in their lives than that time." Everybody had been wearing the same clothes for months and eating communal stew, so the first thing they did was go out to eat up a big storm at the local Howard Johnson and then buy clothes. Abel bought two double-knit jumpsuits and some high-heeled sneakers. He then bought a big kidney belt, like a weight lifter would wear, at a leather store and had his nickname, Tex, hand-tooled on the back of it. "I was a sight," he says.

In February 1972 the band began recording the album at The Village, a big studio off Wilshire Boulevard. With eerie predictive power, at least as far as White Cane was concerned, the outer wall of the studio displayed a mural showing the ruins of an elevated portion of a huge L.A. freeway after an imaginary giant earthquake. Cars were driving off the ruined road into the ocean.

The studio itself was state-of-the-art. The songs the band recorded there that ended up on the resulting album are "Country Woman Suite," consisting of the three songs: "Country Woman" and "Get On Down" written by Rick, and "Time Is My Keeper," by Balkou and Rick.

Also on the album are the slow, bluesy, eight-minute-long, environmentally concerned "Mother Earth," by Rick and Roth, and "Find It" by Rick and Balkou. The album also contains three songs that are rerecordings of tunes already sung by Heaven and Earth: "You Make the Magic," by Rick and Mike McKinnon, and "Don't You Worry" and "Big Showdown," both by Rick.

Abel says that because Rick had been playing with Neil Young and Bruce Palmer just before they pole-vaulted to superstardom, the band's songs were heavily influenced by the styles adopted by both musicians. "You listen to that album," Abel says, "and you hear a lot of 'Country Girl' [a Neil Young song performed by CSNY]. It certainly isn't 'Super Freak.'"

Indeed, on first listen, the tunes on *The Great White Cane* seem to be standard rock 'n' roll songs of the era with some psychedelic and reggae sounds mixed in. But they contain hints of the sound that would make Rick famous, including a sarcastic whine he would later develop into his signature style.

The recording process was chaotic. During the early stages, "Rick kept getting carried away," and the band would lose track, Balkou says. "We'd be jamming out the song, and start off with one thing, and then halfway through it would go someplace else." Balkou says the band "thought that was wonderful because we were so high and didn't know any better, and by the time we came back around to the song, we forgot what the song was about." While the band members "all thought it was fantastic," the result "just never really translated into a recorded song."

At this point, Rick's growing thirst for women, and his willingness to act on it, began to emerge. The band had a communal Volkswagen Beetle, and Balkou says Rick once asked him to use it to drive him to the house of "a couple of ladies in Pasadena." Rick had sex with one, and then the other, while Balkou waited in another room. "I kept asking, 'Where's the fun for me?'" Balkou says, but he never pressed the point.

Another time, the band members were in a restaurant before beginning a recording session. "There was a poor waitress there, in her midforties, maybe fifty," Balkou says. "Rick took her to the back . . . and he did her in the kitchen. Our instructions were to watch the restaurant." Balkou points out that Rick wasn't famous then, and had never met her before, but he did have charisma.

In an attempt to put Rick's sexual exploits in context, Balkou talks about "a Puerto Rican drummer who played with me for a number of years. His name was Mike, he could barely talk, he had a stutter, and he couldn't keep time to save his life. He would start playing and become a runaway train by the end of the song, so we'd get through a set fast. . . . He'd sweat, and he never wore a shirt. But he had a body we'd all kill for, the abs and six-pack." This drummer, Balkou says, would walk up to a group of girls in the audience, sometimes sweating, and say, "Hi, my name's Mike, I'm the drummer, you wanna fuck?'" and often, one of the women would say yes. "He was so cocksure of himself," Balkou says, "yet Rick was one hundred times worse. He knew he was all that and a bag of chips."

Although in later years Rick was accused of abusing women, one musician who lived with him for a year at around this time said he saw no instances of physical abuse. The two men shared a room divided down the middle by a bamboo curtain. From what he could discern through the curtain, this musician says, Rick was "very physically gentle . . . like a lamb" with his female guests. Rick's bandmates were very surprised when they heard much later that Rick had been arrested and charged with abusing women.

In an effort to prep the public for the release of the upcoming album, White Cane soon began touring as an opening act for blues master B. B. King, joining him on his thirteen-city tour. Abel, as a road manager for a mostly white band, wondered why the band was on a B. B. King tour, especially on a bill that also included Gene McDaniels, an older R&B singer. As Abel remembers it, the tour hit the major stops on the so-called Chitlin' Circuit throughout the South, in states such as Mississippi and Alabama. These weren't typical venues for white rock 'n' roll bands, and the usual audience was mostly older black people with just a scattering of white kids. The tour took the band to, among other places, Tacoma, Seattle, Salem, Salt Lake City, Charleston, Jackson, Toledo, Toronto, Providence, Roanoke, Greensboro, Chattanooga, and Vancouver.

Abel admits that the audience "kinda liked" White Cane's performance. He notes, however, that the band's reception was more enthusiastic in major southern cities than in the region's smaller towns.

When the B. B. King tour reached Vancouver, Rick, apparently blind to obvious audience preferences, made a strange mistake. With Rick leading the band, White Cane did their first song, the crowd applauded enthusiastically . . . and then the trouble began. Rick insisted that the group's second song be an a cappella version of the Bob Dylan song "The Times They Are A-Changin'," with the crowd clapping in support. But as Ed Roth noted, it was a B. B. King crowd; people weren't there for folk songs. People refused to clap.

Rick said, "All right, everybody clap their hands!" the musician says. "And no one would clap. He'd say, 'C'mon, put your fuckin' hands together,' and nothing would happen."

After the show, King's road manager visited the band and said to Rick, "Please don't do that," and "Please don't talk like that." Rick's response was, "Don't tell me what to do."

As the tour progressed, the musician says, Rick did exactly the same thing. "It was *Groundhog Day* in slow motion," the person says. "We played every night, and it happened every night, and I don't know how many gigs we did before Toronto. We played Massey Hall in Toronto, which should have been a thrill, but it was the same shit, with him doing that one thing. We'd start with one number that always got a great reaction, and then he'd do this. We'd ask him '*Why* are you *doing* this?' and he'd say, 'Don't tell me what to do.'"

A partial answer to that question may be Rick's feelings about King. Rick complained to Weisman that when King "[came] onstage and start[ed] singing . . . all these old ladies, they [took] off their panties and they [threw] them up there." Weisman's conclusion: Rick was jealous.

Another theory came from Doughty. "Everybody was smoking pot," he says, "but Rick liked the powder [cocaine]." His growing use of the drug may have been swelling his ego at the cost of his rationality. Doughty speculates Rick figured the folk song would hit one night and enable him to become a solo star, which was, after all, his dream. If his plan had worked, according to Doughty, "he'd have cast us off in a minute. With Rick, it's like the first night in a Turkish prison. You've got to watch your back all the time."

But years later, after Rick was a big star, he still occasionally performed such self-destructive singing stunts. A video of Rick performing his later hit song "Super Freak" before an elite music business audience shows him going silent in the middle of the tune. While the background music continues, he then *woop-woops* like a police siren into the microphone and attempts to get the members of the audience to *woop* back. Cameras on the audience show them looking puzzled and not sure what to do. The song and the video then end. "He was like the angel and the demon all in one person," another musician says of Rick. "You never knew which one was going to show up."

Other moves Rick made with White Cane seemed familiar to his associates in previous bands. He had hired Sarns as the band's equipment manager on the tour, and with the last week of that tour approaching, Rick told him, "You don't really expect to get paid for this last week, do you?" Sarns says he "hemmed and hawed" so Rick pocketed Sarns's final check.

Nevertheless, all the band members, including Sarns, stuck with Rick. "Although he went very low, you know that somebody who just keeps pushing like that is . . . going to make it big," Doughty says.

MGM seemed to think Rick and White Cane were on the way to the top. The company made a sincere effort to sell the *Great White Cane* album, sending courtesy copies to numerous media outlets. Its ads for the album called the band "enormously powerful" and "full of thunder and spirit." The ads also touted Rick as "a singer of limitless drive and fire." MGM told *Billboard* they planned to release the tune "You Make the Magic" to promote the album.

The tour, aimed at paving the way for the album, was also going well, in spite of Rick's insistence on trying to convince every audience to clap along. But when the band members reached New York City, spent the night, and gathered at that city's Port Authority Bus Terminal for the Pennsylvania leg of the trip, Rick wasn't there. He had deserted the band, leaving it without a singer.

Weisman was especially frustrated by Rick's disappearance. White Cane "had all the money behind them, the promotion was going on, the album was about to be released, and I think they would have made it to the top this time because that was a hell of a band," he told writer Nick Warburton.

What had happened was that someone had discovered Rick had sold some of the tunes on the MGM-financed album to another record company. "We were all slack-jawed on that one. How could you possibly think you could get away with that?" Doughty says. This wasn't the last time Rick signed contracts for the same music with two or more different companies during his career, a maneuver that pushed this intelligent, ambitious man back toward the bottom of the greasy pole he had been exerting all his energies to climb. The only possible explanation is that he needed the money to feed his drug habit, which had grown into an obsession now that he was using cocaine.

Balkou estimates that by the time Rick disappeared, MGM had already sunk at least $100,000 into the band to press the album, promote it coast-to-coast, and support the band's tour with King. In the end, MGM actually put out very few copies of the album.

Because of commitments already made, the tour continued as planned, without Rick. "Being twenty and naïve," Doughty says, "we figured there's got to be some way to work it out." Balkou says that from then on, he did all the vocals. He says, "The band actually sounded fantastic because we went back to the way we actually rehearsed the songs." But the tour ended in Mississippi and, in Balkou's words, "that was the end of us [as a band]." Along with the rest of the band members, Doughty went home to Toronto. "I don't play in a band anymore," he says.

This ending seemed particularly cruel to the remaining band members, because during the tour, their songs had begun to get airplay, a sign that the album might well have succeeded and elevated them to big-time status.

Rick never took the blame for the mess. In 1978 he told an interviewer that the MGM album and a cross-country tour with B. B. King remained "some of my best musical experiences to this day." He told author David Ritz that Jimmy Ienner, the album's producer, "massacred the band's music," and that production costs, rather than Rick's own nose, had eaten up the $250,000 advance. He said when the album appeared it failed miserably, and MGM president Mike Curb had dropped the band.

Rick also told Ritz that when the record came out in 1972, the music magazines said the band had potential but production of the record sucked. In reality, MGM—aware that Rick's desertion would be fatal to the band and that a functioning band was needed to promote the album—released only the minimum number of album copies required by the contract plus a few promo copies for DJs.

Although cuts from the album are playable on YouTube, many of the album copies now available for purchase are stamped SPECIAL DISC JOCKEY RECORD. NOT FOR SALE.

16

Rick Continues the Pursuit of Glory

We are the music makers, and we are the dreamers of dreams.

—Arthur O'Shaughnessy

Rick soon decided to vary at least part of his pattern by recording his tunes in Toronto and then trying to ride them to fame in the United States. In January 1973 he recorded four songs at the Manta Sound studio in Toronto: "Grim Reaper," "Your Old Man," "Rock and Roll Baby," and "Sally Walker," about Bruce Palmer's wife. It's not clear who played the background music on these recordings, and there's no indication they were ever released.

Rick also became a regular at Daniel Lanois's basement recording studio in Hamilton, Ontario. He sang backup vocals on advertising jingles, then traded his work on the jingles for studio time that he would use to record demos of tunes he was writing. In spite of Rick's somewhat low economic status at the time, he greatly impressed Lanois. Working three hours with Rick, Lanois told the *Los Angeles Times*, was "like five years in a university studying record-making. Inside of 40 minutes you'd have a fully finished production."

Rick also tried his hand at concert promoting. In September 1973 he signed up Kool & the Gang and the Ohio Players to do a concert in Buffalo. These bands were popular at the time, and the planned concert should have done well. But a week prior to the concert, somebody got shot in the theater where the groups were going to perform. Because of that, Weisman says, "mothers would not allow their daughters to go see Kool & the Gang, and the place was half empty."

Rick did only slightly better with his next project. He spent some time in a recording studio, and then called Artie Wayne, an A&M Records executive in Los Angeles, in early 1974 and asked if he could bring in a demo to play for him. "I didn't know him," Wayne wrote in his book *I Did It for a Song*, "but he had been so engaging on the phone that I agreed to listen to his music. I put the needle on the steel acetate, and when the intro started I leaped out of my seat onto the dance floor." (At Stevie Wonder's suggestion, he said, he'd installed a dance floor in his office.) "I could have danced on the ceiling," he wrote.

The record was a bouncy upbeat single called "My Mama." Written by Rick, it included admonitions from his mother that Rick apparently believed with all his heart, such as, "Mama told me to try . . . you can make it if you try." Wayne and A&M executive Kip Cohen immediately offered Rick a record deal and a five-year exclusive songwriting contract.

At this somewhat upbeat point in his up-and-down career, Rick married his girlfriend, Kelly Misener, on April 14, 1974, in a ceremony at his mother's house in Buffalo. Rick's mother put on a big wedding feast. "It was the first time I ever tasted collard greens," Weisman says.

"My Mama" was released shortly thereafter, backed by the funky instrumental "Funkin' Around." The record didn't chart, and there's no indication Rick offered A&M any more tunes.

Rick told author David Ritz that when he recorded these songs, it was the first time he played bass during a session. He also said the single died quickly because he wouldn't agree to sign an exclusive deal with A&M until they guaranteed him an ad budget. Therefore, "they stopped all promotion."

"My Mama" was very popular in England, Germany, and France for a while, Rick also told Ritz, "so I got my ass in gear, put together a four-piece band, and flew over." He said he found a promoter who booked the band on a nice tour and in good-sized clubs.

Rick and Kelly told author Nick Warburton that Rick toured Sweden around 1974 and 1975 with keyboardist Billy Preston. Rick also told several authors he lost momentum because he began having ménage à trois sex with a mother and daughter in Stockholm. Rick said he stayed abroad for a year. When he returned, he was unable to get along with Kelly and moved out of the house they shared in Toronto and into his own apartment. He told David Ritz that "marriage killed the happiness" between him and Kelly.

His next step was to write three new tunes and take them to a casual Toronto friend named George Semkiw, who would become Rick's producer and manager for the next two years. Their first project together was producing two versions of a bouncy dance tune titled "Hollywood Star." One version was longer than the other, and the two parts appeared on opposite sides of the same disc. The lyrics of both, written and sung by Rick, detailed his ambitions more explicitly than any of his previous tunes. "Tell Momma it won't be long," he sang, "everybody here gonna sing my song." He boasted, "I'm gonna be a Hollywood star, riding the hills in a long fine car."

The record label credits the performance of the tune to "Rick James and Hot Lips," implying that Rick had organized a new band. Semkiw says the members of Hot Lips were actually studio musicians he'd hired on a one-time basis.

Rick and Semkiw followed up "Hollywood Star" with "Sweet Surrender," a disco-style love song, and "Changes," a well-done love ballad that included such lines as "Meditating on the thought of you." Rick sang the lead on "Sweet Surrender," backed once again by studio musicians, plus Semkiw, who played guitar and bass. Rick also was lead singer on "Changes," and backed himself on the song by playing drums, bass, and keyboards, Semkiw says. Quality Records, a Canadian company, recorded and released all the tunes in 1976, crediting Rick as the writer of all three. But although Rick was also the vocalist on every song, he was credited as the vocalist only on "Hollywood Star."

This was apparently due to one of the self-defeating aspects of Rick's personality rising to damage his career once again. After Quality released

"Hollywood Star" (with an instrumental B side), but before it released the record with "Sweet Surrender" and "Changes" on it, Rick told Semkiw that Quality couldn't release those two records with labels naming him as the vocalist because there was "legal action against him" in the United States. What Rick probably meant, Semkiw says, was that he was "contractually tied up" with another company. In other words, Rick probably had sold his recording of the songs and had pocketed the advance the other company had given him.

Quality "wasn't too happy," Semkiw says, partly because it immediately faced the task of reprinting the record labels on two records. The company tried to salvage what it could from the situation by coming up with the name Gorilla to replace Rick's name as the vocalist on the record labels, although it was far from anyone's ideal name for a singer of two romantic songs. The company released the records but, worried about putting its weight behind the tunes for fear of possible legal consequences, it let them die. Once again, Rick had outsmarted himself. (Rick told author David Ritz that Quality "didn't know shit" about distribution or promotion, and that was why both songs tanked.)

From then on, Semkiw says, his relationship with Rick went downhill. "Things started to come apart because he'd been lying to me. Rick became an asshole, bugging me for money and drugs," he says, sometimes calling at 3:00 AM. "I told him, 'Our deal is for us to produce a record, not for me to support you.'" Rick soon stopped calling Semkiw or contacting him in any way.

Rick could have formed another band. Instead, he took it easy for a while, singing with already established local groups rather than forming one of his own. He remained an excellent musician and a great entertainer, but due to his double-dealing and his constant need for drug money, he was back where he'd been years before: riding the velvet rut in Toronto.

It was the proverbial darkness before the dawn, because Rick's next record made him a success. This time, however, he had some highly questionable help.

17

Shadowy Investors Make Rick a Motown Star

Gonna find my way to Heaven
'Cause I did my time in Hell . . .

—"Before They Make Me Run," Rolling Stones,
by Mick Jagger and Keith Richards (1978)

While hanging at the Penny Farthing, an old club in Yorkville, Rick met a white Canadian named Tony Nolasco. Rick stood out at the club because he was wearing a cowboy hat and a red bandanna. Although both men were musicians (Nolasco was a drummer and vocalist), they were at the club that night chasing women instead of performing on its stage. "He liked blondes and I liked black girls," Nolasco says, "so we had a nice little balance there."

He and Rick "hit it off instantly," Nolasco says, and often cruised numerous clubs in tandem. "Rick would say, 'Clothes get pussy,'" Nolasco remembers, "but I began to notice that he was wearing a lot of clothes that hadn't been dry-cleaned in six months, so obviously dirty clothes got pussy too." Beyond Rick's success with women, Nolasco also noticed that "musicians really respected Rick's talent." When he walked into a room, "his presence was felt," he says, but because of Rick's various financial antics, "he was never really well-liked."

According to Nolasco, Rick could and would create music with a guitar with a string missing or with a broken keyboard leaning on one side of his leg. He "was a poet with words," Nolasco says. "He could come up with the melodies and the hooks, he had the personality, he had the mic moves down, and he knew how to dress." At three in the morning "with a little reefer going, Rick would be recording and writing some awesome stuff. He was ready for prime time." In fact, Rick seemed to be writing more original material than ever before. He claimed the reason was that living in Europe had given him a worldlier outlook and more exposure to different kinds of musicians.

Before meeting Rick, Nolasco had been a member of the band McKenna Mendelson Mainline, which had toured England, found success on the stage there, and recorded an album titled *Stink* on Liberty Records in 1969 before returning to Toronto. When the lead singer of McKenna Mendelson Mainline left the group, Rick was invited to sing on some of the band's scheduled gigs. He "did a great, really dramatic job," at a performance at Ottawa University that garnered the band a sixty-second ovation, Nolasco says. Soon after that, the group broke up.

Nolasco then raised money from what he said were shadowy sources "to do a major project" to make Rick a star in the United States. On this project, Nolasco would serve as Rick's agent, manager, and fundraiser. The two men agreed, Nolasco says, that they were going to get Rick off the ground and then work on Nolasco's career.

Nolasco recruited a friend, South African guitarist Aidan Mason, who later became the guitar player for Canadian superstar Anne Murray, to work with them. Rick and Mason wrote a tune that sounded commercially viable, and Rick put words to it and sang lead. Mason played the guitar, Peter Cardinali played bass, Ed Roth played the keyboard, and Nolasco did the drumming. The song was called "Get Up and Dance."

This bouncy, minor-key song sounds much more like the Rick who became legendary than any of his previous songs, with hints of his soon-to-be-famous sarcastic whine and lines that in those days probably shocked a few listeners, such as "Feel like gettin' your rocks off?" and

"Is the music got your body wet?" Late in the song he sings, "I feel like doin' it to you."

Although Rick told the *Toronto Globe and Mail* in 1982 that the profits from "Get Up and Dance" enabled him to record the first version of his first album, *Come Get It!*, Nolasco says he and Rick had begun receiving money from what Nolasco calls "the dark side." (In 2004 *Vibe* magazine referred to the *Come Get It!* album as "independently financed.")

Nolasco started a label called Mood Records to press 45s of "Get Up and Dance," the company's first and last product. After Mood had made about ten thousand copies of the record, Nolasco says, he loaded the trunk of his black Cadillac Eldorado with about two thousand of the records packed tightly into cartons and headed for the US border. A US customs officer told Nolasco he couldn't bring the records across the border because they didn't say MADE IN CANADA on them. So Nolasco turned around and drove back to Toronto, stuck on new labels, and took the records across the border to Buffalo in 1978.

Nolasco then opened a Mood Records office in Buffalo to promote their product. He also rented apartments there for Rick and himself. Nolasco created a logo and printed posters, and soon the record was playing on WBLK, Buffalo's hot soul station. Disc jockeys in the nearby cities of Syracuse and Rochester began playing it as well. "Get Up and Dance" became a top 10 song in western New York State. Pretty soon, Nolasco says, "Rick was hearing himself on the radio. He was really buzzed. 'I'm on the radio!' he kept saying."

Nolasco says he had a great time "because I'm in the element of black music," which is something he was raised with. "Rick was prancing around the clubs . . . he's got a song on the radio." Nolasco himself was "getting sick [with happiness] because I'm hearing a lot of bands that I love." Among these bands was Sabata, a local band, and the Cause, a Buffalo band featuring Rick's friend Levi Ruffin. Soon there was an interview in the *Buffalo News* about how hometown boy Rick was doing real well, illustrated with a photo of Rick, his high school buddy Luther Rutledge, and a young woman running down the street.

But Rick reverted to form by trying to sabotage the entire effort for his own immediate benefit. Without notifying anyone, he flew to Montreal with the demo recording of "Get Up and Dance" and signed a record deal with Polydor Records for an extended-play 12-inch version of the song. As part of the deal, Polydor gave Rick a $5,000 advance. This was, of course, the same trick Rick had played previously on other groups and companies numerous times.

When Nolasco found out, he was mortified. "I wanted to punch his lights out," he says. When he confronted Rick, Rick said, "Well, man, I was gonna tell you . . ."

"We could have just canned the whole thing right then and there, but we didn't," Nolasco says. Instead, he contacted attorney Stanley Weisman in Toronto and asked him to speak to Polydor. When Weisman pointed out to Polydor that Rick already had a contract with Mood Records, Polydor agreed to drop the whole matter and write off their $5,000 as a loss, since Rick had already spent it.

Having sidestepped a major hassle, Nolasco decided to move ahead with Rick on their next step: making an album. Nolasco had noticed the talented musicians playing their hearts out in Buffalo nightclubs and hired saxophonist Jay Beckenstein, one of the founders of the group Spyro Gyra, which was beginning to get exposure on WBLK at the same time as Rick's tune. Nolasco also flew the renowned session musicians the Brecker brothers—saxophonist Michael and trumpeter Randy—in from New York City. The group started cutting tracks at Cross-Eyed Bear Studios in Clarence, New York, near Buffalo, where Spyro Gyra also recorded its tunes. "It sounded really good," Nolasco says. "Not because I was involved but because I thought it was the best Rick had sounded to date." Among the songs they cut was "You and I." The album they made became *Come Get It!*

They decided to take their act to Los Angeles with the hope of signing a record contract there. Before they flew to L.A., however, Rick took two other out-of-town trips, both grudgingly authorized by Nolasco. First Rick went to New York City because in order to make a smash in L.A., he said, he needed a new wardrobe. "He blew a few Gs, and I was aware of it and I let him do it," Nolasco says. "Then, because he needed to clear his head because he was under a lot of pressure, he wanted to go to Bogota. . . . So he went to South America and partied it up and snuck back an ounce of coke in a hairbrush." Nolasco was again mortified.

On their subsequent flight to L.A., where they planned to spend only one week, Rick kept pledging his fealty to Nolasco. "'You're my man,' he kept saying. 'You decide now. I don't do that shit' [make management decisions]." Rick had told Nolasco that he had a couple L.A. contacts: Ralph Seltzer, a former Motown staff attorney, and Lanny Sher, a public relations man with record industry connections.

Seltzer listened to the whole album twice, loved it, and told Rick and Nolasco he'd shop it around town if they wanted. "We figured this is great," Nolasco says. "This guy's connected [with the record industry], he's bona fide, he's the real deal, we've got a record that we think sounds great, we have the charts, we've made a little bit of noise in a secondary market, it's all good."

They saw Lanny Sher a day or two later. "He listens to the album and he's all excited," Nolasco says. "'I know somebody at Fantasy, I know somebody at Warner's, geez, I'd love to shop it,'" he says.

"I pull Rick aside and say, 'We can't have both these guys [Seltzer and Sher] walking into the same offices.' Rick says, 'Naaaaaa, just let 'em go.' I said, 'Rick, that's not the way you do stuff,' but we didn't have a tiff over it. I thought, 'We'll just sleep on it and maybe we can revisit it.'" By now Nolasco had spent a rather large amount of shady money.

When their week in Los Angeles was up, he and Rick were driving to the airport when Rick said he wanted to stop in at Motown. (Motown had moved its headquarters from Detroit to Los Angeles in 1972.) "I said, 'Why didn't we do that before? We've gotta go. We're gonna miss the flight,'" Nolasco says. But they stopped at Motown and went in, and "as fate would have it, the elevator door opens and there's [Motown producer] Jeffrey Bowen" and his then-wife, Bonnie Pointer of the Pointer Sisters. Rick and Bowen recognized each other from Detroit days.

Rick jumped into Bowen's Rolls-Royce with him and Pointer, Nolasco stayed in the rented car behind them, and they all drove to Bowen's house, with Rick playing the album in the car for his companions. By the time they all got to Bowen's, Bowen was really excited and wanted to play the album for Berry Gordy. "I'm thinking, 'This good trip just got better; we shouldn't be worried about making the flight,'" Nolasco says.

Rick, Nolasco, and Bowen made an appointment to see Gordy the next day. A Motown representative met them back at the hotel and told the hotel, according to Nolasco, "Everything's on Motown. Give them whatever they want.' Rick and I look at each other sitting on the two double beds and say, 'Let's order some alcohol and some lobster.'"

Nolasco continues, "[I said,] 'We gotta shop every label in town.' But Rick said, 'I don't want to shop anything now.' This was the first indicator of noncooperation [from Rick], but I didn't think anything of it. . . . It was a typical Rick response." Nolasco told Rick now was the time to create a bidding war. "Unique artists come along every once in a while and that's when they're willing to open the vault," he says he told Rick.

When the two men went to Motown on Monday to negotiate, however, "there was nothing to negotiate," Nolasco says. Nolasco feared that Rick would accept less money from Motown than Nolasco and his backer wanted because Rick wanted to be a Motown artist and Motown's negotiators knew it. Bowen and Motown executive Lee Young Jr. jumped on Nolasco "like wolves on the jugular vein," Nolasco says.

One of Nolasco's financial backers flew down, and he and Nolasco visited a high-end music-industry attorney in Beverly Hills, who told them, "If you don't sign a deal with Motown and get some money, you're getting no money. Get what you can and get out . . . or they'll drag you through court for years."

Back at the negotiating table, Nolasco says, Motown offered him $30,000 and promised him that if the record went gold—that is, if it sold five hundred thousand copies—they would pay him and his backer another $20,000.

The record did go gold, and Motown ended up paying the extra $20,000. "The problem was $50,000 didn't come even close" to covering Nolasco's debt to his backer, he says. In Nolasco's words, "That was lunch money."

He noted that Motown paid an especially low price, considering they were handed a complete, ready-to-play album. And as Nolasco predicted, "You and I" became a hit, and the album *Come Get It!* would go on to become the second-biggest-selling album in Rick's career. "Common sense in business would have told you to shop around," Nolasco says.

Aside from what Motown paid Nolasco, the company paid Rick $250,000, Rick claimed in *The Confessions of Rick James.* And as the sales of his later records and his wealth indicate, Motown was good to Rick.

Years later, Rick told a radically different version of these events to *Oui* magazine. When he and Nolasco took their sales trip to L.A., Rick said, "Motown was my *last* choice of label for the *Come Get It!* album because I knew they wouldn't like it." However, he said, he ran into an old friend there, who telephoned Motown executive Suzanne de Passe, and "they signed me." Nolasco says this version of events is totally untrue. De Passe herself told VH1's *Behind the Music* that her reaction when she heard Rick's *Come Get It!* album was that "we've got to meet him and we've got to sign him." She called his music "very infectious" and "very hot."

When Rick called Levi Ruffin and told him he would sign with Motown, Ruffin remembers saying, "Damn it, Rick, why? What about Warner Brothers?" and Rick saying, "Motown gave us a good deal." But, Ruffin adds, Motown "was the greatest black record company in the history of mankind, and most of my heroes were with Motown: the Tempts, Stevie, all those. So I said, 'Damn, this should be fun.'"

Rick went on to music biz glory, leaving Nolasco behind and in deep financial trouble from which it took him years to recover. Nolasco had succeeded, however, where Rick and others had failed: in placing Rick in the position to become the superstar he then became.

18

The Emergence of the Stone City Band

Well I came upon a child of God, He was walking along the road,
And I asked him tell where are you going. This he told me:
Said, I'm going down to Yasgur's farm,
Going to join in a rock and roll band.

—"Woodstock," as performed by Crosby, Stills, Nash & Young,
written by Joni Mitchell (1970)

Many of Rick's early Motown songs were great dance
tunes, and Rick had become an expert at writing dance music.
He was so good at it that sometimes, in songs he wrote that had both
original, relevant words and excellent dance music, the latter overrode
the former.

One of the reasons Rick's early dance music was so good was that
much of it was created by his Stone City Band. Led by Levi Ruffin Jr.,
Rick's longtime friend, the band included Clarence Sims, Al Szymanski,
Oscar Alston, and Lanise Hughes. Its horn section, added later, included
Danny LeMelle on saxophone plus LaMorris Payne and the brothers
John and Cliff Ervin. Many others joined and left the band over the next
decade. Most of its members were black, with the most visually obvious
exception being the very white Tom McDermott, whom Rick referred
to as "my light-skinned brother."

Ruffin remembers the day Rick recruited him for the band. "Rick came by the house and said, 'Hey, Levi, who's doin' it? Who's the hottest shit happening right now?' And at the time I was playing in Bootsy's Rubber Band, and Rick sits there and says, 'Levi, we can do better than that,' and I said, 'Are you kiddin' me?' And he says, 'Man, we can do better than that. Are you in?' And I said, 'Hell yeah.' And that started it right there."

Rick said he named his band the Stone City Band in honor of Sly and the Family Stone. He told the Associated Press that he wanted his group, like Sly's, "to be an integrated group" and hoped "it would catch on with both black and white people." This ambition certainly fits in with Rick's ability and desire to work creatively with white people in Canada.

Stone's version of black music, which the book *Rock of Ages* called a combination of "ominous bass guitar lines, intricate implacable rhythms, and a polemicized edge" influenced Rick's music and lyrics. And both Stone's music and Rick's were a much different form of soul music than what the book cites as the "chipper, choreographed, commercial form" that Motown had developed.

Rick kept having his fun by telling various interviewers that the *Stone* in Stone City Band referred to him and the band being serious, or to something serious, as in the phrase "stone blind." But, LeMelle insists, "Sly was Rick's muse. It was going to be Rick James and the Stone City Band like it was Sly and the Family Stone."

Not only did Rick want to follow Sly's musical path, he wanted to follow the success that Sly had had until his original group had disbanded in 1975. As Rick put it, "After the demise of Sly and the Family Stone, I thought I could have a group as big as his." He was very aware that there hadn't been any black superstars in rock since Jimi Hendrix and Stone. Rick admired both Motown and Sly for building a massive audience by attracting both white and black listeners. He noted in 1979, "Right now, there's no black group that can go onstage and be like the Rolling Stones. This racism thing that comes down blows my mind. A lot of black and white crowds still have trouble mingling. In a lot of cases, whites won't go into a black show."

The *Sydney Morning Herald* said that Rick was a modern version of Sly, America's first black rock star. It also noted that onstage, Rick acted flamboyant, cocky, surly, and bawdy, just like Sly had. But just as Rick saw Sly and the Family Stone as his career model, Rick's many critics saw his chronic tardiness, dishonesty, drug addiction, and general irresponsibility as reminiscent of none other than Sly. Rick, however, still relatively unencumbered by his drug use, would eclipse Sly with his very first album.

19

Rick Creates Punk Funk

"Punk funk" means to be one with yourself. To be rebellious, aggressive, and able to do and say what you feel at all times, without inflicting mental or spiritual pain.

—Rick James

Rick had sold "You and I" and *Come Get It!* to Motown, but he still had doubts about both the album and the song. He told one interviewer he saw them mainly as products "that might sell well enough to at least get me a deal good enough to do another album."

And as the *New York Times* noted, although the *Come Get It!* album was well done, its music was far from original. The sound resembled that of Parliament/Funkadelic, also known as P-Funk, a music collective led by George Clinton. During the 1970s, P-Funk and many other African American groups played funk music, a mixture of rhythm and blues, soul music, and jazz, described by the *New York Times* as "swaggering, bass-heavy dance music."

The lyrics of many of Clinton's tunes, however, described *Star Wars*–like space epics. One critic said that by the time Rick appeared, Clinton's lyrics had alienated "anyone over nine years old." Rick, on the other hand, believed that song lyrics should be based on real life, not on science fiction.

And, as Rick noted, other black musicians at the time didn't do much with the words of the songs they sang, even if they avoided space epics. "Lyrically, they're saying nothing," Rick said. "'I feel all right,' 'Can you feel it?' 'Get it on the good foot,' 'Get up and get down,' 'Oomph!' 'Good God!' 'Get up and boogie'—over and over." Rick wanted to do more with his lyrics than emphasize the rhythm of the underlying tunes. While admitting his debt to Clinton and others, Rick insisted his lyrics made his music superior to Clinton's. "I took George's stuff to a higher plateau," he told a *Washington Post* interviewer. "The babble that existed on top of their music was out of this orb. I just added sensible—and sexual—lyrics, entendres and innuendoes." He also stopped imitating Mick Jagger, Neil Young, and other white musicians.

Rick told *Rolling Stone* he was confident that telling it like it is would become a trend among other new music groups "instead of George Clinton science fiction, or doo-wop choreography, or turn-around-and-lick-the-eyebrows."

By adding down-to-earth lyrics to his songs, Rick, like almost all other Motown artists, was following Berry Gordy's dictum that a good song tells a believable story and tells it in the present tense, allowing the listener to connect with it emotionally. But Rick went further than Gordy in the direction of lyrical realism. "We're just gonna talk about the street. It'll be a real deal," Rick told *Rolling Stone.* By using such lyrics in his tunes, and by adding a disco beat to some of them, he extended the popularity of funk music, which was dying, and laid the foundation for rap and hip-hop, which were about to enter their vigorous youth.

The lyrics Rick wrote for "You and I," and for much of his best music from then on, also included his heartfelt accounts of his own personal experiences, blended expertly with his deep emotional reaction to them. At this moment in his life, he inserted himself into his art and would never completely remove himself from it. "Success didn't come to me until I went back to the real of what I was about," he told an AP interviewer.

For the rest of his career, every time he moved away from the reality of his life and experience, his songwriting declined. Every time he moved back to those roots, it improved, sometimes dramatically.

In his songs from this point on, "Rick brought in tenement slums and corner bums, reluctant housewives and lascivious underage girls," the *Guardian* noted. They were nonfiction descriptions of life in the ghetto, including frank descriptions of sex. One reviewer called such lyrics "lewd, adult fun." No Motown artist had ever gone so far, or would go so far again, in the use of pornographic and semipornographic lyrics.

These lyrics inspired Rick to call his music punk funk. The word "punk" in his neighborhood referred to a rebellious, young person, Rick said, "who doesn't necessarily beat up anybody but believes in expressing what is on his mind," which certainly might be sex.

On another occasion, however, Rick said his use of the term "punk" came from poor, white British rockers he'd heard during his time in England "whose only vehicle for escaping suppression and economic stress" was their music. Rick's music wasn't the nihilistic music of England's Sex Pistols and other similar groups, though. It was rather what the *New York Times* called "a seamier version of the freewheeling street-party atmosphere" that Sly and the Family Stone had created years before with their own funk music, epitomized in their 1967 hit single "Dance to the Music."

Motown executives, realizing how danceable "You and I" and *Come Get It!* could be, asked Rick to rerecord both the song and the album to make them even more compatible than they already were with the ongoing disco craze. As a result, "You and I" became a disco hit at both black and white disco clubs.

Rick had released *Come Get It!* at just the right moment in history. Many Americans were tired of the culture wars of the 1960s and '70s and just wanted to escape by dancing to a throbbing beat and snorting a line or two of cocaine, which many still thought harmless.

In fact, so many people were dancing to disco at the time that new high-quality disco music was always needed. In Rick's words, "I was lucky because the first album came out at the time when negroids and whiteroids were doing some serious dancing. There were negroids, whiteroids, jewroids, then there were assholes and hemorrhoids . . . all the 'roids' were really dancing and listening at the time. . . . The disco situation helped break the record."

But "You and I" wasn't just run-of-the-mill disco. As one reviewer noted, "There was enough funk bubbling under the surface" to distinguish "You and I" as something relatively new and make the song a crossover success in pop and R&B as well.

Rick cinched its popularity by adding a spectacular saxophone solo. The *Los Angeles Times* called it the best disco saxophone solo "since the marvelous break in the Average White Band's 'Pick up the Pieces' a few years ago." Many of Rick's future records would be highlighted by such sax solos, many of them by Daniel LeMelle.

Surprisingly, Motown released only a small number of copies of the rerecorded single, on their Gordy label. According to Ruffin, he and Rick had to become its promoters. "You and I" wasn't getting any substantial air play, Ruffin says, until they asked a gay man named Tony, "How we gonna bust this out?" Ruffin said Tony and his friends introduced it in gay bathhouses in Atlanta, where they "danced that shit and spread that shit all over the damn South."

Then the song and the album were massively aided by Rick's appearances on *Dick Clark's Live Wednesday* show on NBC-TV. According to Rick, Clark had asked Gordy if Diana Ross could appear on his show but Gordy would only allow it if Rick could appear as well. This was at least the second time that Gordy had influenced Clark on behalf of an act that Motown favored. Early in the Supremes' career, when they were being derided as the "no-hit" Supremes, Gordy had offered them to Clark for his 1964 Caravan of Stars US tour for $600 a week, much less than what Gordy was charging Clark for other Motown acts. The Supremes broke out into mass popularity during that tour.

Rick appeared on Clark's show with two background singers and performed "You and I" and "Mary Jane" with them, fortified by a pre-show hit of coke from the miniature Coke bottle he wore around his neck. While Clark tossed softball questions at Rick between the two performances, Rick's cogent answers were disrupted only by his constantly running nose, which caused him to spend much of the interview sniffing and wiping.

Some of the more naïve members of the audience may have thought Rick was crying. But he had nothing to cry about. The *Come Get It!* album, released on April 20, 1978, did very well. Coproduced by Rick and Art Stewart, it hit number 3 on the R&B album chart and stayed on the chart for forty-seven weeks. It also rose to number 13 on the pop album chart and remained on the chart for thirty-six weeks.

Not only were "You and I" and *Come Get It!* successful, but to the amazement of many, both hit the top without a supporting tour. Rick told one interviewer he was preparing a tour when "You and I" roared to the top. But, he said, "The show wasn't the way I wanted it and I didn't want to go on the road with a show that wasn't ready."

Then the honors began. *Come Get It!* was certified gold by the Recording Industry Association of America on August 22, 1978, meaning it had sold at least five hundred thousand copies. (In 1978 Motown had not yet joined the RIAA, but after the success of *Come Get It!* as well as the Commodores' *Natural High* album, also released in April 1978, it asked the association to audit the company's sales of both, and both were certified gold. In 1980, after twenty-one years of nonmembership, Motown finally joined the RIAA, thus allowing that organization to certify all its record sales from then on.)

In a 1986 suit against Rick in federal court, decided in 1989, Motown said *Come Get It!* had sold 913,250 copies through mid-1988, meaning that it had almost reached platinum status, or one million copies sold. In 1978 Rick won *Cash Box* magazine's Top New Male R&B Vocalist Award for both the album and the single. *Record World* magazine named "You and I" the Top Record Feature by a Male Vocalist.

Rick's sister, Camille Hudson, says her brother's burst of fame took her by surprise. She hadn't been in contact with him but happened to be in a club, heard the song played, and thought, "My God, that sounds like my brother." She was confused when the song was announced as a Rick James tune, because she had called him Jim when they were both children, and knew him later as Ricky Matthews. Soon afterward she got in contact with him, congratulated him, and joined his office and administrative staff.

With "You and I" and *Come Get It!*, Rick had succeeded in his third attempt to become a Motown star, and his seventh attempt to become a recording star on any label. The climb had consumed fourteen years of his life—without even counting any of his musical activities in Buffalo.

Levi Ruffin was ecstatic with the success of their first professional venture together. "I loved Rick because he gave me a chance at the big time," he said. "I've done things and played places I used to dream about as a kid." In 1978 Ruffin was thirty years old and, as he says, "Here we are on the radio all over the country, we go to clubs, don't have to buy no drinks, cocaine is free, bitches want to give you ass."

On the album cover, a guitar-carrying Rick, sporting long, braided, and beaded hair, is wearing a sleeveless black jacket with red-and-white-spotted lapels, a large fanciful collar, pants decorated with a lightning bolt symbol, and winged black-and-silver boots. He also has on a large winged heart bracelet. The winged heart logo appears again in the upper left corner of the album cover, and is emblazoned with the names RICK JAMES and STONE CITY BAND.

Carrying a guitar, and stepping toward the right, Rick is extending a hand leftward in the direction of a supine, lightly clad woman, former *Playboy* playmate Anne Marie Fox. She is lying on stage looking very distressed, presumably at the thought that Rick seems to be leaving her. On the back of the album cover she is lovingly clutching one of Rick's booted legs.

20

Rick Helps Save Motown

Mr. James was widely credited as the savior of Motown Records.

—*Washington Post*, August 7, 2004

Rick said he was surprised and pleased when Motown signed him as a vocalist on the basis of "You and I." He'd thought the music he was creating at the time was "too raw and unslick for them," but they gave him "a very good deal." There was absolutely no doubt in Rick's mind, however, that Motown needed him. "They've got to cater to the people in the streets. All the old Supremes fans are winos with false teeth." This was an obvious exaggeration, but the company's declining sales supported his theory.

From 1962 through 1971, Motown had dominated black music with Smokey Robinson, the Supremes, Marvin Gaye, Stevie Wonder, Diana Ross, the Four Tops, the Temptations, Mary Wells, the Marvelettes, the Jackson 5, and many others.

It had shown other larger and richer record companies—all of them white-owned—how profitable black music could be. Those firms responded by luring away Motown acts and hiring or creating new black acts of their own. Meanwhile, the soloists and groups that remained with Motown were no longer the hit makers they once were and would soon leave the company.

And while Motown was still a profitable business in the late 1970s and early '80s, it was less profitable than it had been in the 1960s and earlier in the '70s. But the arrival of Rick James and the Stone City Band changed all that. Suddenly there was a new hit maker, and he was garnering interest from the younger generation.

Rick would help Motown survive under its original ownership until 1988 by writing, producing, and recording his own funky dance music, topped with his own semipornographic lyrics and semipornographic onstage antics. Almost simultaneously, he began writing and producing hit songs for other Motown groups, including the fabled but fading Temptations and some new Motown groups he himself created, including the Mary Jane Girls.

Motown president Berry Gordy, after selling Motown in 1988, credited Rick retrospectively with "taking our music in a totally new direction." Music historian Rickey Vincent said that Rick "moved Motown records out of the 1960s for good." Rick also helped loosen up the company's choreography. Later on, Joanne McDuffie Funderburg, the leader of the Mary Jane Girls, was asked about all the wiggling the scantily clad band did onstage. "We weren't like the Supremes, the Marvelettes, everybody with the same hairstyles, same dress, same gloves, we weren't doing that, with just our arms moving, that wasn't what Rick wanted. He wanted it to be different."

And Rick made it different. He wore his hair in long, beaded braids, often performed shirtless, and groped and dry-humped women from the audience who ventured onto the stage. He smoked huge marijuana joints while performing, urged the audience to do the same, and challenged the cops to arrest him and everyone in the venue. He staged nonstop cocaine parties at his house and sang songs about how much he loved drugs and oral sex. He was indeed a new breed of Motown star.

Motown's final rise actually had begun in 1977, the year before Rick produced his first Motown hit for the company, when the Commodores broke the company's musical mold with their hit song "Brick House." With its obvious reference to the phrase "built like a brick shit house," used to describe a statuesque woman, it shattered the company's puritanical strictures.

Rick took it from there, becoming Motown's penultimate superstar. (Shortly after Rick arrived at the company, Lionel Richie, one of the Commodores' lead singers, quit that group and in 1986 leapfrogged over Rick to become Motown's final solo superstar.)

21

Rick Writes a Song about Himself and Kelly

You and me, we are as close as three-part harmony.

—"You and I," by Rick James (1978)

"You and I," the first in a line of increasingly sexy punk-funk classics, was a bouncy, sparkling tune about love and affection. Its lyrics matched the mood its music created, including the line, "You and me, we are as close as three-part harmony." The song also included the line, "Our love has greater wealth than Hughes himself," a reference to eccentric multimillionaire Howard Hughes.

The only clue the song gave to Rick's future career as a raunchy songwriter and the only punk-funk lines it included were "We'll be together 'til the six is nine"—a glancing and juvenile reference to oral sex as well as to the year Rick and Kelly had met—and the obvious "When you need me, I never hesitate, I always come, It's so much fun, yeah."

Rick told David Ritz he'd been thinking about Kelly when he wrote the song. He told another interviewer that Kelly was "the main woman in my life for many years." He said he wrote the song to emphasize that they were and would be a longtime couple. The song, in fact, said the couple would "be together eternally," but Rick later told an interviewer that lyric line was "crazy, because as we broke up the song became a hit."

This recollection is contradicted by Los Angeles County Superior Court records, which show the couple's official date of separation as October 30, 1976, more than a year and a half before "You and I" hit the charts on May 20, 1978. It's possible, however, that periods of reconciliation may have occurred after the stated separation date.

Rick really did want to reconcile. According to Levi Ruffin, one day "Rick was getting dressed—it was the afternoon, and Rick didn't get dressed in the afternoon unless it was something very important . . . and he said, 'Man, I'm going to meet Kelly, man.' And I said, 'Rick, what's up?' And he said, 'I think we're getting back together.'"

Rick, Ruffin says, "was smiling from ear to fucking ear." But Kelly "came in with lawyers" who put divorce papers out to be signed, "and it was like someone had stabbed" Rick when he returned. "Broke his fucking heart, man."

Weisman says the divorce was "very bitter." Ruffin claims Kelly "made a big mistake" by getting divorced when she did, because if she'd waited until after Rick had achieved stardom, her settlement might have been much greater than the $50,000 she received. "She and I talked about it later, and she said, 'Levi, I didn't give a fuck . . . I couldn't deal with him anymore.'"

Daniel LeMelle, who knew Kelly during her relationship with Rick, calls her "the best person for Rick ever." He says there was "unbelievable love" between them, and "when I was there, he respected her."

But by the time Kelly left, the relationship apparently had deteriorated. Rick "used to treat her so bad, browbeating," Ruffin says. "Whatever she did was wrong, whatever she had on was wrong. Rick would say, 'You could have done this.' 'Why didn't you do this?' 'Why didn't you do that?' Your feet are too big.' Just anything. He knew that she loved him so I guess he figured she would never go away, so he could be this asshole. And one day she quit, and it broke his heart."

Rick and Kelly were divorced on May 28, 1979. At the time, according to court papers, the couple's monthly expenses were $8,300. That meant they were spending, and presumably earning, approximately $100,000 per year. It was a very respectable amount for 1979, but a drop of water in the immense ocean of sparkling moola that would soon engulf Rick.

That was partly because the song Rick wrote about their relationship did much better than their marriage. "You and I" appeared on the *Billboard* R&B chart on May 20, 1978, and soon hit number 1, remaining in that position for two weeks and on the chart itself for twenty-two weeks. On August 5, 1978, true to Motown's ability to make white hits out of black music, it entered the *Billboard* pop 40, peaked at number 13, and stayed on that chart for ten weeks. Although Rick's career would continue for decades, he never came closer to attracting an equal number of both black and white listeners than he did with this song.

About three and a half years later, Kelly married Wayne Shanahan. They celebrated their thirty-first anniversary in 2015. Today she owns La Rumeur Affamée in Sutton, Quebec, an upscale food shop with an outstanding bakery and more than 150 kinds of cheeses. Ruffin says he talks to her often on the phone and that she's happy, has a nice middle-class life, and travels a lot. One of her sons plays in a reggae band. (Kelly refused a request for an interview for this book.)

22

Hash and Cash

I'm in love with Mary Jane.
She's my main thing.
She makes me feel all right.
She makes my heart sing.

—"Mary Jane," by Rick James (1978)

The *Los Angeles Times* panned the *Come Get It!* album, calling it "massively flawed" because it consisted of "a great disco song, 'You and I,' flanked by numerous mediocre tracks." As it turned out, however, another tune on the album, "Mary Jane," became one of Rick's most famous songs, and remains today the second-most-popular tune he ever recorded.

Everyone assumed that the tune was about pot, and they were right. Rick, saying he was "not afraid to admit it," proclaimed marijuana "the greatest thing since ice cream" in several interviews. He also said the reason he sounded like he was singing about a girl when he was singing about marijuana was that he wanted to treat the drug "like it was a girl, because I look at it like it's a girl."

The subject of the song reminded many of "Cocaine," written and recorded by J. J. Cale in 1976 but made famous in 1977 by Eric Clapton, who covered it for his album *Slowhand*. Cale's tune was a love song to that drug, which he dubbed a female, and included such lines as "If you want to hang out, you've gotta take her out / cocaine" and "She don't lie, she don't lie, she don't lie / cocaine."

Rick told one interviewer, "Marijuana hasn't made me crazy, it hasn't lowered my IQ, nor has it been detrimental in any way, shape or form." Rick also claimed that taking drugs could lead to a greater appreciation of music. When people protested that his audience for the song included children, Rick responded that "kids are no longer kids. They are able to decipher and decide what they want. You can't sit down and tell a thirteen-year-old anything about anything because they pretty well know what's going on. Their brothers and sisters were junkies and/or prostitutes, they've been through the marijuana trip, and they may even smoke it."

To those who complained that smoking marijuana was illegal and sometimes harmful, Rick argued, "I don't propagate anything. I don't say, 'Everyone smoke grass.' I say, 'I love Mary Jane.'

"Mary Jane" climbed to number 3 on the *Billboar*d R&B chart and stayed on the chart for seventeen weeks. On the pop chart, it rose to number 41, just short of the Top 40.

"Dream Maker," another notable tune on *Come Get It!*, begins with a spoken-word poem and becomes a sensitive, self-abnegating love song from a man to a woman that starts softly, reaches an energetic peak, and then trails off slowly, ending with the sound of a woman's orgasmic moaning. One reviewer who may not have listened to the entire song hailed "Dream Maker" for its "ethereal sensitivity."

In the song "Hollywood," a mournful, seven-minute-and-twenty-seven-second ballad, Rick sadly tells his parents that he's leaving the ghetto to "do good in Hollywood." The song includes repeated unconvincing assertions that he "won't be lonely, won't be lonely, won't be lonely." It's the polar opposite of "Hollywood Star," Rick's previous song about the neighborhood, which Quality Records released in 1976. That song was a happy, bouncy tune in which the singer is standing at the corner of Hollywood and Vine in the bright sunshine and exulting in what he's sure will be his future fame and fortune.

With "You and I" and *Come Get It!*, Rick finally achieved the fame and fortune for which he had hungered for years. His first royalty check from Motown was for $1.8 million. Unfortunately, as Rick later told California court-appointed psychologists, he used that check to buy "all the drugs [he] could afford."

23

Rick Uses White Slang to Bust Out

We're bustin' out of this L-seven square
Freaks like you and I could never funk from there

—"Bustin' Out," by Rick James (1979)

Rick's second album, *Bustin' Out of L Seven*, described by author Rickey Vincent as "a slow-grinding funk monster," was based on white slang lifted from one of the whitest movies ever made, a 1965 film called *I'll Take Sweden*. In that movie, Frankie Avalon played a guitar-strumming beach bum courting a young woman played by Tuesday Weld. Avalon told her father, played by Bob Hope, that most daughters think their fathers are "L seven," or "square." (Written close to each other, "L7" can appear to be forming a square.)

Expanding creatively on the theme, the album cover displays a drawing of Rick, accompanied by three scantily clad African American Wonder Women, bursting through a hole in a stone wall. The wall surrounds a large modern penitentiary with two names on it: "L 7" and "Serious Joint," with "Serious Joint" simultaneously indicating a place where people take normal life seriously, a prison that is difficult to escape, and a large marijuana cigarette. The drawing gives Rick a muscle-bound physique he never acquired in real life, and he brandishes an electric guitar.

Rick must have been pretty busy during the album's production, because he is listed as the album's coproducer and the rhythm arranger for all the songs. He also is credited with playing the clavinet, bass, key-boards, congas, and bongos heard on the album, as well as the percus-sion, harmonica, and acoustic six- and twelve-string guitars.

The *Los Angeles Times,* while noting there was no knockout track on this album comparable to "You and I," nevertheless called *Bustin' Out of L Seven* a much better album than *Come Get It!* and said Rick's ability to sing and compose ballads had improved. The paper, which had called Rick's *Come Get It!* ballad vocals "flowery" and "leaden with excesses," said Rick had learned a lot about sustaining dramatic tension in such songs.

Although none of the other tunes on *Bustin' Out* soared as high on the charts as the previous album's "You and I" or "Mary Jane," the album spawned three hits: its title track, "High on Your Love Suite/One Mo Hit (of Your Love)," and "Fool on the Street."

The *L.A. Times* loved "High on Your Love Suite," a funky dance tune, which it called a "furious, conga-dominated track," and in 1978, Motown released a 12-inch version for dance clubs.

"Fool on the Street" is a brisk dance tune that slows down unex-pectedly to a crawl around the middle, and stays there. In a spoken word conversation at the end of the song, which is also at the end of the album, Rick meets a male buddy on the street and the two share a joint.

Released in January 1979, *Bustin' Out* hit number 2 on the *Billboard* R&B album chart, remained at that position for six weeks, and stayed on the chart for thirty-four weeks. It rose to number 16 on the pop album chart and stayed on that chart for twenty-seven weeks. It was Rick's second Top 40 pop album, and over the next nine years it sold 537,878 copies, according to court papers.

For this album, Rick was among the writers and publishers the Amer-ican Society of Composers, Authors, and Publishers (ASCAP) honored for high achievements in their field in 1979.

24

Rick and Teena Marie
Make Beautiful Music Together

Teena Marie was a waif Rick rescued from Motown's compost pile.

—*New Times* magazine

One of the traits that marked Rick as an above-average rock star was that he began producing records early in his career with Motown. He'd coproduced his first album at Motown, *Come Get It!*, with Art Stewart, and soon after that album became a hit, he continued to produce or coproduce his own albums. He also began producing other Motown vocalists.

The company was so sure of Rick's skill as a producer that soon after *Come Get It!*, he found himself committed to producing a tune for Motown's former superstar, Diana Ross. Then, according to music legend, Rick was walking down a Motown hallway one day when he happened to hear vocalist Teena Marie playing the piano and singing in a rehearsal studio. Surprised at the quality of her music, which pierced the wall that separated them, he stopped to listen. "Never in my life had I heard such a range with so much passion in a white voice," he wrote in *The Confessions of Rick James*. Rick asked to be relieved of producing Ross, whose career was in decline, and to be allowed to produce Teena instead. His request was granted. (It may have been a loss for Motown that Rick didn't at least design the cover for Ross's album. He wanted Ross, wearing ripped-up jeans and leather, to be looking at another version of herself, dressed as a Supreme, lying in her coffin.)

The pairing of Rick and Teena was ironic: while he was known as a black R&B singer who sometimes sang white rock 'n' roll, Teena Marie (born Mary Christine Brockert in 1956) was a blue-eyed white woman who sang black R&B. In fact, when Rick first heard her music through the wall, he assumed she was black. Even after getting to know her, he told author David Ritz he "couldn't believe she was white. Her essence, her spirit, her life was black. She seemed a divine example of reincarnation." Berry Gordy once remarked that "the only thing white about her was her skin," and Teena's black fans called her Vanilla Child. She was flattered that her recordings were played almost exclusively on black stations.

Teena had grown up only two blocks from a black Los Angeles neighborhood, Oakwood, and had many black friends. They gave her the nickname "Off White." She told one interviewer that when she started her career, she would tell people she was white, but they would assume she was trying to pass. Because of this, she had to sing R&B before she could sing pop, the near-universal fate of black vocalists.

Motown signed Teena in 1975. Her first album wasn't released until 1979, however, because until she found Rick she hadn't been able to find the right Motown producer. It was Berry Gordy's niece, Iris Gordy, then a Motown vice president, who thought these two fish-out-of-water musicians were perfect for each other. Teena said she marveled that Rick "[didn't say,] 'This is a white girl. I can't produce her.' He doesn't think in those terms." She may not have known that Rick had been working with whites musically for the previous decade.

With Rick's participation, Teena eventually produced four of her own albums for Motown, and they did well on both the pop and R&B charts. Rick and Art Stewart coproduced her first one, *Wild and Peaceful*, which was released after *Bustin' Out of L Seven*.

Rick wrote four of the songs and sang the lead vocal with Teena on "I'm a Sucker for Your Love." (He had written it for Diana Ross before switching his musical intentions to Teena.) One *Los Angeles Times* reviewer called the song an "up-tempo, bass-powered, horn-blasted" hit, saying that Teena "growled and purred her way through its salacious grooves," indicating beyond a doubt that it was a Rick James production. It rose to number 18 on the R&B chart and remained there for twenty-six weeks while rising to only number 94 on the pop chart. It also became only the second of Rick's tunes to appear on the British chart, where it reached number 43. Rick also wrote three other songs on the album, including "De Ja Vu (I've Been Here Before)." The same reviewer called "De Ja Vu" a monument to "pure gospel-pop exhilaration."

The album cover for *Wild and Peaceful* featured a seascape with clouds but no picture of Teena. In its early days, Motown hadn't put the faces of its artists on its album covers because it feared that record stores in the southern United States would refuse to stock them. This time, however, Motown didn't put Teena's face on her first album for fear of turning away those buyers who wouldn't listen to her if they knew she was white. To further disguise her ethnicity, Motown execs also considered changing her performing name to Tina Tyson.

Nevertheless, the partnership of Teena and Rick was a hit. For one thing, Teena was as dedicated to music as he was. She was an insomniac and hated it, but told an interviewer, "I'd go without sleep for eight weeks or eight months before I'd give up music. What else would I do?"

25

The Magical Funk Tour

Mr. James was an explosion of decadent excess.

—*Washington Post*, August 7, 2004

In March 1979 Rick and his now-thirteen-member Stone City Band embarked on their first Motown odyssey, the Rick James Stone City Band Magical Funk Tour. This forty-city trip, his first as a Motown artist, was the beginning of the series of tours that would make his reputation as an unforgettable stage performer. Rick's recently acquired manager, Shep Gordon, had booked him for the four-month coast-to-coast excursion.

The group, described by the *Cleveland Plain Dealer* as "outstanding, peerless, first-rate instrumentalists," comprised the same musicians who had recorded Rick's songs with him in the studio. Back then, in an industry in which the studio band was not necessarily the touring band, this gave the group what another Stone City Band member, Daniel LeMelle, calls a "home-grown sound" that appealed greatly to concert audiences.

After *Bustin' Out of L Seven* was released, Rick had decided to add a horn section to the band. LeMelle, who honchoed a horn section, remembers that in 1979 Norman Whitfield, a Motown producer, put Rick in contact with him. When Rick and LeMelle and their groups first met, Rick pointed out that he and his associates all dressed like rock stars, while LeMelle and his group, which included LaMorris Payne and brothers Cliff and John Ervin, "were all Joe College." Nevertheless, he invited them over to his house, telling them he wanted to "see what you West Coast boys can play."

Stung by Rick's sneering attitude, LeMelle decided to play a trick on him. As he recalls, "I went to the record store, bought *Come Get It!*, and we learned every part on every song." LeMelle says once they were at Rick's house, when Rick asked them to play something, "We started making noise, honking, and playing stupid stuff. They were looking at us like 'What the fuck?'" But when Rick then asked them to play the first song from *Come Get It!*, "We did beyond well. We played it like we had recorded it." They were hired instantly and dubbed the Punk Funk Horns, with LeMelle as their leader.

When hired, they joined a band whose members all imitated Rick's general style of dress. Every male onstage usually wore glitter-spattered braids and shirts unbuttoned to the waist, silvery thigh-high boots, skintight lamé bodysuits, leather pants, rhinestone belts, and silk shirts on occasion.

The band's costumes, along with the falsetto voice Rick often used and the somewhat feminine look of his hands-on-hips stance, played into the gender-bending androgyny that was popular among bands of that era. As Eddie Murphy's brother Charlie Murphy remarked on *Chappelle's Show* years later, with only some exaggeration, "The most feminine guys in those days got all the girls!"

Guitarist Tom McDermott appeared to be pushing androgyny to its outer limits. With his clear-white hairless skin, much of it on display, his long blond hair, and his sometimes feminine gestures and expressions, he often seemed ready to jump the gender barrier at the earliest possible opportunity. When Rick and the band performed Rick's song "Love Gun" on *Soul Train*, for instance, McDermott wore a tight, figure-hugging top that bared one underarm and exposed his other shoulder completely. His explicitly bulging crotch, while alluding to the title of the song being performed, may have suggested to some that this was a performance for gay men. Except for the female backup singers, who wore dresses, the other band members were similarly attired. At least one apparently gay male couple danced enthusiastically in the audience.

All this fit into an ongoing transition in R&B from musicians like James Brown, Wilson Pickett, and Otis Redding to singers like Rick, Prince, and Michael Jackson. As writer Nelson George has pointed out, while Brown, Pickett, and Redding were tough-looking macho men, these newer vocalists were softer guys with long hair, baby faces, and glittery costumes.

Onstage, Rick unmistakably and frequently indicated his enjoyment of performing oral sex on women by holding his fingers in a V in front of his mouth and thrusting his tongue back and forth through them, a gesture his macho predecessors would never have considered. His stage costumes combining the 1960s hippie look with '70s disco wear provoked comparisons to P-Funk and Sly Stone. Rick was cunningly using his considerable onstage charisma and his exuberant style to make up for his less-than-stellar voice.

He conducted chants, told stories, and developed himself as a flamboyant onstage character. He also concentrated on the concerts themselves, which soon became outrageous extravaganzas that included fireworks, lasers, flashing lights, colored smoke, confetti bombs, phosphorescent costumes, spark-spraying rockets, and scantily clad women dancing and rolling around onstage in front of twenty-foot-high papier-mâché joints that belched smoke. A mist created by dry ice floated overhead.

Ruffin said he invited his father to one of these concerts and remembered that the older man's reaction was total amazement at all the activity onstage. "He had thought it would be just like a giant jazz combo sitting there grooving," Ruffin said, "but we were flying all over the stage. There were explosions. I'd jump on a trampoline, and pretend I was flying an airplane. . . . My father didn't understand how we could work that hard for an hour and a half." Ruffin would lose so much weight while touring, he said, that when the tour was over people would look at him and say, "Where's your ass?"

The giant joints, plus real drug use onstage and by audience members, only added to a perception that Rick and his audience were in a gigantic bong. At almost every concert, Rick lit up a joint onstage. He'd also kneel and accept joints from fans, especially while or after performing "Mary Jane."

At one concert, one of Rick's warm-up groups, Cameo, told audience members to "light a match, a lighter, your fingers, or a joint" and let those lights shine while they danced. According to a *Greensboro (NC) Daily News* review of one of the performances, the arena was "aglow with jiggling and bouncing lights as marijuana smoke filled the air."

All that pot smoking would have mellowed out most people, but not Rick. Another concert review said that despite his drug use, Rick "had enough ribald humor and fierce energy to maintain a first-rate performance," and the review praised his "knockdown stunts with the microphone" à la James Brown.

Rick's hair was also an onstage attraction. Offstage he often wore a Jheri curl, a permed hairstyle that gave him a loosely curled look. Onstage, however, he often wore a beaded cornrow hairstyle with Cleopatra-type braids, saying it was inspired by the African warriors of the Maasai tribe—and the rock band KISS. Later he traded in the braids for a full shoulder-length Louis XIV–type hairstyle.

Rick's hair had to compete for attention with his clothes. One outfit, which a critic for the *Rockford (IL) Register Star* said made the singer look like a "flamboyant Viking," combined a black-and-white shimmering hooded cape, a red-and-silver sequined jumpsuit, and knee-high platform boots, all decorated with flying hearts and lightning bolts. He often changed up his look by appearing in tight Spandex or leather pants for one song, then wearing sandals, jeans, and turquoise jewelry and looking very much like a 1960s hippie for the next. On some occasions, as the theme from *Superman* echoed through the hall, Rick played the part of the inner-city superhero, wearing a blue suit with red hearts as he strutted and dived across the stage. He made at least three costume changes during an average performance, with his stage wear depending on the song he was performing and the album he was promoting. When singing his later song "Big Time," for instance, he wore a top hat as a prop.

Performances also included skits based on Rick's most recent hits, some so elaborate that they relegated much of the music to the background. In one skit, for instance, Rick and company employed a lamppost, a fire hydrant, a mural, and a complete cardboard automobile to simulate a street scene while he sang his song "Mr. Policeman."

Rick's concerts were sexual as well as pyrotechnic extravaganzas. He often used his microphone as a phallic symbol, boasted about his sexual triumphs, strutted arrogantly, and swung his hips. He hoisted female fans onto the stage, climbed on top of them, and pretended to have sex with them. Meanwhile, as the *Miami Herald* pointed out, "male and female silhouettes would writhe behind triangular screens in mock lovemaking." Rick told one crowd that his biggest thrill in life was "to hear a woman scream in ecstasy," and spent a lot of time onstage either preening or stroking a female singer while the two sang a particularly suggestive duet.

Often Rick would appear before audiences displaying his tongue in the manner of Gene Simmons of KISS, whose signature move in concerts was to waggle his tongue wildly at the audience. Rick's tongue movements, along with the lyrics of some of his songs, recalled oral sex more vividly than Simmons's, however, especially when Rick flashed his tongue in and out of his mouth like a lizard and thrust his pelvis back and forth. Don Waller of the *Los Angeles Times* called Rick "a marvelously greasy vocalist and a frank performer whose bumps 'n' grinds, not to mention his gladiator smirk, would have brought out the town marshal in years past." Author Gerri Hirshey noted that Rick's "X-rated lyrics would have caused '60s young America to swallow its retainer plate."

The *Philadelphia Inquirer* decided it was Rick's "considerable achievement to have made sleaziness into an alluring stage persona" and complimented him on his ribald humor. Rick, onstage, made sex seem less serious and more like fun.

As another reviewer put it, in Rick's lyrics, women were sex toys— the younger the better—drugs were fun, and life was one long, overnight party. The *New York Times*, however, described Rick's embodiment of himself onstage as "a leering stage persona" unrivaled even in the age of Prince and George Clinton. It called his voice on some of his records a "salacious whine" and said his hits were "paeans to debauchery and the women who made it possible."

Asked years later about his onstage sex antics, Rick told one interviewer that "Things were simpler. . . . We didn't have to worry about too much sex because there was no HIV. We didn't have to worry about anything other than getting into discos and dancing and having fun and whose body we were going to jump on that night."

Rick loved performing. "I get higher than I ever got on any drug when I'm onstage," he said. When asked about his performing preferences, Rick replied, in a profound understatement, "I'm very energetic. I'm not your organic, laid-back tree." As he said near the end of his life, "I tried to make the audience forget all their problems." He said he wanted his performances to free his audiences "from themselves, and from space and time and consciousness."

Rick may have been more successful at doing this than he thought. In 1982 a Boston city official, Richard Sinnott, who was in charge of granting entertainment licenses, said that after attending rock concerts by Rick and the Who, he "was reduced to a shell of myself, barely able to function." Sinnott did not mean this as a compliment.

Most audience members reacted to the concerts even more strongly than Sinnott did. Many got up to dance, and many security guards tried to prevent them from doing so, causing a reviewer for the Baton Rouge *Morning Advocate* to write that "to require an audience to sit passively in its cramped seats while the star on stage is trying to incite a marijuana-soaked dance orgy seems ridiculous." Sometimes the guards didn't bother to try.

One of Rick's concerts was enlivened not by his onstage behavior but by a commercial dispute. As a result of a charge that Rick allegedly owed $250,000 to a concert-related business, ten police officers were sent to serve a summons to him at a concert in Dallas. While they were there, the police threatened to arrest him if he did what he usually did onstage:

smoke a real joint. When Rick told the audience about the threat, they screamed out that they'd riot if the cops carried out the threat, and the officers decided to wait until the concert was over to confront him. Informed of their plans, Rick changed clothes during a break in the show, put his braids under a Rasta hat, and walked out of the arena unrecognized and unserved.

Meanwhile, Rick's crew put one of Rick's aides in a hooded costume and sent him out onstage at the end of the show. The police went to arrest the aide but drew back when they noticed that unlike his boss, the aide was bald. Rick completed his escape, but the incident led to several printed rumors that Rick—who prided himself on his real, long, and frequently braided hair—was bald. Fifty thousand dollars worth of equipment was seized, the next night's concert had to be canceled, and equipment had to be borrowed for the night after that—but what most annoyed Rick were the erroneous reports that he was bald.

His opponents in the dispute had "defamated [*sic*] my character and professionalism, saying I had a bald head," Rick told the *Washington Post*. Rick spat out the words "bald head" while tugging at his braids to show they were real. His enemies, he said, "were wrong, and they're going to suffer for it. That tears down my character, anybody says I got a bald head." The monetary dispute was eventually resolved.

On this tour, Rick was finally able to accomplish what he had been trying to do on his tour with B. B. King: get the audience to participate by clapping their hands. He did this by encouraging the crowd to slam their right hands on their left hands while imagining that their left hands were either the Ku Klux Klan or Ronald Reagan.

Some of Rick's onstage effects were a little too over-the-top, however. He created a lot of his pyrotechnics with "flash pots," powder-filled containers that were lit up to create a big flash, smoke, or sparks. According to Rick Abel, Rick's road manager on several tours, Rick "wanted this stuff going off all the time. Bam! Bam! Bam! Bam! Bam!" Abel hired his best friend, a Vietnam vet named Paul who loved explosions, to handle this part of the production. The problem was that Paul would overdo it by putting too much powder in each pot. This was dangerous, Abel says, "because if you put powder in them after they've just been ignited, they'd go off on you." But according to Abel, "Rick kept saying 'Do it again! 'Do it again!' 'Do it again!'"

Rick and Paul would get carried away, and several times during the course of a tour the pots would ignite while Paul's hands were still in them. The burning phosphorous would get under Paul's skin and, Abel says, "He'd be screaming. It was insane. I'd have to take him to the hospital."

Rick described his own concerts as "like going to a concert on the Fourth of July." He noted that while rock groups like KISS had brought their pyrotechnic performing style to white kids, most black kids hadn't been exposed to such extravaganzas until he brought it to them. Although the audiences at Rick's concerts were somewhat mixed, his big stage productions were aimed particularly at black people. He believed that because most black musicians at the time favored conventional attire and relatively conventional onstage performances, their mostly black audiences never got to see the type of go-for-broke spectacle that white audiences saw.

Fans lined up for hours to gain entry to Rick's performances. In April 1979 several hundred people who had been unable to squeeze into his show when it played Boston's Orpheum Theatre allegedly broke store windows and assaulted Boston police officers in frustration. The problem was that the only way to enter the theater was through a small entrance at the end of a narrow alley. Rick wrote in *The Confessions of Rick James* that he watched mounted police officers "beating on Black sisters and brothers from their horses and just cried. I felt responsible and promised myself from then on I would only play places that could hold the kind of crowds we were getting." The *Boston Globe* called the incident a "wild melee." Rick didn't return to Boston until 1988, when he performed at that city's Channel nightclub without incident.

This police clash with Rick's fans, who were mostly black at the time, undoubtedly scared off some white attendees, but Rick wanted white fans as well as black ones and tried to attract them. One white reviewer, calling the onstage Rick "pure kitsch" and "a cartoon," wrote the persona Rick presented was that of "a lovable goon who poses a minimal threat to Caucasian life." All Rick seemed to want to do, this reviewer wrote, was "take his freaky chick to Hollywood and smoke a couple of tons of reefer."

All this was a big change for Motown. Referring to most of Motown's previous hit-making groups, Rick said, "Black musicians no longer have to put on suits and sing doo-wop, with all of them doing the same choreography and same robotic moves." Putting on his new choreography required a lot of energy, however. According to LeRoi Johnson, Rick would work out for months before leaving on tour, stretching, playing basketball, and jogging up and down hills. This preparation was definitely necessary.

Occasionally, like all creative efforts, Rick's shows failed. The *San Diego Union* called Rick's 1983 performance in that city "unimaginative" and said it was the sort of concert that "doesn't engage the crowd so much as divert it." According to the paper, too many of Rick's songs "seemed to peter out or segue into other tunes before they could generate more than a perfunctory impact." The paper also noted that Rick seemed to be sharing the stage "with a harried stagehand" who kept running out to adjust mic cords and stands. The *Union* ended this condemnation by noting that the only showstopping moment belonged to one of Rick's male backup singers, "whose extraordinary falsetto packed into a few bars all the piercing, crowd rousing emotionalism Rick himself couldn't generate all night."

And Rick Abel insists that Rick "didn't know how to leave people wanting more." Near, at, and beyond the scheduled end-of-concert time, Abel says, he'd be flashing Rick the "five minutes left" sign again and again, and Rick would ignore him and try to get the audience to sing along. "He'd keep doing it and doing it," Abel says, "but of course you could never critique the show because it was his invention. I'd say, 'Rick, maybe only do that once or twice?' and he'd say, 'What the fuck do you know?' He couldn't look at it from a perspective of building up slowly to a peak, then maybe bringing it back down for a short period of time, then kicking it back up for the final installment."

When everyone was working together, however, Rick's concerts were gigantic crowd-pleasers that made lots of money, with the max as high as $250,000 per event. This was an "unheard-of" total during the 1980s, according to Rick's accountant, Dick Romer. He says expenses for a $250,000 concert were about $100,000, leaving Rick's earnings for the evening at $150,000 before taxes.

That trend continued for Rick, and in 1985 Motown announced that his recent concert tours had grossed more than $50 million.

26

A Bottomless Pool of Female Flesh

Yeah, we're goin' to Surf City, 'cause it's two to one
You know we're goin' to Surf City,
gonna have some fun, now
Two girls for every boy.

—"Surf City," sung by Jan and Dean, written by Brian Wilson
and Jan Berry (1963)

From his earliest days in the music business, Rick had always worked at attracting as many women as possible. In Toronto, Stan Weisman says, he and Rick would walk down Yonge Street, where there were all kinds of interesting stores, including leather and clothing shops. Along the way, Rick would "walk into every door and talk to the sales lady, and chat them up all the way down the line, getting their phone numbers."

As Rick's star rose, attracting women became progressively easier. When Weisman was visiting Rick at Motown headquarters on one occasion, he says, a Motown mail clerk hauled out two huge canvas bags of mail for the singer. Rick invited him to open some of the envelopes at random. "I pulled out a couple of letters, and it's all from women enclosing nude photos of themselves and their home phone numbers." The nude pictures Weisman saw were mild demonstrations of affection compared to the female frenzy on view at Rick's concerts. Hundreds of women would throw crotchless panties onstage or otherwise indicate they wanted to have sex with the singer. The problem for Rick became how to select the best-looking women from this mob for his own enjoyment.

Sometimes his trysts with willing women were handled discreetly. As Rick's accountant, Dick Romer, describes it, the procedure for hooking him up was for some security people to "go out and give some of the better-looking women backstage passes. The best of them got the opportunity to meet Rick." After the weekend, these women would "get a plane ticket back or clothing or whatever. Rick was always very generous with the women who hooked up with him."

Outside of a very small handful of serious relationships, "Rick had a bimbo of the week," says screenwriter Richard Wesley, who worked on a film project with Rick. "He never allowed the same woman into his hotel room twice. His attitude was 'I'm in town to do a concert for three days, and for those three days it's me and you. But next time I come back, I don't know you.' It was one trip and you're done."

Rick loved getting high and having group sex with two or three women at a time. This was not exactly unusual among rock musicians—or anyone else who could manage it—during this era. As Peter McGraw, one of Rick's fellow Toronto musicians, remarks, "Every musician had experiences with two or three partners. . . . It's rock 'n' roll." Somewhat more unusual was Rick's enjoyment of cunnilingus, especially when he could inspire a woman to produce so much fluid in response that she would squirt it out. He also enjoyed ordering an excited woman to insert her hand in her own wet vagina and then insert that soaking hand in her own mouth.

Rick was so voracious that the problem for the members of his entourage became how to keep some of the best-looking women for themselves. Just as interested in sex as Rick, the members of his entourage engaged in what LeRoi Johnson calls "a two-minute rap" contest. You had to be able to get a girl as fast as you could snap your fingers. He says, "I would see a girl I wanted and I would send somebody with the key to my room, and I'd say, 'Take this key to her and I don't care what you say, she had better be there.'"

Even if the gambit succeeded, however, Rick often "would send his security people to take the women for himself, because Rick felt that everything belonged to him," Johnson says. On one tour, Johnson remembers, he and two other members of Rick's entourage were in a hotel room with three girls. One man was in the bathroom with one girl and Johnson and the other man were in the bedroom with two other girls. Rick's valet, nicknamed California, came around, and a few minutes later "Rick's security people kicked the door in and took the two girls and left," Johnson says. "We said, 'Fine, we've still got this one who's in the bathroom' with guy number one. Ten minutes later, however, the security people came back, announced that 'California said you had three girls,' and took the other girl."

Another contest over a woman occurred on tour in the 1980s, at Leviticus, a club in Manhattan. A fellow staffer pointed out a woman who "looked like an angel," Johnson says. "She was absolutely drop-dead gorgeous. She was with a guy about six foot five." Johnson walked up to the woman, told her he had to talk with her, separated her hand from her companion's, and took her aside.

"One of the security guys saw me, and went back to Rick and said, 'Roi's got this gorgeous girl,'" Johnson says. Rick ordered security to drag Johnson out of the club and take the girl. "The next time I saw her we were on the bus, on the road," Johnson says. "Rick had had her in the back, and she came out in a negligee—a negligee! I wanted to kill Rick. This girl was a once-in-a-lifetime beauty, but once any girl went with Rick, she was finished for me."

Rick didn't restrict himself to the girlfriends or sex partners of his entourage. As Rick's friend Peter Kelly says, "Rick took everybody's girl."

Rick restrained himself in some situations, however. He once met a girl at a farm owned by one of his former band members, Stan Endersby. Shortly thereafter, the fifteen-year-old began flirting with Rick at a bar. Rick immediately shooed the girl away, then phoned Endersby and asked him to drive over and pick her up. He also wrote in *The Confessions of Rick James* that he "stayed away from married chicks. I practiced that art with a lot of fortitude, maybe because of my Catholic upbringing, maybe because my Dad cheated on my mom." He violated even this rule on occasion, however.

Even years later, when Rick was out of shape, no longer making hit records, and rarely touring, women would still migrate to his house wherever he was living and join the large party that was always going on (likely partly a result of the masses of cocaine Rick kept on hand). When Rick wanted one of the women, he would just step out of his bedroom and point at her. After he'd finished with her, he'd point at the next woman he desired.

27

Rick Writes a Song about His Penis

Hold it straight and hold it steady. When you shoot me I'll be ready.

—"Love Gun," by Rick James (1979)

Rick's next album, 1979's *Fire It Up*, featured the hit song "Love Gun." Rick told author David Ritz, "You don't have to be Sigmund Freud to figure out that 'Love Gun' was a penis." In the song, Rick attempted to attract the female he was addressing with lyrics such as "Put your finger on the trigger / When you pull it back I'll figure / That now you're ready for the fire," "Fire me up girl and we'll have big fun," and "I'm gonna shoot you with desire."

During a performance of the song on—of all TV programs—Dinah Shore's *Dinah and Friends* on September 19, 1979, the two female background singers added such lyrics as "Give me a shot, of your love gun" and "Ahhh, bang bang! Ahh, bang bang!"

Billboard liked "Love Gun," noting that "taunting background female vocals" added to its "hyperactive air." Although another reviewer, William Ruhlmann, found it "just smutty" rather than provocative, the song rose to number 13 on the *Billboard* R&B chart, and stayed on the chart for twelve weeks. Rick called it a "monster hit" and made it a permanent part of his repertoire.

Prince, who later became one of Rick's rivals, gave "Love Gun" the ultimate compliment a few years later by having his girl group Apollonia 6 imitate it in their 1984 song "Sex Shooter." Prince's song included lyrics such as "I need you to get me off . . . / I need you to pull my trigger, baby / I can't do it alone . . . / Come on, kiss the gun / Guaranteed for fun."

Fire It Up appeared only nine months after the release of *Bustin' Out of L Seven*, and Rick was credited with writing, arranging, and producing every tune on the album. Rick had told an interviewer he was going to "record it, mix it, and master it" in just two weeks. He justified this speed by claiming he was no longer "experimenting" with his music but was doing "exactly what I want to do," which was adding spicy ghetto lyrics to funky dance music. He also said he had already spent a lot of time on preproduction.

It's more likely, however, that Rick's real motivation was to capitalize on his success with *Bustin' Out* as fast as possible by issuing another album. One of the ways he did this was by imitating other groups: "Love Gun" resembled the song with the same title released by the white rock group KISS the year before, which hadn't charted. The title aside, each song referred to the penis as the "love gun," used the phrase "love gun" numerous times, and urged a woman referred to as "baby," to "pull the trigger" of the love gun involved.

Rick's accelerated strategy worked for "Love Gun" but not for the album itself. While the *New York Times* neutrally described *Fire It Up* as a blend of rock, jazz, and funk, Vladimir Bogdanov called it "dull and formulaic" and a "holding action," and criticized it as "the usual mix of rock and R&B."

The song "Come into My Life" was the only other single on *Fire It Up* that charted, rising to number 26 on the R&B chart but not charting as a pop song. A rousing dance tune, it included such hard-to-understand lines from Rick as, "Girl, when push comes to shove and it's me you want to love / Come / Don't be afraid to hesitate, I won't hurt you or make you wait / If you come," backed by female backup singers repeatedly and musically spelling out "C-O-M-E."

This was Rick's least popular album so far and also the one that appealed greatly to black people but attracted relatively few white listeners. Nevertheless, *Fire It Up*, released in October 1979, rose to number 5 on the *Billboard* R&B album chart and stayed there for twenty-nine weeks. It hit number 34 on the top pop album chart and survived on the chart for twenty weeks.

In a 1989 suit against Rick in federal court, Motown said *Fire It Up* had sold a disappointing total of 357,569 copies through mid-1988, down from sales of about 900,000 of *Come Get It!* and 500,000 of *Bustin' Out*. A poster that was based on Rick's image on the cover sold almost as many copies as the record itself.

On the inner sleeve, Rick dedicated two of the songs on the album, "Stormy Love" and "When Love Is Gone," "to my X love K [Kelly Misener]. May you find Peace, Love & Happiness." Rick told Ritz that "Stormy Love" was "the most emotional thing I ever wrote." The couple had "come to the end of the road," he said, and "I was hurting. This was my farewell."

"Stormy Love" is a spoken-word poem about loss and regret recited by Rick over a musical background. It includes lines such as "Until this day the gods have not forgiven me for betraying" and "To think that for years to come / I must live alone without you / The only one I've ever loved." The second song, "When Love Is Gone," is more musical but is otherwise similar. When both songs were released, Rick and Kelly had been apart for three years and divorced for six months.

Already depressed about losing Kelly, overindulging in liquor, pot, and cocaine, Rick was even further knocked off his feet when he was hospitalized for hepatitis in late 1979. Once he recovered, however, his appetite for drugs and sex was even stronger than before his hospitalization. But now there was a new artist emerging who would challenge Rick as the king of sex: Prince.

28

Rick and Prince Duke It Out
for Sex and Glory

Everyone has a rock bottom.

—Prince

In a way, the clash between Rick and Prince was all Rick's fault. He made the mistake of booking Prince (born Prince Rogers Nelson in 1958) as one of his opening acts in 1979 on his *Fire It Up* tour and on subsequent tours, giving the musician his first national exposure and reinforcing the younger man's apparent belief in the potential of pornographic flamboyance. One of Rick's motives may have been that Prince reminded Rick of himself. The problem was that pretty soon Prince was more famous than Rick.

Even on their first tour together, to Rick's great annoyance, Prince started imitating some of Rick's trademark moves. This would have seemed mere flattery if Prince weren't directly preceding Rick onstage, making Rick look like the copycat. Prince, although not a Motown performer, appeared to have stolen a page from Diana Ross's playbook. When Ross and her fellow Supremes were warm-up acts on the Motown Revue tours in the early 1960s, Ross would sit in the audience after performing and memorize the trademark moves of the tour's stars. She'd then perform their moves in her own act the next day before the stars appeared, making them look imitative and ridiculous.

The resulting hostility of some Motown artists toward Ross was nothing compared to that between Prince and Rick, who went on to spend years harassing and imitating each other. Each accused the other of being second, rather than first, with every innovation each made. "Everything that Prince did, I've already done," Rick once told Richard Wesley. "He was always biting off me."

Despite their obvious dislike for each other, it became apparent that neither man covered his ears in the presence of the other man's performances. For the rest of Rick's career, he and Prince competed intensely to see which of them could produce the most pornographic song.

Almost immediately, Prince won this race to the bottom (in all senses) with his 1980 album *Dirty Mind*, which included the song "Sister," with such lines as "I was only sixteen, but I guess that's no excuse / My sister was burnin' to love me, and loose . . . / Showed me where it's supposed to go / A blow job doesn't mean blow / Incest is everything it's said to be." Rick's songs seemed tame by comparison. The problem with "Sister," as with all Prince's semipornographic songs, was that he was too serious; he didn't lighten his shocking message with Rick's winking humor.

Rick had a serious problem with this particular song, calling it "dangerous for the race" and linking it in *The Confessions of Rick James* with songs about devil worship or gangsta rap. Black writers and recording artists, he said, should be more concerned with the influence they have on younger generations. Having sex with your own sister was going too far even for Rick. Rick's references to cunnilingus on many of his songs were similarly outdone by Prince's ode to oral sex, another song on his *Dirty Mind* album, fittingly titled "Head." In it, Prince meets a woman who is not only technically a virgin but on the way to her wedding ceremony. She takes a gander at the singer, talks for a couple minutes, and then tells him, "You're such a hunk, so full of spunk, I'll give you head." Prince, or the character he's singing about, then "came on her wedding gown," forcing her to admit she wants to go to bed with him, and she marries him instead of the man waiting at the altar. Then, according to the song, *he* gives *her* head.

Prince upped the ante while singing onstage in London, switching viewpoints between seducer and seduced, woman and man, something Rick would have done only if the alternative was slow castration. As the *Washington Post* noted, Rick's idea of singing about sex was to "pander to sexual fantasies by exaggerating traditional gender roles," while Prince's sex songs, along with those of Boy George and Chrissie Hynde, blurred those roles.

Some of Prince's songwriting ideas may have been stimulated by the Hollywood environment in which both he and Rick moved. Ruffin recalls an occasion on which Rick took him to his first Hollywood party, a wedding reception. "It was beautiful!" Ruffin says. "The couples were fantastic-looking. . . .There's drugs, but there's also caviar. . . . I'd never been a part of this kind of atmosphere." He continues, "Next thing I know, the husband and wife are dancing, they're so cute, then they break off and they each go to their partner, him to his boyfriend and her to her girlfriend, and begin slapping tongues [French kissing]. I said, 'Rick, get me the fuck out of here.' Rick said, 'Levi, we just can't walk out, come on, man.'" They eventually left.

Rick had been teased for the sexually ambiguous nature of some of the outfits he wore on his album covers, but Prince went him one better early on when he wore only black jockstrap-type underwear, an open overcoat, and a scarf on the cover of his *Dirty Mind* album. He also occasionally wore panties and high heels when performing.

Prince may have produced purer porno, but Rick's semipornographic tunes were generally more popular, since radio stations shied away from Prince's more explicit songs. *New Musical Express*, in fact, awarded the prize in the Rick v. Prince competition to Rick. Reviewing one of Rick's onstage performances, *NME* claimed that Rick "took on Prince man-to-man, trampling over the short-legged one's plastic sensuality with a labial lasciviousness which somehow managed to equate cold blood with wild freaky sex." That must have been quite a show.

Creem magazine disagreed, arguing that Rick was less perverse than Prince. When Rick sang about being "kinky" or "freaky," the *Creem* reviewer wrote, he was probably referring only to oral-genital contact. He added that "Prince's bizarre [sexual] scenarios don't occur to him, and if they do, he keeps them out of his music."

To say the least, none of Prince's activities pleased Rick one iota. Rick "was obsessed with Prince and thought himself in a rivalry" with the younger man, according to screenwriter Richard Wesley. Each man harassed the other. At one of Rick's concerts at the Universal Amphitheatre in Los Angeles, Prince was seen entering the amphitheater just before Rick came onstage. Rather than sit down and wait for the show to begin, Prince, a small man, leapt into the arms of his own burly bodyguard, a typical Prince feminine act, and had the man carry him to his seat. This attracted so much attention that Prince's fans began swarming around him, driving him to decide to leave the auditorium. Rather than just walk, however, he jumped onto his bodyguard's back and rode out piggyback style, arousing the crowd once again. Rick was appropriately furious, calling Prince's actions "a pathetic attempt to steal the show."

Rick took his revenge by humiliating Prince in public whenever he had the opportunity. Once, taking Prince by surprise, Rick grabbed his hair, pulled his head back, and poured liquor down his throat, causing the younger man to choke and spit.

But Prince beat Rick in the larger arena. As early as 1983, the *Baton Rouge Morning Advocate* pointed out that Prince was in better physical shape than Rick, provided a flashier show, and "served his raunch in a more literate and melodic dish." He also became a more popular performer than Rick had ever been, and lived longer, dying in 2016 at age fifty-seven.

29

Rick Takes a Nap in the Garden

We are stardust, we are golden We are billion-year-old
carbon And we've got to get ourselves
back to the garden.

—"Woodstock," performed by Crosby, Stills, Nash & Young,
written by Joni Mitchell (1970)

As a relatively young musician at thirty-two, as well
as an ambitious one, it was natural for Rick to want to stretch himself musically. Stevie Wonder "can do anything musically, and people
will love it and accept it," Rick told an interviewer that year. "I think
that will come with me, with time, where I can extend my music."

Rick was so ready to make a change, he told another interviewer, that
he was ready to drop the funk label and call what he did just "music." To
inspire himself, he and the Stone City Band moved to Miami, hired a
yacht, and drifted around the Caribbean while Rick strummed his guitar
and composed a bunch of new songs.

Rick had been talking for years about his desire to sing ballads, so it
shouldn't have been much of a surprise to anyone when his next album,
Garden of Love, released in July 1980, featured mostly ballads. Five of the
tunes' titles, which one writer called "flowery," said it all: "Island Lady,"
"Gettin' It On (In the Sunshine)," "Don't Give Up on Love," "Summer

Love," and "Mary-Go-Round." Rick was credited with producing, writing, and arranging every song on the album except "Big Time."

Years later, the *Los Angeles Times* noted astutely that Rick's real weakness in creating ballads was his inability to arrange the emotions they contained into any kind of pattern. He expressed unmodulated feelings throughout each ballad, the *Times* said, causing listeners to lose interest halfway through. The *Philadelphia Inquirer* complained, also accurately, that Rick's "slower melodies tend to bring out the sap in him: his brazenness melts and he gets all gooey."

Author J. Randy Taraborrelli, referring to the songs on this album as "mood music," accused Rick and the Stone City Band of "wandering somewhat aimlessly" on tunes such as "Don't Give Up on Love" and "Island Lady."

Another more sympathetic reviewer opined, however, that the ballads on *Garden of Love* may have been "too esoteric for the masses." And an even friendlier writer called the songs "first rate," and said many listeners heard them as "wimpy" because they were so used to Rick's usual "hard and rowdy funk."

Rick reacted angrily to criticism that the songs were sappy. "Well, damn it," he told an interviewer, "I should be able to musically come from my total makeup as a person and have it accepted. People want more than three-chord funk these days." Before issuing *Garden of Love*, however, even Rick had expressed some worries about his ability to write and sing ballads. "I don't know if I'm ready to do what Lionel Richie and the Commodores have done: stun my audiences with an overabundance of sensitivity," he told an interviewer. As it turned out, he was right.

There was another problem with the album. It included only six songs, although Motown execs, according to an eventual suit against Rick, wanted more. It also did not help Rick's Motown career that the sole hit on the album, "Big Time," was the only song he hadn't written.

A drawing on *Garden of Love*'s jacket shows Rick in a blue bodysuit with braided and bejeweled hair, accompanied by three women in modest outfits. All of them are in a pleasant-looking patch of seaweed and sea anemones. On the back of the album, sea sprites and butterflies dance in the foliage on the shore of a lake.

Garden of Love rose to number 17 on the *Billboard* R&B album chart and stayed on the chart for fifteen weeks. On the pop album chart, however, it rose only to number 83 and dropped off the chart completely after ten weeks. *Garden of Love*'s lackluster reception caused Rick to cancel the Funky Island Tour he had planned for America and Europe. Court papers indicate *Garden of Love* sold only 146,774 copies through mid-1988.

It was a long fall from producing a near-platinum album to one that didn't even make the Top 10 on the R&B chart. Again, the only tune on *Garden of Love* to garner any positive attention was "Big Time," written by Leroy Burgess, James Calloway, and Sonny Davenport; it rose to number 17 on the *Billboard* R&B chart and stayed on the chart for seventeen weeks. Even that tune didn't make the pop chart, however.

Rick said "Big Time" was the first tune he'd recorded that wasn't completely or partly one of his own compositions. He'd heard it when he visited his friend Kenny Morris, who played it for him. "I *had* to have it," Rick said, adding that he removed a couple tracks he'd written for *Garden of Love* to make room for it. He'd turned down previous offers of tracks written by other people in order to keep his own compositions on his albums, "but this one was too good to pass on." Its musical quality aside, it's possible Rick loved this song because it proclaimed the central driving force of his life: his ambition. In such lines as "I'm in the Big Time, Big Time / And I know success is all mine, all mine," "Big Time" proclaimed that Rick thought he had finally made it. But he hadn't.

Motown later tried to cover Rick's decline by announcing in 1985 that *Bustin' Out of L Seven*, *Fire It Up*, and *Garden of Love* had sold a *total* of more than five million copies. More than 4.8 million of these sales, however, had been of *Bustin' Out* and *Fire It Up*.

Rick was shocked by *Garden of Love*'s failure. "I found out with *Garden* that success could end at any time, and you're only as good as your last record," he wrote in *The Confessions of Rick James*.

After the album's failure and the tour's cancellation, Rick made yet another mistake. Afraid his career was over, he flew to Hawaii to recover.

While there, he ate dinner with his manager, Shep Gordon, at Gordon's house on Maui. Salvador Dali, the famous surrealist, was the other guest at dinner. Dali told Rick he had great lips, and asked if he could do a sketch of the singer on a napkin. Rick said yes, and when Dali finished the sketch, he gave it to Rick, who put it in his pocket. Not thinking of the value of the drawing, Rick later jumped in the ocean with the sketch in his pocket, ruining it.

Rick wasn't happy when he realized how much the item he had taken for an inadvertent dunk was worth. At this low time in his life, however, he was cheered by the continuing success of his protégée, Teena Marie. Because Teena's first album, *Wild and Peaceful*, had sold so well, and because she'd learned so much from him, Rick had told her she should be the sole producer of her next album. Not feeling she was quite ready for that responsibility, Teena Marie had chosen Richard Rudolph, husband of the late vocalist Minnie Riperton, as her coproducer. She selected him because she had admired Riperton for her innovative music and singing. The resulting album, *Lady T*, entered the R&B chart on March 8, 1980, rose to number 18, and remained on that chart for twenty-six weeks, equaling the chart success of *Wild and Peaceful*, except that it rose higher on the pop chart, to number 45. Her next Motown album, *Irons in the Fire*, came out shortly after *Garden of Love*, on July 6, 1980, and rose to number 38 on the pop chart and number 9 on the R&B chart. For now, Rick's only success was vicarious.

But that would soon change.

30

Rick Absolutely Hits the Freakin' Top with *Street Songs*

It had long since come to my attention that people of accomplishment
rarely sat back and let things happen to them.
They went out and happened to things.

—Leonardo da Vinci

Rick's reactions to the failure of *Garden of Love*, while somewhat drastic, were very rational. "I realized how fickle the business
is," he told *Jet* magazine. "The phone didn't jump off the hook. My ego
was at stake."

His friends' advice after *Garden of Love*'s failure inspired him to take
immediate action, Rick wrote in his autobiography, *The Confessions of
Rick James*. "All my friends said 'Rick, you got to get back to the Funk,
the streets. You got to get hungry again.' Everyone said the same thing.
It was like a broken record. I had gotten too rich, too fast. I had lost that
thing, that ghetto tiger, which had fueled me in the beginning. . . . I was
in the California sunshine, not the ghettos and black snow of Buffalo.
Life had become easy and I had become lackadaisical."

Rick dropped his manager, Shep Gordon of Alive Management
(who also had managed Alice Cooper and Teddy Pendergrass), saying Gordon "wasn't going in the right direction" with his career. Years

later, LeRoi Johnson criticized Gordon more pointedly: "Shep's focus was Teddy, and Rick was second, and Rick didn't like that at all. Teddy was a big star in those days, but Rick wasn't playing second to anybody." After Rick dropped Gordon, Johnson entered Rick's management team and soon became his manager, staying on in that job until drug abuse overwhelmed Rick a few years later.

Rick also moved back to Buffalo with a vengeance, saying his creativity had suffered when he'd pulled up his roots and ended contact with his fellow ghetto freaks. "I wasn't seeing none of those crazy people," he told an interviewer, "and I couldn't find nothing to write about."

Rick's mother had been living with him in L.A. in one of William Randolph Hearst's old homes in Beverly Hills, although Rick said "it wasn't even comfortable," even though, or perhaps because, it featured a sunken living room. A serious earthquake had scared her back to Buffalo. Shortly thereafter, Rick sold Hearst's former house and followed his mother, buying a twenty-six-room suburban ranch house on thirty-seven acres in what had been the all-white Buffalo suburb of Orchard Park. Because the previous owner, a black doctor, had been refused admission to the local country club, he had built a pool and tennis court for his children on the property. According to Rick, the next owner wanted to make the house a home for people with intellectual developmental disorders but was refused permission. His revenge was to sell the home to Rick. The property also featured basketball courts as well as facilities for Rick's ten snowmobiles, Arabian horses, and numerous luxury cars.

Inside, the house included a tropical paradise room (with colored lights, a sauna, and plants) and a living room with a big fireplace and space for all Rick's albums. There also was a room furnished only with ancient Chinese objects, and one that served as Rick's bedroom, which featured its own fireplace and a big brass bed with a silken, tentlike canopy. In 1980, soon after arriving, he also bought the house next door.

Rick's new digs had many advantages. In the winter he could ride one of his snowmobiles on his property, a sport he could hardly pursue in L.A. In better weather he rode his Arabian horses, including a black stallion named Punk. And he could keep and drive one of his dozen cars while wearing one of his three hundred pairs of shoes with one of his 365 suits. But the real advantage of the move was the boost it afforded his creativity. In his words, "The shit just started coming. The real basic shit."

In addition to changing his home base, Rick also changed his recording goals. "The quickest way to lose touch with your black base is to go out there and start writing pop hits for the white market," he told an interviewer. "That's what Stevie [Wonder]'s doing, and the Commodores. Lionel [Richie]'s writing his ass off, but it's the white market. Black people don't buy those 'Sail On's' and 'Three Times a Lady's.'" Of course Rick realized the white record market was bigger than the black one. But he knew that in white America, where he lived and wanted to prosper, a black vocalist had to be a hit with black people first before becoming a hit with white people.

Rick also told an interviewer that on his next album, he wanted to imitate another black performer, Marvin Gaye, by producing songs along the lines of Gaye's *What's Going On* but with more of an emphasis on sex. And that's exactly what he did. As Rick Abel puts it, "This is when Rick literally found his voice in terms of the type of person he was." Rick's next album, *Street Songs*, which emphasized not only sex but police brutality and changes in society, certainly resembled *What's Going On* thematically, returning funk to its inner-city roots. One reviewer later wrote *Street Songs* represented "the social and political climate of black America in the early '80s in the same way that recordings by Marvin Gaye, Stevie Wonder and Curtis Mayfield . . . captured the zeitgeist of the '70s."

Rick also changed his approach in another important way. Although his version of disco had first brought him to public attention, in this album Rick woke up from his disco nap and started talking about reality. Aligning himself with the majority of record listeners, who were by this time revolting against disco music, which they criticized as meaningless and repetitive, Rick also denounced it, calling it "just another mechanical form of music." In a major turnaround, he said that disco was "cool in the castles where it was played, but not so cool in the minds of a lot of people in the street."

Street Songs, released on April 7, 1981, rose to number 3 on the *Billboard* pop album chart, the highest position held by any black artist that year, and spent seventy-four weeks on the chart. "I was no longer a black artist," Rick gloated. "I had officially crossed over." The album also rose to number 1 on *Billboard's* R&B album chart, and stayed there for twenty weeks, tying the record for that position held by Stevie Wonder's album *Songs in the Key of Life*.

The *Los Angeles Times* ranked *Street Songs* number 7 among the Top 10 albums produced that year, and *Billboard* called it the year's most successful soul LP. *Street Songs* also won *Billboard's* number one album award for 1982. As a result of the record's strong sales, Rick became one of Motown's bestselling acts ever.

On July 7, 1981, the RIAA certified *Street Songs* as a platinum album, meaning it had sold at least one million copies by that date. In court papers filed in 1989, Motown said *Street Songs* had sold 2,376,714 copies through mid-1988, making it a double-platinum triumph as well as Rick's bestselling album ever, and justifying its designation as a mega-smash. (The album has since achieved triple-platinum status.)

Rick insisted to *Oui* magazine in 1982 that the album sold ten million copies, including four and a half million in the United States. "God and I had a very good conversation, and He *listened* to me," he said. He was exaggerating the numbers, but there was no question that *Street Songs* sold more than sixteen times as well as *Garden of Love*, his previous album, giving him every reason to go crazy when discussing its success.

Street Songs also earned Rick a Grammy nomination for Best R&B Vocal Performance, Male, but the award went to James Ingram for the track "One Hundred Ways," from Quincy Jones's album *The Dude*. Nevertheless, *Billboard* ranked Rick as 1981's top soul album artist, promoting him from number 27 to number 1 on its combined singles/album listing.

As Motown executive Suzanne de Passe told *Behind the Music*, with this record, and some of his earlier albums, Rick had come to embody "all those urban street values of being fly and having women and the right clothes and the right ride. . . . It was all about being fabulous."

31

"Super Freak"

Most people don't realize they're a freak until it's way too late to change it.

—"Meredith Grey" on *Grey's Anatomy*

"**S**uper Freak," the highlight of *Street Songs*, is the most famous song Rick James ever wrote, becoming a major hit shortly after it was released and a major hit again nine years later, when MC Hammer reworked it as "U Can't Touch This."

As Rick told the *Times* (London), the tune was born when "[I] was listening to the tracks, just riffing on my bass, and I hit on this punky-funky sounding line. The song came together, I had the Tempts singing behind me, and next thing I know it's a smash." This may be the greatest simplification in pop music history.

One of the song's strengths was indeed Rick's use of the Temptations to sing background, an effective homage to one of the most famous and long-lived acts to precede Rick at Motown. (The Tempts had left Motown in 1976 and did not return until 1980.) Rick said he chose the Tempts because they were "probably the most important vocal group in the history of black music."

Rick may have been unique among Motown stars in using long-established predecessor acts at the company when recording his own songs. He did it not only with the Temptations but with Stevie Wonder, Smokey Robinson, and others. This habit indicated the depth of his gratitude for finally becoming a Motown star after three tries, as well as the depth of his admiration for the most successful black music company in American history.

To make sure the audience knew who the backing singers were, Rick introduced their contribution to "Super Freak" with the words, "Temptations, sing!" In the video of the song, the footage of the Tempts singing is in black-and-white, while footage of Rick and his backup singers is in color—a clue that he saw the Tempts, at the top from 1965 to 1973, as part of the historical past. However, his reverence for them is real and apparent, with the Tempts portrayed in one of their patented bend-down, front-scoop, side-turn, side-clap moves. In an additional show of respect, Rick's five female fellow performers repeat the Tempts moves a few second later.

"Super Freak" was complex in many other ways. Much of the song's popularity, including its strong erotic appeal, was its opening line: "She's a very kinky girl." Reviewers called this the best opening lyric ever; its obvious strength is that it entices listeners to keep listening to find out why she's kinky. At least one songwriter, Christopher Ward, ranked "She's a very kinky girl" in the same class with the Beatles lyric "She was just seventeen, you know what I mean," which began their 1963 song "I Saw Her Standing There" ("What *do* you mean?" the listener asks). Ward also linked it with the lyric "I heard the news today, oh boy," which opened the Beatles's 1967 song "A Day in the Life." ("What news *did* you hear?" the listener wonders.) This was only the beginning of English influence on the song. It could almost be said that "Super Freak" was an English song that happened to be written and recorded by African Americans.

But the lyrics listeners have come to know and love were not the ones he originally penned. Rick wrote in *The Confessions of Rick James* that the original lyrics he wrote for the song "were nasty, to say the least—too nasty for radio." He became aware of this when he sang the tune to his friend Alonzo Miller, a DJ and program director at KACE-FM, an L.A. radio station. "After hearing the lyrics, he just shook his head and said, 'Rick, they'll never play it on the radio.'" Among the lyrics Miller objected to was the line "She will never let your spirits down / Once you get her in the sheets." He suggested that Rick change it to "Once you get her off the street," which Rick agreed to do. Miller added that he'd always thought Rick was slicker than his lyrics and that that was what separated Rick from Prince. Convinced by this argument, Rick and Miller cleaned up the lyrics, and Rick gave Miller 10 percent of the song's publishing royalties for helping him "see the light." (Miller is credited as a cowriter of the song.)

LeRoi Johnson told Rick it was a great song and different from the other songs, but Rick kept criticizing it as "too English technopop," and too "new wave." MTV had just started broadcasting shortly after "Super Freak" was released, at that time as a channel that played many new wave videos twenty-four hour per day and inadvertently popularized the new wave technopop sound, thus contributing to the popularity of "Super Freak," Rick's biggest hit. That MTV later refused to broadcast the "Super Freak" video makes this entire progression highly ironic.

"Super Freak" referred to its new wave status in its own lyrics. One of the lines in the song is, "The kind of girl you read about in new wave magazines." Many US listeners unfamiliar with new wave music thought the reference was to *Newsweek* magazine. And, in fact, the first time the background vocalists sing it in the recorded song it does sound much more like *Newsweek* than "new wave."

Rick told author David Ritz the song came about when he came up with a line that reminded him of "how punkers look funny when they try to dance. I heard it as a goof and never dreamed it'd take off." Because Rick and his fellow musicians thought of this song, which they themselves had written, as an English song, someone in the group suggested to Rick that he use an English cockney accent when recording it. Rick sang it not only with a slight cockney accent but in a high, cartoonish voice that made him sound smarmy and leering when he sang the slightly risqué lyrics. This added to the song's erotic appeal.

Rick thought the lyrics to "Super Freak" were silly. "The line about 'she's the kind of girl you don't take home to mother' was jive," Rick said. "I could take any girl home to mother." LeRoi Johnson says he actually had to talk his brother into including the song on the album. When asked if Rick ever acknowledged that he was right about "Super Freak," Johnson says he'd occasionally tell Rick, "You were wrong about 'Super Freak' and then he'd give me that look, that 'So what?' look, a look that said, 'OK, you were right once, but so what?'"

As it turned out, the "Super Freak" lyrics, when combined with its music, were extremely catchy. Once people heard Rick sing "That girl is pretty kinky," and the background singers reply, "That girl's a super freak" it became hard to forget the song, especially because in those relatively innocent days, its words were startling. One reviewer described them as "raunchy groupie lyrics." Reviewers also liked the song for what the *Washington Post* called its "mysterious, frenetic energy," probably due to the combination of its sexy lyrics with a thumping bass line.

Another odd thing about "Super Freak" was that after Rick and Miller edited the lyrics, it wasn't as obscene as many people thought. Rick was right when he said the song wasn't meant to have an especially bad connotation. While it was considered erotic and scandalous at the time—and the smarmy voice Rick sang it in added to that impression—it contained only two unarguably erotic references. Referring to the woman who's the subject of the song, Rick sings, "Three's not a crowd to her" and quickly adds "ménage à trois."

But Prince had already one-upped him the year before by singing about such trios in his song "When You Were Mine," on his *Dirty Mind* album, which includes the line, "I never was the kind to make a fuss / when he was there / sleepin' in between the two of us." Prince's lyrics indicated that the participants in his intimate grouping included at least two males, one of them himself. This is not a ménage in which Rick would willingly have participated.

The second unambiguous sexual reference in "Super Freak" occurred when Rick sang "I really love to taste her, every time we meet." This obvious reference to cunnilingus may have been pushing the boundaries a little, but was cunnilingus really that freaky in 1981?

The song's lyrics also contained the line, "Room 714, I'll be waiting." To those in the know, the line indicated that the couple in the song was planning to use drugs, because 714 was a widespread slang term for quaaludes.

The "Super Freak" video only added to the song's erotic appeal and general popularity. In it, an in-shape, clear-eyed Rick appears wearing a sequined vest with a V-shaped opening, black pants with lightning bolt decorations, and high black boots. Physically as well as musically at the top of his game, he moves swiftly from one of his five female coperformers to another while singing, smiling, winking, smirking, and outlining a female form in the air, flicking his tongue in and out of his mouth, playing his guitar, and briefly using that instrument as a phallic symbol.

The four women onstage are a multiracial group: two whites, one African American, and one Asian American (Cheryl Song, who danced on the TV show *Soul Train*). In two brief scenes another African American woman appears. The sexy women use every publically presentable trick in the book to hold the viewers' attention, including winking, pouting, looking astonished, sticking out their tongues, flipping their hair back, wiggling their hips, and shaking and thrusting out their breasts. They also stick out their tongues, flip their hair back, wave their hands and arms in the air, giggle with their hands over their mouths, dance with their nearly naked backs to the camera, move their hands near Rick's crotch while gaping with astonishment, briefly flip up their skirts to reveal their own mostly naked legs, and move their heads back and forth with their arms straight up in the air. When they gesture at Rick to come hither, they look pleased but cover their mouths ineffectually with their hands in an attempt not to reveal their delight.

In an exceedingly sexy move, after the African American female performer dances for a moment with her mostly naked back to the camera, Rick dances butt to butt with her while playing his guitar and singing. And in an exceedingly democratic move, twice in the video Rick has everyone on the set dance in place behind him while he sings, including average-looking men and women in office-type outfits. At the end of the song he also introduces saxophonist LeMelle's vibrant tenor sax solo with the words "Blow, Danny, blow." (Rick gave LeMelle a similar verbal acknowledgment at the end of several songs he wrote later in his career.)

"['Super Freak'] was about all the girls I know," Rick told *Right On!* magazine. "The girls with green and white hair, slits all the way up their butts." He said its title "wasn't meant as a bad connotation" but instead was "complimentary. It just means being sexually open and not constricted. To me, a freak was an uninhibited woman." Yet the title came to be widely applied to Rick himself. The *London Daily Telegraph* speculated this may have happened because "the song's loping bass line brought to mind a pimp out for his evening strut." There was a deeper reason than that, however.

"Super Freak" meant "heavy drug user" to many listeners, and the song finally told the truth about the effects of Rick's most ruinous pastime. By this point in his life, LeMelle says, "drugs pretty much consumed and controlled him" (although they had not yet cut as deeply into his abilities as an entertainer and a sexual being as they would later). By continuing to stand day after day, night after night, and year after year in the middle of the heavily traveled intersection of desire and availability, Rick eventually destroyed himself. But not before creating an extremely memorable pop song.

Journalists perceived the connection. Near the end of Rick's life, one critic wrote that "the idea of Rick James calling anybody freaky is, face it, fascinating." The *Washington Post* said that Rick's "brash, boisterous, self-destructive life epitomized the title of his greatest hit." And *Newsday* said that despite the many songs Rick had recorded before "Super Freak," his "flamboyant outfits, chaotic personal life and sexually charged songs made him *synonymous* with this one song." Although the subject of the song was the kind of girl "you don't take home to mother," Rick could easily have said the same thing about himself. And his listeners recognized and responded to this deeper meaning.

Although Rick didn't receive a Grammy for "Super Freak" in 1982, his performance of that song made him the first black artist ever nominated for a Grammy for Best Rock Vocal Performance, Male. He was up against Bruce Springsteen, Rod Stewart, Gary "U.S." Bonds, and Rick Springfield, who ultimately won the award for "Jessie's Girl."

Nevertheless, Rick James was featured on the awards show performing another song from *Street Songs*, "Give It to Me Baby."

Rick had kept "Super Freak" on the album despite his dislike of it partly because, while he never wanted to lose his black audience, he believed "Super Freak" would increase his popularity with white fans. He told one interviewer he wanted to have something "that white folks could dance to" on the disc.

Those white folks not only danced but helped make the record a hit. A crossover tune par excellence, "Super Freak" almost instantly changed the racial composition of Rick's audience from mostly black to one-third white. Rick, "even more than Prince, has managed to bridge the distance between black and white audiences and idioms alike," Don Waller of the *Los Angeles Times* said afterward. "The last time that happened, they had to invent a new name for the result—'rock 'n' roll.'" This couldn't have made Rick happier—a rock 'n' roller was exactly what he wanted to be.

Adding compliment to compliment, in 1995 Jim Henke, chief curator of the Rock and Roll Hall of Fame and Museum in Cleveland, in conjunction with a group of rock critics and historians, added "Super Freak" to the hall's list of the five hundred songs that shaped rock 'n' roll.

"Super Freak" appeared on the top R&B singles chart on August 1, 1981, rose to number 3, and stayed on the chart for seventeen weeks. Partly as a result of its rock 'n' roll quality and its appeal to whites, it made the pop top 40 chart on September 5, 1981, rose to number 16, and didn't drop off completely for ten weeks, becoming an across-the-board smash. From its release in 1981 through mid-1988, according to Motown, it sold 2,376,714 copies in all formats. Over the ensuing decades, it has kept selling: in 2006, the RIAA awarded a gold certification to its digital version, meaning that that version alone had sold more than five hundred thousand copies.

"Super Freak" was used in the film *Doctor Detroit* and in numerous other movies and TV shows, all of which were required to pay royalties to Rick. In addition to a great deal of money, the song also provided Rick with something else very important—a theme song.

It also caused the groupie scene surrounding Rick and his associates to rocket into the stratosphere, propelling him into affairs with various well-known and attractive women, including movie stars Elisabeth Shue and Linda Blair, model Janice Dickinson, and Marvin Gaye's estranged wife, Jan Gaye.

His fame also caused him to be paired with vocalist Grace Jones as an award presenter at 1982's American Music Awards. Jones was wearing a magnificent, but gigantic, transparent, Japanese-style, black-ribbed, inverted-bowl hat. Rick, acting very frisky with Jones, moved in on her under the hat, and ad-libbed to the crowd that he was "trying to get some." Jones laughed and replied, "Some of what, may I ask?" and Rick said, "Some of this hat." Jones replied, "I see. I get it," and added, with a smile, "Well, that's all right. Stay under there."

A minute or so later, Rick said, "Stevie Wonder, you should see this hat." Wonder, who is blind, was in the audience. Commentators criticized Rick for his remarks to both Jones and Wonder. Jones seemed unfazed, however, and at Rick's funeral some years later, Wonder told the mourners that he "loved" Rick for "the laughter I had" at Rick's remark. Wonder said he interpreted the remark as meaning "Wow. Look at that hat. It's so big Stevie can see it." Over the years Wonder has demonstrated that, counterintuitively, he enjoys jokes about his blindness.

Rick may have been acting frisky at the ceremony because of his affair with Jan Gaye. He knew the affair had angered Marvin, and his nerves were twanging with the thought that he might have to put himself within Marvin's punching range onstage in order to hand an award to the vocalist. Rick's fears were partly realized when Marvin won the prize for Favorite Soul/R&B Single for—of all tunes—his song "Sexual Healing."

However, when Marvin moved close to Rick onstage to accept the award, he merely told Rick, "Take good care of her," obviously referring to Jan. A little more than two years later, in April 1984, Gaye—who had been struggling with his own drug addiction, poverty, and sometime homelessness—was shot dead by his own father during a vicious argument.

32

"Fire and Desire" Highlights Rick's Messy Relationship with Teena Marie

I have a different mentality when it comes to catering to a man. I just won't allow it. Don't get me wrong, I'll do for you but I'm not taking care of no man and catering to him for life; he better be bringing something to the table.

—Teena Marie

Several songs on the *Street Songs* album besides "Super Freak" became major hits as well as subjects of widespread controversy. Among them was the ballad that Rick and his protégée Teena Marie performed on the album, "Fire and Desire," which one reviewer called "stunning" and "first rate" and Connie Johnson of the *Los Angeles Times* called the best tune on the album.

Vibe magazine rated the song number four among the 50 Greatest Duets of All Time. After hearing Rick and Teena perform the scorching ballad, the *New York Times* said the couple had "sustained a level of erotic intensity seldom seen in a large arena." *Slate* magazine, referring in part to "Fire and Desire," complimented Rick on his ability to craft the kind of "slow-grind ballads that cause birthrate spikes."

In the song, Rick and Teena impersonate a former couple meeting by chance. Rick tells Teena he has a new girlfriend, that he regrets the way he behaved with Teena, and that she changed him by showing him so much "love and sensitivity."

Irony, plus a dramatic incident, underlies the great success of this song. Many reviewers had criticized Rick for hitting the peak too early on the ballads he himself sang. Apparently unable to apply this criticism to himself, he passed it on to Teena Marie, telling interviewer Brian Chin that his new protégée made *her* songs peak too soon. "I wanted to teach her to tell the story. First let people hear the story of what you're trying to sing . . . then you can give them your stuff. It was very hard for her to get that, but she did." As Teena put it, "He taught me how not to give everything to everyone right away, how to build up to a climax."

Considering the success of "Fire and Desire" as Rick and Teena sang it, it's surprising in retrospect that Rick hadn't intended to record it with her. "I didn't ask Teena to sing on it," he wrote in *The Confessions of Rick James*. "In fact, I had found a local girl with an amazing voice who was going to record the female vocals. Teena was . . . sick with a fever of 108 degrees, but when she heard I was going to use somebody else she immediately got out of her sick bed to sing on the track."

Rick said he was grateful to Teena for performing on "Fire and Desire" and for helping to make the song a hit. Nevertheless, Teena's excellence on the track backfired on him. *USA Today* said her "soulful bellows outshine Rick's" on the tune.

Teena, doe-eyed, five feet tall, and somewhat chunky, was a dazzling onstage performer. She ended many concerts Rick headlined by performing her songs "I'm a Sucker for Your Love" and "Square Biz," as well as singing backup on many of Rick's songs and performing with him on "Fire and Desire." Reviewing one of her 1981 appearances, the *Los Angeles Times* noted that "her fervent, frenzied performance sent the crowd into ecstasy." The paper noted that while it was rare to see a young black audience "treat a white performer with such reverence, it was certainly deserved. A tiny young woman with a powerful voice, Marie is a terrific singer and, quite frankly, better than nearly all her black competitors." Rick seemed to agree: "White people should be *real proud* of her," he said.

The *New York Times* reviewer seemed determined to go the *Los Angeles Times* one better in his praise of Teena, calling her "the most powerful white female soul singer that this observer has ever seen" and saying she was "capable of executing great whooping melismas in perfect pitch." The paper said "this tiny redheaded woman passed one of the ultimate tests for a pop singer in being able to deliver a ballad in a large arena and keep the audience riveted." With her strong voice and unabashed sensuality, Teena anticipated Madonna.

Although Rick hadn't written "Fire and Desire" about Teena, but rather about an Ethiopian woman he'd had an affair with on a visit to Paris, rumors of a Rick-Teena romance started immediately after they began singing the song together. Rick didn't seem enthusiastic about the idea. "T and I are like brother and sister," he told *Jet* magazine. "I do love her and she loves me but it's a musical love; we don't have a hot and heavy romance." From a male point of view, this was understandable. Rick's preference in women ran to lanky supermodels with nuclear-grade looks; Teena, although a great and determined artist, didn't make that bar. Rick wasn't above adding to the speculation, however. He told one interviewer, "If there was a woman I would choose to be my wife, one of the first ones on the top of my list would be Teena Marie. She's a lovely lady." He also called Teena the one woman who could quite easily slip into his "space of craziness" and understand him.

So it was to the surprise of absolutely no one that the two hot-and-heavy vocalists did yield to love and lust shortly after "Fire and Desire" became a hit. *Ebony* magazine wrote that Teena dated Rick for a year around this time and was engaged to him for two weeks. Interviewed in Las Vegas in 2013, Levi Ruffin said Teena lived at Rick's house in Orchard Park "for a couple of months." He said he and the other band members rehearsed at the house for months, and that his wife and daughter socialized with Teena.

One day, Ruffin found out that Teena "was talking to my daughter and wife about what kind of bridal shit she was going to wear," he said. "She just *knew* she and Rick were getting married. You could see it in her soul." Ruffin said he told her that Rick wasn't ready for marriage, and one day Rick finally told her the same thing "and broke her heart."

Teena told *Vibe* magazine in 2004 that Rick was her best friend, and said, "We made the mistake of having a relationship." She said there "were too many women" around Rick, and while "I always knew that I would be number one, I didn't like that there would be a number two, three, four, or five."

Teena told interviewers later that she and Rick broke up in mid-1981, either temporarily or permanently, on the first night of their *Street Songs* tour. That meant they still had to sing "Fire and Desire" to each other onstage, projecting major positive emotions, for the next several weeks. Paradoxically, this added to the performance, because in Teena's words, "we'd be fighting onstage, and the audience thought it was part of the act." She said "the theatrical part of both of us saw how that was working [by making our art] even more intense each night." *Right On!* magazine seemed to agree. "Their voices blend and their bodies lock together in tight embrace, leaving little to the imagination, and the sparks that fly onstage are not just the lights reflecting from their sequin costumes," the magazine said.

While the lyrics of "Fire and Desire" were not about Rick and Teena's romance, some other songs were. The first song either of them wrote specifically about their relationship was a song Teena composed in 1981, "Portuguese Love." (She was part Portuguese, and the song describes a lovemaking session in Pittsburgh.)

Referring in *Confessions* to the lovemaking session that inspired the song Rick wrote, "[Teena] told me I was the first one ever to give her an orgasm. She came like the pouring rain." The later tunes "Casanova Brown" and "Square Biz" are also about Rick and Teena. With verses such as "You made love to me like fire and rain / Ooh, you know you've got to be a hurricane / Killing me with kisses, oh, so subtly / You make love forever baby / You make love forever," "Portuguese Love" certainly qualified as a love song. According to one source, Rick contributed a brief, uncredited vocal to the piece.

In his 1997 song "Good Ol Days," Rick sings that he and Teena "were burning up with Fire and Desire," but that he "just couldn't hang around."

33

Rick Sings about Sex and Poverty

Give it to me
Give me that stuff
That funk
That sweet
That funky stuff
Give it to me, give it to me.

—"Give It to Me Baby," by Rick James (1981)

"**G**ive It to Me Baby" became Rick's second single to reach number 1 on the *Billboard* R&B chart, after "You and I." It spent five weeks of its twenty-five-week stay in that position. It was less popular with white audiencess, however, never reaching higher than number 40 during its two weeks on the top pop 40 chart.

"Give It to Me Baby" referred to just what you think it does. As one wry reviewer in the *London Daily Telegraph* noted, the song "was not a request for dinner." It was so popular because, as Rick pointed out, many men "can relate to being too high or too intoxicated and your old lady don't want to make love to you . . . all you can say is just 'Give it to me.'"

Some feminists were shocked by the song, since it seems to be about men demanding sex from women who don't want to give it to them. Many women would say this approach encourages rape and that instead of demanding sex the man involved might try cajoling them into cooperating, or just go ahead and pass out. Present-day rock lyrics, to say nothing of rap lyrics, have long eclipsed such verbal violations of feminine preferences, however. At the time, Rick got away with the lyrics partly by modifying his description of the situation to create sympathy for the man involved. "You [the man] can't [have sex] because you're too bent," Rick said of the song on several occasions. He told one interviewer that the song "is really about impotence—being too high to make love." In an interview with *Right On!* magazine he said the tune "was basically meant to be funny."

The video of the tune makes the song more acceptable by paying attention to the details of the situation it describes, beginning with the song's introductory lyrics: "When I came home last night, you wouldn't make love to me." A character played by Rick comes home still drinking champagne as he exits his limousine, but far from drunk, so the viewer can assume that the song is referring to the previous night, not the night portrayed in the video. Rick's gorgeous young African American wife, played by Jere Fields, at first looks disgusted at Rick's demand for love because they'd had an argument the evening before. She responds not by locking him out of the bedroom, however, but by changing from her nightgown into her bikini and enticing him to join her in a midnight swim. Rick strips down to his Speedo and joins her in their private pool, she becomes more and more loving, and at the end of the video he carries her inside in his arms. They're obviously about to make love consensually.

The other hit tune on this album, "Ghetto Life," was about Rick's return to the city of his birth. In some ways that experience had been a downer: most of Buffalo's factories had closed and the city's remaining supply of good union jobs had evaporated. "There was no hope for making any kind of a living," author Craig Werner wrote. "So you could see the hustling culture developing at the time. And Rick catches that beautifully."

On the *Street Songs* album jacket, Rick described what had become a permanent ghetto, including, he told Werner, the area's "pimps and hos, dope dealers, getting high, having a good time and dancing, crying, making love . . . the police and the player haters."

"Ghetto Life" rose to number 38 on the *Billboard* Top R&B Singles Chart and stayed on the chart for ten weeks, but never rose above number 102 on the pop chart. It obviously appealed to black people much more than it did to white people.

A UK reviewer, noting that Buffalo, even in its prime, hadn't been that good for Rick or many of its other residents, called "Ghetto Life" Rick's description of "his deprived childhood over an infectiously grinding disco beat." Elsewhere in the song Rick sang about "Tenement slums and corner bums / playing tag with winos was the only way to have some fun." As these verses hint, unlike many other artists who tackled the subject, Rick sang about both the lows and the highs of American slums, instead of depicting people wallowing in unrelieved misery. The song also, very realistically, indicated the ghetto's staying power: "One thing 'bout the ghetto, you don't have to hurry / it'll be there tomorrow, so people don't you worry," Rick sang.

Author Jonathan Lethem, writing about "Ghetto Life" in the *New York Times* after Rick's death, said that "here's where the promise of punk-funk is kept." With the tune's "ragged, furious guitars, blended with Rick's ragged, furious voice and ragged, furious lyrics . . . genuine pride and defiance are impossible to mistake."

34

Rick Denies He's Gay
and Confronts the Cops

Me and all my women laugh at it.

—"Below the Funk (Pass the J)," by Rick James

Rick fended off accusations that he was gay and attacked the police in two other songs on *Street Songs*, "Below the Funk (Pass the J)" and "Mr. Policeman." Although neither song hit the charts, they both revealed a lot about Rick, his attitudes, and his friends.

"Below the Funk (Pass the J)," with "J" meaning "joint," was about Rick's dislike of being called gay by his Buffalo homies. They appear to have done that because of his stage attire, hair, frequent falsetto tones, occasional hands-on-hip posture and, according to Rick, envy of his wealth. "Now the players hangin' 'round the main strip," Rick sings, "Actin' like they're on a trip / if they had my cash they could be hip." His response, which he sings next, was, "They call me a faggot / me and all my women laugh at it," one of the few defensive statements in any of his recordings. In *The Confessions of Rick James*, he added a nonmusical coda to this defense by saying that whenever he and his band members heard rumors about James being gay, "we'd laugh our asses off. We'd say, 'Yeah, if Rick is gay, bring yo Mama on in to find out.'"

In the remainder of "Below the Funk," Rick criticizes Buffalo as "zero degrees below" and "too damn cold and funky," but his defense against the accusation of homosexuality is the song's only memorable feature. It has a good beat, but no real melody, and in most of it Rick sings so poorly he might as well be talking. He sounds drunk or stoned, which makes sense because he keeps asking the homies allegedly around him to pass the joint.

A lively and aggressive tune titled "Mr. Policeman" inspired the back and front covers of the *Street Songs* album. On the back, a white uniformed cop is pictured on a dark and otherwise deserted ghetto street frisking Rick and a brunette woman, while another woman, who is white and blonde, watches. Rick is dressed in black except for red thigh-high boots. On the front cover, Rick holds an electric guitar and leans against a lamppost while a cop leads the two women off down the street, apparently having arrested them. The album jacket photos were based on one verse in the song: "I see you walkin' on your beat / searchin' strangers on the street / especially the whores you meet."

Rick and his entourage performed an onstage skit about this search and arrest of the prostitutes during the *Street Songs* album tour, beginning each appearance with it. The policeman appears, strutting on his beat and looking ominous. Gesturing to the audience, he mimics smoking a joint, and then pulls out his nightstick, obviously a warning that he's looking for a pot smoker to arrest. He spots the women, but when he starts to harass them, the two women and their apparent pimp beat him and drag him away.

Rick lamely denied that he was encouraging people to beat up cops. "I don't tell them to *do* that. . . . I don't tell kids to kick policemen's asses," he told *Creem* magazine. "In not *one* record have I told people 'Kick Policemen's Asses.'" Many found this argument unconvincing.

The photo insert for the 2002 CD reissue of *Street Songs* shows Rick dissing the police by riding on the same cop's shoulders while smoking a cigarette or joint. Rick's red boots, dangling down from the cop's shoulders, are almost exactly the length of the cop's entire torso. Another photo shows Rick with his arm around the brunette woman while the blonde white woman raises her knee in front of his crotch.

In spite of the stage skit and album illustrations, "Mr. Policeman" was mainly about the police shooting of one of Rick's friends, Rick told *Right On!* magazine. The friend "was hanging out on a corner with some other cats. He was wanted. When the police came, the guy started running and they shot him. He wasn't armed." One verse in the song goes: "Hey Mr. Policeman / I saw you shoot my good friend down / He was just havin' fun, checkin' out a one and one." (A "one and one" is a bag containing both heroin and cocaine.) Referring to the cop, Rick sings, "It's a shame, such a disgrace / Every time you show your face / Somebody dies, man / Somebody dies." Considering a recent spate of unprovoked police killings of black men in the United States, this song retains its relevance today.

Rick gave "Mr. Policeman" a reggae flavor, mainly because he'd loved Jimmy Cliff's 1972 movie *The Harder They Come*, which was partly about police repression of the poor in Jamaica. And he added insult to semirealism by having the officer calling into his precinct in the song identify his vehicle as "car number fifty-four," a reference to *Car 54, Where Are You?*, a TV sitcom about bumbling cops from the early 1960s.

"Mr. Policeman" was one of several songs Rick wrote and performed to protest society's ills, even though he believed the ghetto residents who were and still are among the major victims of the wrongs he cataloged knew the score anyway, and that songs wouldn't help the situation.

Although *Street Songs* was produced, written, and arranged by Rick alone, Stevie Wonder played harmonica on "Mr. Policeman" and Ja'net DuBois, an actress on the TV series *Good Times*, made the moaning sounds on "Make Love to Me." DuBois recorded her contribution with no trouble, but Rick said Wonder refused to play the harmonica the way Rick wanted him to. Rick told interviewer Brian Chin that Wonder was "doing his own trip, playing Stevie. Who am I to argue with Stevie, right? The engineer stopped me in the studio. He said, 'Rick, come on, you have to take hold of this song, or Stevie's gonna run with it!' I said, 'You're right, this is my fucking song,' and I stopped the tape and said, 'Stevie, stop playing that shit! We're gonna pick the harmonica up a couple of keys and do this shit right.'" Wonder played it the way Rick wanted him to, but resentment undoubtedly lingered.

35

The *Street Songs* Tour

We believed anything worth doing was worth over-doing.

—Steven Tyler

Street Songs **launched Rick** and his entourage, which included Teena Marie, on a sold-out fifty-eight-city American tour featuring what Rick's press releases called his "flash, funk and furious energy." After he drew thirty-five thousand people to two shows at the Capital Centre near Washington, DC, in 1981, the *Washington Post* dubbed Rick the top black concert attraction in America. Conservative estimates were that Rick's *Street Songs* tour earned him and his promoters $10 million before expenses, putting him just behind the Rolling Stones as the nation's biggest concert attraction.

His stadium appearance in Greensboro, North Carolina, in August 1981 sold twelve thousand seats and also attracted an additional sixty fans who, ticketless, tried to break in through the backdoor before they were dispersed by police.

Later that month, when Rick brought his act to Baton Rouge, Louisiana, several four-foot-high loudspeakers toppled into the audience, triggering a stampede that led to the show's cancellation. The show's sponsors had expected only fifteen thousand spectators, but close to twice that number showed up. There were no serious injuries, but a line of cars stretched for six miles on the road to the arena, and a woman caught in traffic gave birth to twins during the concert.

He performed two separate two-night engagements in Los Angeles within two months of each other—at the Long Beach Arena, where he broke Elton John's attendance record, and at the Forum—and sold out all four concerts.

At the Mid-South Coliseum in Memphis, Elvis Presley's hometown, Rick even exceeded Elvis's attendance record, a feat never previously accomplished.

Many of the people attending these performances were African American. "Rick opened up all these big venues for blacks," LeRoi Johnson says, adding that Rick was one of the few black performers able to fill giant stadiums such as the L.A. Coliseum, the Superdome, and Philadelphia's Veterans Stadium.

"We were doing two shows in one day in different states. . . . We would do a show, get offstage and get on a jet," Teena told *Vibe* magazine. When landing at their next location, she said, "They would fly us into concerts with 120,000 people" in the audience and land the helicopter on the hotel roof. It was estimated that Rick was grossing $369,000 a night on this tour.

At every stop, Rick made his entrance as an inner-city superhero wearing the same shimmering hooded cape over the red-and-black jumpsuit and knee-high red boots he wore on the *Street Songs* album cover. When he dropped the cape, women in the audience would scream. During later concerts, he doffed the jacket too, displaying glitter-spotted skin to the accompaniment of more screams.

When Rick sang "Super Freak" and lit up a joint, the audience would erupt with screams and continue to scream until Rick left the stage. Before doing that, he would always sing a duet with Teena Marie. She would end each concert alone by performing her two hits, both produced by Rick, "I'm a Sucker for Your Love" and "Square Biz."

36

Cocaine Begins to Take Its Toll

Pile it up! Pile it up! Pile it high.

—"Shattered," Rolling Stones, by Mick Jagger and Keith Richards (1978)

We would eat dinner and do cocaine. We didn't know anything about
the Betty Ford Clinic then. The biggest mistake I made is that
I tried to become my alter ego. I wanted to be . . . wild man,
party machine, lady slayer, and the cocaine told me I could.

—Rick James, *Detroit News*, 2004

Rick had been smoking pot and snorting cocaine for years, but in 1981, just before his *Street Songs* tour began, Rick took a step that greatly increased the damage his drug use would do him. In that year, he and LeMelle met Sly Stone.

Stone had been their "rock god," LeMelle says, "but when I saw him, he was just a dude sitting in the corner of his dressing room freebasing," who "couldn't even stand up." Rick, realizing that he and LeMelle were watching a man smoking himself to death, told Stone that "the fucking cocaine, man, has darkened your senses. You're not making the music that you used to make." He told Stone that the pipe was the reason for his demise. Stone had deteriorated to the point that he could barely make it onstage and "was late for every bloody gig he did for years. He

demanded coke before he would go on," one anonymous Toronto musician said. In 1970, at the height of his popularity, Stone missed more
than twenty-five shows.

Rather than protest Rick's denunciation of him, Stone urged Rick
not to freebase. According to LeMelle, after the visit, "Rick said, 'We
will never let this happen to us.' And then we hugged." But instead of
following through on that promise, Rick started imitating his musical
hero. He and Stone would lock themselves in a back room and "become
the highest people in the world," LeMelle says. Soon, Rick was spending
more and more time smoking his cocaine pipe—and hundreds of thousands of dollars a year keeping it filled.

Freebasing was "when the hideousness of my addiction really
started," Rick told the *Washington Post* in 1998. "When I was snorting I
was in trouble, but I wasn't in that much trouble." He said he went from
spending $200,000 a year snorting cocaine to between $300,000 and
$400,000 a year smoking it. "I soon had a guy traveling with me who I
hired just to cook it up for me. And then I was gone."

Snorting cocaine was widespread in the music business. Legitimate
record companies gave out little coke mirrors, from which coke could
be snorted, as promo items. Framed gold records were dusted with coke
and partygoers invited over to use straws to snort up the drug. At the
time, snorting coke was thought to be harmless, but freebasing was a
different matter, and was seen as such.

Rick told several interviewers that he snorted and smoked cocaine
to "fill the empty hole" inside him and to ease the terrible pain of loneliness. When Rick met a beautiful TV actress who also smoked cocaine,
he noted in *The Confessions of Rick James*, "She was in a lot of pain, just
like me. She had everything she could want, yet she was as lonely as
could be. . . . She and I were duplicates. Soul mates in pain."

Smoking cocaine is rapidly addictive, as convicted stock manipula-
tor Jordan Belfort describes in his book *Catching the Wolf of Wall Street*:
"I put the glass pipe to my lips. . . . I took an enormous hit and held it
in for as long as I could. An indescribable wave of euphoria overtook
me. It started in the base of my aorta, shot up my spinal column and

bubbled around the pleasure center of my brain with a billion synaptic explosions." Belfort makes the first few seconds sound amazing, but any Stone City Band member would disabuse you of the notion that this kind of drug use was glamourous. "He used to stink," Levi Ruffin says of Rick. "You could smell him a mile away." When Rick's mother asked Ruffin why Rick's bus stank, he told her, "That's what cocaine does—it comes out of your pores. She was crushed."

Those who loved Rick tried to protect him. LeRoi Johnson remembers beating up a drug dealer in the Peabody hotel in Memphis, Tennessee, who was trying to get to Rick. "But after a while," Johnson says, "you ask yourself, 'Why am I out here doing all this when somebody's not protecting himself?' You can't fight all the drug dealers." Ruffin says Johnson would ask him to stop Rick from freebasing, and his reply would be, "How are you going stop a multimillionaire from doing what the fuck he wants to do?"

A few Stone City Band members half-seriously insisted that the only way to protect Rick was to smoke up all his dope. A few band members tried that when they were on tour in Dallas and on other occasions, but after they finished, Rick would just want to order more. As they left, Rick would be looking for more coke on the floor and they'd have to tell him, "Rick, that's not coke, that's lint."

In an interview with *Soul* magazine, Rick blamed his increased consumption of drugs and alcohol on the responsibilities that had come with success. "A lot of people's lives were suddenly in my hands—the band, the crew, the record company," he told *Soul*. "Those people have to eat by the things that a performer does. If I'm not doing anything, they starve. Success is a big responsibility and I've never been a very responsible person."

Rick would spend day after day, week after week, closeted in his room at his house in suburban Buffalo while freebasing thousands and thousands of dollars of coke and allowing no one in. His housekeeper would leave meals outside the door for Rick to eat, but he would rarely open the door to receive them. On one occasion, when his hunger returned with a vengeance after an extended freebasing session, he gobbled down a plate of bacon and eggs that had been sitting outside his door for four or five days, his friend Peter Kelly says. Years later, Rick tried to explain to California court psychiatrists that "doing coke was not a social thing with me." He said he did it by himself in a back room a lot of the time. "I felt like I had a big hole inside me and getting high seemed to fill it for a while," he said.

But as Peter Kelly also points out, Rick often combined dope and sex. "He wanted girls to get high with him and get involved in a ménage à trois," Kelly says, although he adds that on some occasions, "Rick would get so fucking high and was so hyped he couldn't talk and couldn't have sex."

When Rick and Jan Gaye, Marvin Gaye's estranged wife, formed a romantic attachment soon after Rick's *Street Songs* tour, Rick was often able to talk to Jan but unable to have sex with her because smoking cocaine had rendered him impotent. In her book, *After the Dance: My Life with Marvin Gaye*, Jan Gaye writes that after one such incident, Rick "was embarrassed, but I reassured him. God knows that each of us had had enough sex to last a lifetime." It's doubtful that Rick felt the same way. Rick later acknowledged to an interviewer during one of his periodic attempts at giving up drugs and alcohol that his sex life had suddenly become "much better."

But worse than some embarrassment over impotence were the times Rick would overdose, collapse, come very near death, and wake up in a hospital. Johnson remembers this happening on numerous occasions starting on the *Street Songs* tour. Once, Johnson says, Rick OD'd so badly at the Sunset Marquis Hotel in West Hollywood that "he was probably dead, and his security and everybody panicked. We called 911, stood him up, and put him in the shower, and although he was blue from OD'ing, we got him back. I can't remember exactly how many times we did that." Johnson says he and Rick's two other brothers rescued him from similar near-disasters at the Plaza Hotel in Manhattan, the Chateau Marmont in Los Angeles, and L'Ermitage in Beverly Hills.

Freebasing, and drug use in general, soon began wounding Rick's career in the same way it had hurt Sly Stone's. Abel, Rick's road manager, remembers when Rick signed on to play at the San Diego, Houston, Atlanta, and Philadelphia appearances of the Kool Jazz Festival tour that R&B star Teddy Pendergrass was headlining. Seven or eight acts had been scheduled for the San Diego performance. "It was a real tight setup," Abel says, "because each act had only a half hour or forty-five minutes to play. . . . Basically you came on, played, and got off. No extending the set, no stretching it out; you had to follow the clock."

Before Rick's scheduled appearance time, Rick noticed Pendergrass's tour bus in the parking lot and began chatting with him, and Pendergrass invited him to visit with him in the bus before his appearance. Abel said to himself, "Oh, shit, Teddy's a big coke guy."

When it was time for Rick to go onstage, Abel knocked on the bus door but couldn't get anyone to answer. Without Rick, the show simply went on to the next act. When it was time for Pendergrass to go onstage, however, he kicked Rick out of the bus, Abel says, and went onstage and performed. Rick, meanwhile, "stumbled out an hour and a half after his appearance had been scheduled" and his act was canceled.

Two weeks later, when Rick was scheduled to appear with the same tour in Houston, Rick wasn't ready to go onstage. "He just blew it off," Abel says. "He didn't want to go on until he was ready, and he thought they would make room for him. But instead they said, 'We're done. He's not doing anymore.'"

On a later tour, in Winston-Salem, North Carolina, Abel was assigned to visit the box office after the show to collect $23,000 in cash due Rick and the band. It was too late to deposit it in a bank, and Abel, nervous about keeping it in his room overnight, hid it above the false ceiling in his motel room. Abel says he was nervous not only about thieves, but about Rick, because it was Abel's job to pay off the band and crew members the next day, and he needed most of the money to do just that. He knew, however, that Rick would want to spend an undetermined portion of the cash on coke and wouldn't care what other, more legitimate, uses for it Abel had in mind. Rick, however, found a way to access that money anyway. He accepted a delivery of coke from a dealer, then told the dealer to visit Abel in his motel room. "So it's one AM and someone's knocking at my door," Abel says. He opened the door, keeping the chain on, and the dealer said, "Rick sent me to you to get my money." Playing dumb, Abel said, "Money for what?" and the dealer put his finger up to his nose and sniffed. Abel gave him the appropriate amount.

These sorts of scenes became more and more common as Rick's addiction spiraled out of control.

37

Rick Scores as a Minor TV Personality and Dreams of Hollywood Stardom

Sequels are for when a writer runs out of ideas.
If I run out of ideas I'll stop work.

—Jeanette Winterson, 1985

After hitting the top as a musician in the early 1980s, Rick himself, actors playing Rick, and Rick's animated image began appearing in a series of television performances. Rick played himself on *Miami Vice*, appeared on an episode of *Seinfeld*, and was on an episode of *Lifestyles of the Rich and Famous*. On the TV show *The Midnight Special*, he hosted Evelyn "Champagne" King, Linda Clifford, and Cheryl Lynn. He appeared with the Four Tops on *Dick Clark's New Year's Rockin' Eve '82*. He appeared on *Real Time with Bill Maher* with Jerry Falwell and others, on the TV documentary *Studio 54: Sex, Drugs & Disco*, and on the A&E documentary *Uncut: The True Story of Hair*. He was a character on one episode of *The A-Team* and *One Life to Live*, and appeared on *The Tonight Show Starring Johnny Carson*, *Entertainment Tonight*, and *Saturday Night Live*. He also appeared in cartoon form on *South Park*, as a plaintiff on *Judge Joe Brown*, and in the movie *Life*. He rarely did as well on the screen as he'd done on the stage, however.

Early on, a growing problem with dope, plus a case of hepatitis, almost ruined Rick's scheduled performance of "Give It to Me Baby" on *Saturday Night Live* on November 7, 1981, according to Levi Ruffin. "I suggested he cancel the goddamn gig 'cause he was really sick," Ruffin says. "Rick was fucked up so high he couldn't remember the 'Give It to Me Baby' lyrics." Ruffin, in in the stage area, wrote cue cards for Rick with big letters on them in the hope that they'd help the drug-addled performer remember the words of the song.

Ruffin says he then left the stage area and returned to the waiting room. Rick followed him in, bringing his dope dealer and telling two women there to get up so the dealer could sit down. Furious at Rick for kowtowing to a dope dealer, Ruffin decided to walk out. As he approached the door, Rick "looked at me and said, 'I'm Rick Mother-fucking James.'" (Later, on *Chappelle's Show*, the Rick character often made similar statements.) Ruffin opened the door, Rick told him that if he left he'd be fired, and Ruffin kept going. In spite of this tense confrontation, Rick managed to get through the performance somehow, and it looked fine on TV. The two old friends later made up.

Although Rick's in-person TV appearances didn't always go well, he often talked about producing and starring in movies. "I'm getting bored with the music industry," he told an interviewer in 1982. "I need something else to kind of stimulate me." His desire to try something different also reflected his in-depth knowledge of how risky and brief many rock 'n' roll careers could be. According to screenwriter Richard Wesley, who worked on Rick's movie ideas, Rick "wanted to go into music-based movie dramas in a big way. He saw that as the next plateau. He was not going to spend the rest of his career writing risqué lyrics to R&B music."

What he really wanted was to write and produce films. He specifically mentioned making a movie called *Dr. Jekyll and Mr. Jive*, and said he wanted to redo the Elvis Presley movie *Jailhouse Rock*. Rick also talked for years about doing the score for a film or a Broadway production of a musical he dubbed *Alice in Ghettoland* for Motown, adding that it would be about "the experiences of a white girl in the ghetto." He told author David Ritz that when he'd been with Salt 'n Pepper he'd written a song called "Alice in Ghettoland." Instead of falling down a rabbit hole, Alice "falls into a trash can and winds up on the chocolate side of town dealing with gangstas and pimps."

Initially, Rick said, Teena Marie would star in *Alice in Ghettoland*, but then he appeared to have second thoughts. In later interviews, he said merely that Teena and Richard Pryor would contribute to the project in one way or another.

This *Alice* idea was likely at least subconsciously inspired by Motown's 1978 production of *The Wiz*, starring Diana Ross. The story lines of both films were similar: young female characters were dropped into worlds both familiar and strange to them, met strange but familiar characters, and either managed to go home or adjusted to their new environments. Rick Abel says he remembers Rick talking to two writers about the movie early in Rick's Motown career: "Alice would be taken to a Ghettoland, and she'd be kind of like Cinderella, but instead of the mean stepsisters she'd be beaten up by the colored girls." He insists that none of Rick's movie ideas were pipe dreams, at least in the beginning: "People were paying attention when Rick really had some juice." Rick never really gave up on this project and talked about producing *Alice in Ghettoland* for the rest of his life.

In the early 1980s Rick took a concrete step toward the silver screen by hiring well-known movie producer Jerry Weintraub to manage his film career. Weintraub had produced *Nashville* and *Oh, God!* and went on to produce *Diner*, *Ocean's Eleven*, and other films. Rick told a Toronto *Globe and Mail* interviewer that he and Weintraub were going to make a film called *The Spice of Life*, which would be "an integrated musical with sex, drugs, and funk 'n' roll," adding, not too helpfully, that it would be about "surviving, love, reality, living, learning, losing and winning." Later on he told an Associated Press reporter that *Spice* was a book he himself had written and that he would act in the movie. "It's a hardship story, a guy who makes good—a Cinderella story," and the character he was slated to play would be a musician. When a *Oui* magazine interviewer suggested that the book and proposed film were "about a poor but talented black boy who sings, plays, writes and produces his way out of the ghetto into superstardom," Rick responded, "Well yeah—an autobiography."

Vibe magazine said *The Spice of Life* would be "the story of the tumultuous rise and eventual fall of a black music superstar." Rick was to play a "bold, audacious, sexual dynamo with plenty of cutting-edge music and pretty women in tow." When a *Oui* magazine interviewer asked Rick if his films were going to have black, sexual, or musical themes, he responded: "All three! We really do need to see more black actors up on the screen. And I know I'm no [Robert] De Niro—I can only really play me, which I will in [*The Spice of Life*]. Of course, there's going to be a lot of sex—everything in life is about sex!" Rick also said the film might touch on his youth as a juvenile delinquent in Buffalo who later went AWOL from the navy and fled to Canada.

In the fall of 1982, Rick told *Oui* magazine that shooting on *Spice* would begin in January 1983. He said Richard Wesley, who wrote the 1970s films *Uptown Saturday Night* and *Let's Do It Again*, both starring Bill Cosby and Sidney Poitier, was writing the script. The film would be a Weintraub–Rick James–Motown film. Wesley says the Motown company hired him to write the screenplay for the film based on a short story Rick had written. The story was about a recording artist who has finally reached the pinnacle of stardom but found himself caught up in some illegal activities. In the climax of the proposed film, the recording star would be dramatically assassinated by a vengeful mobster while giving the greatest concert of his life. "Rick knew people in the underworld and people and situations that could be very dangerous," Wesley says. "The characters were based on people he knew, and in a couple of cases, instances that actually happened in his life."

Motown executive Suzanne de Passe gave Wesley a copy of the short story, and although it included some typos and grammatical errors, "as soon as I read it, I understood it from page one all the way through to the end and knew how it could be turned into an active screenplay." One of the better scenes outlined in the story was one in which the protagonist's mother helps him get out of town when gangsters are looking for him. He suggested that actress Mary Alice, who played the mother in the

1976 movie *Sparkle*, would have been great in the role. (*Sparkle*, a film about three young black women who form a famous singing group, was remade in 2012.)

Wesley says de Passe was very much interested in producing the film but that they both objected to the ending, in which the main character, to be played by Rick, would be shot. "I tried to talk him out of it. I said, 'At the moment when the hand goes up holding the gun, someone could pull the hand away,' and he'd say, 'No, No, No, he's got to pull the trigger.' I knew right then that this movie was never going to be made."

According to *Vibe* magazine, Wesley told Rick, "You're the star of the movie. You can't die," only to have Rick respond, "Fuck that. I don't want no fuckin' sequel. No *Spice II* or *Added Spice*." Wesley says Rick believed that if the *Spice* story stood alone, with no sequels, it would make the picture and its story more powerful.

Weintraub joined Wesley and de Passe in disagreeing with the ending and apparently also disliked Rick's proposals for other movie projects. Rick wrote in *The Confessions of Rick James*, "Jerry and I disagreed on everything as far as movies were concerned." Rick's Hollywood dreams died on the vine

38

Rick Scores Big-Time as a Songwriter and Producer . . . for Other Musicians

Rick was probably one of the greatest producers I ever met.

—Berry Gordy

Teena Marie was only one of the artists Rick successfully produced. He also produced individual songs for already established groups that he idolized, such as the Temptations. But what really attracted Rick was producing entire albums by performers he created or discovered himself, such as Teena, his own backup group the Stone City Band, the Mary Jane Girls, Process and the Doo-Rags, and Val Young.

Rick loved producing because he was a control freak who liked being in charge of every aspect of a record. Stan Endersby also notes that Rick took pride in the songs he wrote and enjoyed watching other people perform his work.

And at this time, Rick was also exhausted. As Endersby and other musicians have pointed out, endless touring takes a tremendous toll on entertainers, and Rick already had collapsed and been hospitalized at least twice while touring. But when he produced groups, they could tour without him and he could stay at home "while they were out on the road doing his stuff and he was just getting the check," Endersby says. Rick also was aware that producers usually have much longer careers than vocalists.

Rick loved producing in spite of the fact that when he started putting tunes by his protégés on his albums along with his own tracks, the *Los Angeles Times* noted that he was voluntarily sharing the spotlight "with folks fully capable of singing him off the record." Rick's only problem as a producer, in Ruffin's words, was that "when Rick produces you, who do you think you're gonna sound like when you come out of the room? Rick! Not vocal-wise, but in the way you'd approach the vocal." Others also noted this, but it's impossible to determine if this added to or distracted from the popularity of the songs and albums Rick produced.

Rick worked at a feverish pitch when he was producing. Levi Ruffin offers one reason for this: cocaine. "What kept us going was cocaine. We called it 'producing powder.' That was the name we had for it. 'Cause you had to take it to keep up with Rick," he says.

But Rick came by most of his producing skills naturally. He was demanding, and a perfectionist, as a producer. In an interview for Mike Sager's 2003 book *Scary Monsters and Super Freaks: Stories of Sex, Drugs, Rock 'n' Roll and Murder*, Daniel LeMelle—who from 1979 to 1986 was arranger and director of the Stone City Band horn section, and who worked on nine albums Rick produced—tells a story that perfectly illustrates this. He says that on one occasion, after Rick had put the band through a long recording session, they were all driving on a California freeway, listening to the final cut of a song. Everyone was relaxing when suddenly Rick told the driver to stop the vehicle and pull it off the road. "Did you hear that?" Rick asked. Angered no one knew what he was talking about, he played one section of the song again and again, rewinding the tape each time. They all sat on the side of the freeway for an hour while Rick cursed and threatened to leave the band members beside the road unless they told him what was wrong. Finally, he revealed that for several bars in one portion of the song, the horns, which had supposedly been recorded in stereo, had been mistakenly recorded in mono. This mistake, he told them, would have been pressed into the distributed records if he hadn't caught it, meaning "it would have been out there and it would have been wrong." He concluded by saying, "My shit has got to be perfect."

39

The Mob Comes Calling

Will all your money keep you from madness?

—"Down in the Hole," Rolling Stones, written by Mick Jagger
and Keith Richards (1980)

Now that Rick was a successful producer, the Mob reappeared in his life.

Levi Ruffin says Rick had a habit of telling ambitious youngsters who wanted to become recording artists that if they "got it together," he'd introduce them to influential people in the recording industry and produce their records. Rick rarely followed through, however. Unfortunately, he made the mistake of making this promise to a young white man whose name Ruffin says he can't remember. That young man's father was in the Mob.

Subsequently, Ruffin says, a group of threatening-looking men arrived at Rick's house early one morning and put him in a car. Then they drove over to Ruffin's house and put him in the car as well, and took the two men to breakfast.

"It was like a fuckin' movie," Ruffin says. "This is about six o'clock in the morning, you've got these motherfuckers standin' behind us with suits on, and this older gentleman is saying, 'You owe my son a record, you gonna produce my son.' I was sittin' there scared to fucking death. Rick said 'Fuck you,' and we walked out. But we were shaking."

Like father like son: both Rick and his father (shown here) served in the US Navy. *LEROI JOHNSON*

Rick's mother, Mabel Sims, shows off her dancing costume. *CAMILLE HUDSON*

Buffalo numbers czar Stefano Magaddino.
ARCHIVES AND SPECIAL COLLECTIONS DEPARTMENT, E. H. BUTLER LIBRARY, SUNY BUFFALO STATE, COURIER EXPRESS COLLECTION

All in the family: (left to right) Rick, about to doff a fur jacket, poses with his mom and their relative James Brown. *LEROI JOHNSON*

Sharing a laugh at a swearing-in ceremony: (left to right) Rick's famous cousin congressman Louis Stokes (Democrat/Ohio) and Rick's other famous cousin Carl Stokes of Cleveland, the first elected black mayor of a major American city.
DIANA MCNEES/CLEVELAND PLAIN DEALER

Rick's cousin broadcaster Chuck Stokes interviewing two Michigan congresswomen on his weekly *Spotlight on the News* program on WXYZ-TV in Detroit. *CHUCK STOKES*

Rick's cousin broadcaster Lori Stokes, coanchor of *Eyewitness News This Morning* and *Eyewitness News at Noon* on air on WABC-TV in New York City. *LORI STOKES*

Even though he was a member of the student council, Rick (at far left, second row from bottom) didn't like school. *LEROI JOHNSON*

Braids and earrings made Rick smile. *LEROI JOHNSON*

Rick performing with the Mynah Birds. Left to right: Goldy McJohn, Bruce Palmer, Richard Grand, Rick, Jim Livingstone, and Frank Arnel. (The earlier version of this band included Ian Gobel and Rick Cameron.) *STAN ENDERSBY*

Rick posing with Salt 'n Pepper. Left to right: Gary (Coffi) Hall, Ron Johnson, David Colin Burt, Ed Roth, and Rick. Chris Sarns is not pictured.
STAN WEISMAN/DAVID COLIN BURT

Rick and members of Heaven and Earth decide to rest on a couch they moved into the middle of a Toronto street. Left to right, sitting on couch: Denny Gerrard, Rick, Stan Endersby. Left to right, standing: Gary Holmes, Ed Roth, Pat Little. *STAN WEISMAN*

Rick and the members of White Cane. From left to right: John Cleveland Hughes, Denny Gerrard, Nicholas Balkou, Rick, Ian Kojima, Ed Roth, Norman Wellbanks, and Bob Doughty. *GAB ARCHIVE, REDFERNS, GETTY IMAGES*

A young, smiling Syville Morgan at about the time she first met Rick. *SYVILLE MORGAN*

Syville Morgan, the mother of Rick's first two children, in 2004. *SYVILLE MORGAN*

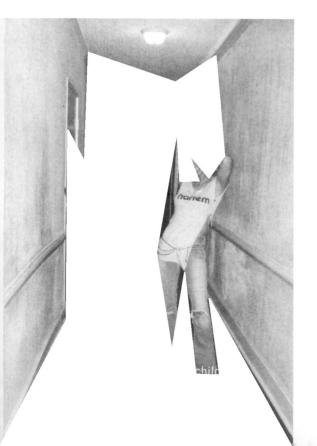

Rick's first wife, Kelly, cuddles the children of Rick and Syville: Rick Jr. (middle) and Tyenza (bottom). *LEROI JOHNSON COLLECTION, LIBRARY AND ARCHIVES, ROCK AND ROLL HALL OF FAME AND MUSEUM*

An imperious Kelly raises her finger. Left to right: Marvin Gaye; Rick's mother; security man; unidentified man; Rick's first wife, Kelly Misener; Rick; and Rick's brother LeRoi Johnson. *LEROI JOHNSON*

Five of the most important men in Rick's life, the members of his Stone City Band. Left to right: Levi Ruffin Jr., Tom McDermott, LaMorris Payne, Danny LeMelle, and Nate Hughes.

Rick performing onstage. *ARCHIVES AND SPECIAL COLLECTIONS DEPARTMENT, E. H. BUTLER LIBRARY, SUNY BUFFALO STATE, COURIER EXPRESS COLLECTION*

Cowboy Rick comes to town.

A smiling Rick plays teen idol while
turning his back on a mirror.

Rick's sometime paramour and the white female soloist he made famous: Teena Marie, as she was about to appear on the cover of *It Must Be Magic*, her fourth Motown album.

The most successful vocal group Rick ever produced, the Mary Jane Girls. From left to right: Candice (Candy) Ghant, Cheryl (Cheri) Bailey Wells, Kimberly (Maxi) Wuletich, and Joanne (JoJo) McDuffie Funderburg.

Rick smiles while Kimberly (Maxi) Wuletich of the Mary Jane Girls searches hopefully for his tongue. *MARK WEISS, WIRELMAGE*

Rick demonstrates one of his favorite sexual moves while posing with the Mary Jane Girls at the 11th Annual American Music Awards, 1984.
RON GALELLA, GETTY IMAGES

The famous and topless Rick hugs the famous and topless Linda Blair.
RICHARD CORKERY-GLOBE PHOTOS INC.

Rick waits happily to appear on the television show *Lifestyles of the Rich and Famous.*

Rick as he was about to appear on the cover of *Street Songs*, his best-selling album.

Tanya Hijazi, later to become Rick's second wife, laughs with him at a party in late 1992.
RON GALELLA, GETTY IMAGES

Rick's second wife, Tanya Hijazi, embraces Tazman, her son with Rick, at Rick's first funeral.
FREDERICK M. BROWN, GETTY IMAGES

Frances Alley tells the jury at Rick and Tanya's trial about the tortures they allegedly inflicted on her.
THE CONUS ARCHIVE

Rick's pants highlight his crotch.

A fiendish looking Rick flashes the sign of the devil.

Rick's post-Motown record producer, convicted felon Joseph Isgro, is arrested again, in 2014, on charges that he helped run a sports book ring for the Gambino organized crime family.
JOHN MARSHALL MANTEL|THE NEW YORK TIMES|REDUX

Comedian Dave Chappelle gleefully playing Rick James on *Chappelle's Show*.

The women gather after Rick's first funeral. Left to right: Tanya Hijazi's mother, Susanne Shapiro; Rick's sister Alberta Johnson; Rick's sister Penny Johnson; Teena Marie; Rick's sister Camille Hudson; and Rick's second wife, Tanya Hijazi. *CAMILLE HUDSON*

Rick lies in his coffin. *CAMILLE HUDSON*

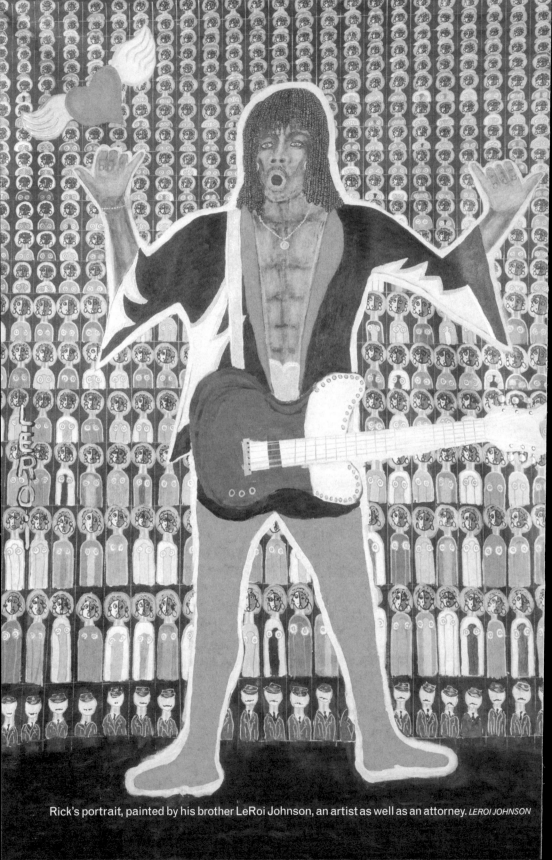

Rick's portrait, painted by his brother LeRoi Johnson, an artist as well as an attorney. *LEROI JOHNSON*

In *The Confessions of Rick James*, Rick wrote that he acted more dip-
lomatically than Ruffin's account would indicate. Before the meeting
ended, Rick said, he told the mafioso to call him the next morning. Then
he stayed awake all night, and when the mobster called Rick merely told
him, "Hey thanks for the offer, but I have to refuse."

No revenge was taken on Rick as a result of this incident, which
Ruffin calls "gangster shit." Ruffin says, however, that as a result of this
incident, he "realized this business ain't worth a fuck, man. It's all about
the money. There's too much money in the [record] business."

40

Rick Denounces the Reagan Recession While Throwin' Down

> Ronnie find the cure, this is just
> too much for us to endure.
>
> —"Money Talks," by Rick James (1982)

Throwin' Down, the title of Rick's next album, had at least two possible meanings. Among them was "throwing a party," which was certainly appropriate, considering the album included mostly dance numbers. Another slang meaning of the phrase at the time was "smoking cocaine." In fact, Rick claimed that he invented that meaning of the phrase. Whether or not that was true, Rick produced the album in a haze of cocaine smoke.

Nevertheless, Rick managed on this one album to attack the sitting president, Ronald Reagan, for his economic policies; collaborate on a major song with the Temptations; and sing three catchy pickup songs. With the most controversial tune on the album, the political song "Money Talks," Rick made an explicit break with his previous musical history, which had been entirely nonpolitical. One critic called "Money Talks" a "verbal assault" on President Ronald Reagan. Rick told an interviewer "Money Talks" was "basically a song about how Reaganomics is screwing up the country."

In fact, it was a lament for how hard it was to make a living during the recession of 1981–82. Unable to avoid a sexual reference, Rick told *Right On!* magazine that the song was a "simple tune dealing with how even working girls on the street" were finding it difficult to make a living, and added, "My heart goes out to" them. The lyrics run, "She works the corner of Twelfth and Vine / Making her tax-free money, pinching every dime / She has to hustle to make ends meet, / Even a workin' lady finds it hard to eat." A reviewer who listened to "Money Talks" noted that Rick not only named Reagan explicitly as the culprit in the song, something that only black artists seemed courageous enough to do, but that the singer also had joined Prince in calling the president "Ronnie" with "unawed casualness."

Rick said that he wasn't happy with "Money Talks" because it didn't tell anyone anything new. "People are already aware . . . because when they wake up they've got to . . . look for a job," he said in July 1982. He also said he didn't plan to write any more songs about current events because "the situation is not going to be better" as a result of them. "People just want to temporarily ease their minds," he said, presumably with nonpolitical music, which he immediately returned to creating. (He later wrote and sang more political songs, however.)

Britain's *New Musical Express* opined that all "Money Talks" did was "lick up the crumbs" of the *Street Songs* tune "Ghetto Life." The magazine also said the song "stumbles over an uninteresting melody and fails completely" because Rick's "shouts of protest" in it are "utterly unconvincing." Rick didn't actually shout in the song, but the melody is so uninteresting that a listener focuses on the singer's voice during most of the recording. In any case, as in many of Rick's songs, the hard-driving dance music in "Money Talks" more or less wiped out its verbal protest message.

"Standing on the Top," Rick's collaborative vocal with the Temptations, became the second-most-popular song on the album. Rick said he was inspired by the fact that by including four of the Temptations among the background singers on his previous single, "Super Freak," he had caused fans to ask, "What happened to them? Why haven't we heard from them?"

What had happened, as the *Washington Post* noted, was that the Tempts had slipped into "the netherworld of nostalgia." Amid numerous personnel changes, they had left Motown in 1976. In 1980, however, Motown had re-signed the latest iteration of the Tempts, consisting of Eddie Kendricks, David Ruffin, Otis Williams, Melvin Franklin, Dennis Edwards, Richard Street, and Glenn Leonard, and assigned them to cut an album appropriately titled *Reunion*.

Rick said that when he heard the album while it was being produced, he felt it needed a hit single. He already had written the song "Standing on the Top" and had planned to record it himself, but the Tempts loved it, and he proceeded to produce, arrange, and record it with them. "Standing on the Top" appeared on both *Throwin' Down* and *Reunion*.

"It was strange producing them," Rick said of his work with the Temptations. "I grew up listening to them. . . . I didn't feel self-conscious; only a little strange in the beginning. But I tried to fit in because it was business. . . . The outcome of it I knew would be so strong that it took away from all the strangeness or emotions."

Adding to the tension Rick felt while producing "Standing on the Top" was the fact that about one hundred people were watching him do it, including Berry Gordy, actor Timothy Hutton, and Jim Brown. It was the largest number of people he had ever seen in a studio, he said, and he found himself surprised that he was still able to teach the Tempts the song.

There were some emotional moments, however. As Rick told one interviewer, he sang all the Tempts' parts onto cassettes and asked them to take the cassettes home and learn the parts. It was evident the next day, however, that two of the Tempts hadn't done what Rick asked. "They didn't know anything," Rick said. "They hadn't even listened to the tune." He said he was "very upset" and "gave them a long speech about how this was their careers and [he was] already rich and [didn't] need this aggravation." They got the message and cooperated from then on.

It could be argued, though, that the song was a dis on the Tempts. This comes through clearly in the video of the tune. When the Tempts sing the words "on the top," they turn and point to Rick, who's literally higher than they are because he's standing on a riser to their right, as if they're acknowledging that their day has passed. They then immediately go on to sing, "We understand it," with "it" presumably being the ups and downs of life.

The Tempts also could be heard as singing about Rick's present or eventual decline. In the song they note that when you're down, people ask you stupid questions, like "What does 'L-7 square' mean?" a reference to Rick's earlier album *Bustin' Out of L Seven*, and "Do you braid your hair?" also a reference to Rick and not the Tempts.

Rick was proud, however, that "Standing on the Top" did well, rising to number 6 on the *Billboard* R&B singles chart. It gave the Tempts their first Top 10 R&B hit in six years, and stayed on that chart for seventeen weeks. It also rose to number 66 on the pop chart.

Although Rick earned some money from "Standing on the Top," he probably took in less than he would have had he recorded the song himself. In contrast to his image, Rick had acted as altruistically in giving the tune to the Tempts as he had in asking them to back him up on "Super Freak." "I grew up listening to them and felt it was an honor to work with them," he said.

This wasn't the only instance of his going out of his way to help out a legendary Motown act. At one of Rick's concerts, his opening acts were scheduled to be Marvin Gaye and the Gap Band, in that order. Rick told the promoter it should be the other way around, with Motown legend Gaye having the place of honor. (The first opening act for a star's concert is traditionally performed by the least popular group, and as the star's appearance nears, more popular acts play.) The promoter refused because Gaye hadn't had a hit record recently. According to LeMelle, Rick said, "This isn't going to happen." With the concert scheduled to open shortly, LeMelle says, "We packed up all our stuff, got in a car, and went to a movie. While we were in the theater, Rick got a call from the promoter, telling him, 'It'll be like you said.'"

Rick also performed with Grace Slick on *Throwin' Down*, with the two musicians singing together on "She Blew My Mind (69 Times)." The tune actually did better than making it to number 69 on the top R&B singles chart, rising to number 62 and staying on the chart for six weeks. It didn't make the pop chart, however. (Although the tune was titled "69 Times" on the album, it was called "She Blew My Mind (69 Times)" on the single.) It might have done better without the titillating title, especially because the pornographic implication is deceptive: mutual oral sex is not the song's subject. The song is actually about a girl who dumps her boyfriend for another guy, thus blowing his mind.

Also highlighting the album were the pickup songs "Dance Wit' Me," "Throwdown," and "Hard to Get." The *Washington Post* claimed that "Dance Wit' Me" "owed more than a little" to Funkadelic's "(Not Just) Knee Deep," with a rhythm guitar pattern and synthesizer riff that were "very similar to 'Knee,'" adding insult to injury by saying that it "lacked the complex arrangement and quality singing of the Funkadelics' single." Some of these specifics were technically correct, but "Dance Wit' Me" is much more energetic and creative than "(Not Just) Knee Deep." Meanwhile, a different reviewer probably made Rick feel better by calling the tune "a funk-laden thumper that exudes fun."

Creem magazine scored some humorous points against Rick with this song by asking how listeners could distinguish a song that starts "Pretty little thing, girl you're looking fine" ("Dance Wit' Me") from the beginnings of two other tunes on the album: "Say little girl, know you're lookin' good" ("Throwdown"), and "Girl, you're cute, you're sweet, you're such a sexy treat" ("Hard to Get"). Critics also noted that Rick sounded distracted on *Throwin' Down* "when the subject wasn't himself, or doesn't lead to the bedroom." The *Washington Post* said most of the songs on the album were "populated with voluptuous women eager to bed down with the singer."

Nonetheless, "Hard to Get" rose to number 15 on the R&B chart without making the pop chart, and "Dance Wit' Me" reached number 3 on the R&B chart and number 64 on the pop chart.

Perhaps Rick should have produced a topical cover for this album, like an illustration of starving zombies stalking the ghetto or the Stone City Band members in rags as a result of the Reagan recession. Instead, the album's cover reeks of druggy fantasy. The cover of *Street Songs* had shown Rick with a cop and party girls on a slum street, emphasizing his origins as a ghetto resident, as did the songs themselves. In other words, the album cover represented something real. But on the cover of *Throwin' Down*, Rick looks like a funk version of Conan the Barbarian. Standing on the steps of a castle amid furs and bones, he is wearing shorts, studded leather boots, a very wide decorated metal belt, and gold amulets around his neck. A skeleton of a human head next to him looks like a person who might have died under a hair dryer in the year 1000 BC. In one hand, Rick carries a metal shield with a godlike face hammered into its center. His other hand touches an electric guitar painted to look like a bloody battle-ax.

On the back of the album jacket, Rick appears to be dragging a Valkyrie-like black woman up the heavy stone castle stairs. She is wearing furry cut-back shorts, a metal bra, a heavy spiked bracelet, and metal wings on her head.

On the record sleeve inside the album Rick is standing and the woman is sitting on the ground between his legs, facing outward. Her arms are chained, and Rick, looking somewhat defiant, is pulling her hair with both hands, although she does not seem to be feeling pain. The design of the whole album package reminded many of George Clinton, whom Rick had criticized for producing albums that were definitely detached from reality.

Rick was credited with writing, arranging, and producing almost all the songs on the album, with the exception of "My Love," for which he shared credit for both the words and music with his brother LeRoi Johnson. Rick called the song "a family affair," not only for that reason but because the "jazz lilt" to the melody reminded Rick of his mother's jazz vocal albums, which he had described to an interviewer as "the musical textbooks of my youth."

Reviewers in general had a field day dumping on Rick's voice and most of the melodies in *Throwin' Down*. The *Post* said his "weak singing undermined every cut," calling it "flat" and "characterless" and accusing him of adding female singers as well as horns and strings to the album to disguise his voice's shortcomings. *Creem*, piling on, said Rick sounded "like a Looney Tunes imitation of Edward G. Robinson."

Despite such harsh critical reactions, *Throwin' Down* rose to number 13 on the *Billboard* top pop album chart, stayed on the chart for twenty-three weeks, and was certified as a gold record by the RIAA. It rose to number 2 on the R&B chart on the same date, and spent thirty-nine weeks on that chart. The album sold 817,591 copies through mid-1988, Motown said in its 1989 suit against Rick. That the album sold this strongly was impressive but was disappointing compared to the 2,376,714 copies *Street Songs* had sold.

Rick admitted to the *Los Angeles Times* in 1983 that *Throwin' Down* wasn't as good as his previous albums, but he blamed it all on Motown. "It should never have been released," he said. "In fact, it should never have been recorded. I made it too soon after *Street Songs*. I was getting pressure from Motown to put out another album." Still, *Throwin' Down* was certified gold. The album also was nominated for (but did not receive) the 1982 American Music Award for Favorite Soul/R&B Album. Rick thought this may have been because he had achieved his goal for this album, which he said was to make people happy: "Right now there is enough heavy stuff going on in the world, and people don't want to hear it in music," he said. "I just want people to have fun and to escape for a little while."

Rick responded to the nomination with a remote broadcast from his home studio in Buffalo. "R&B is as important to black people as life itself," he told the camera in a quiet voice. "It is the foundation of all music today." While his long-haired white dog, Ganja, gazed at him adoringly, he strummed his guitar and sang, "Music is something that will never stop beating, music is something that will never disappear. I want to thank you from the bottom of my heart for all these years." That

Rick thought of 1978 to 1983 as "all these years" showed a lot about his accurate perception of the length of the average rock star's career.

Rick's tour in support of *Throwin' Down* drew huge audiences and was a monster success. In April 1982 at the Grugahalle in Essen, Germany, he performed before the biggest audience any rock artist had ever attracted in Europe: 7,200 ticketholders plus about thirty million TV viewers in other countries. The event was the tenth all-night concert staged by the German TV show *Rockpalast*. Just before the departure of the flight from the United States to Germany, Rick demonstrated his continuing (if drug-related) concern for his Stone City Band members by standing at the door of the aircraft and giving a Quaalude to each one as they filed in. He wrote in *The Confessions of Rick James* that they all wanted the pill because the flight was so long and they, like Rick, were afraid of flying. "I just put it in their mouths, like candy," he wrote.

In Greensboro, North Carolina, a year after his appearance in that city in support of *Street Songs*, Rick attracted 13,500 fans. And in Augusta, Georgia, in July, more than eighty-five hundred people with an estimated average age of sixteen danced in the aisles and on the seats of the sold-out Augusta–Richmond County Civil Center as Rick sang "Ghetto Life," "Mary Jane," and "Super Freak." (It should be noted, however, that none of these songs were from the *Throwin' Down* album.) Wearing long braids and clad in a black skintight suit studded with sequins, Rick doffed his jacket, "baring glittered chestnut skin much to the delight of thousands of his mini-skirted female fans," a local reporter wrote.

A reporter for the *Augusta Chronicle* wrote that Rick "stunned, aroused, insulted and challenged the hyper-ready audience," and used "pantomime, gesticulations and outrageous sexual overtures" against a background of "loud explosions and fireworks" to rouse the screaming audience to "sheer hysteria." After the show, Rick changed into a lounging costume consisting of a tight green outfit, snakeskin boots, and a white safari hat.

This was Rick at his performing peak. But despite his triumphs with fans, there was a warning of troubles to come when he told a reporter immediately after this Augusta concert that this would be his last tour.

"I don't need this," he said. He talked about going into movies full-time and complained that he was "really tired of performing live."

Before long, it became obvious that Rick was pushing himself too hard. Although he had been suffering from abdominal pain for several days prior to a scheduled appearance in Dallas in August, his thirtieth show of the tour, he refused to cancel the sold-out event at the Reunion Arena, where nineteen thousand fans awaited him. Observers said the thirty-four-year-old musician didn't look good before he went onstage. He planned to go to the hospital immediately after the show, and he was given oxygen during a break. Finally, after performing for a total of forty-five minutes, he collapsed unconscious onstage and was rushed off in an ambulance as the audience erupted into pandemonium.

Tests at Dallas's St. Paul Hospital indicated Rick suffered from exhaustion, and he canceled two of his upcoming concert dates. His abdominal pains slowly worsened during his next twelve concerts, however, and after a Denver appearance he canceled the final five weeks of the tour and returned to Buffalo for medical treatment.

Rick later told an interviewer that his drug use was the problem. Even before the *Throwin' Down* tour started, he said, "I was doing too much partying. I'd wake up at noon, take drugs to get myself together, drink cognac, smoke weed and do some other things I ain't too proud of, into the wee hours of the night. I'd drink myself to sleep, and at noon the next day, the cycle would begin again."

Rick said he'd stopped ingesting coke and alcohol after his collapse and that doing so was "a case of live or die." He said his creativity had been heightened and his sex life improved by avoiding both substances. But he didn't stay abstinent very long.

He soon scheduled another tour, including a return to Dallas in October 1983 to perform at what he called a "payback" concert to make up for the one at which he had collapsed. Once again, his audiences responded. And when he went on to Baton Rouge, Louisiana, the *Baton Rouge Advocate* wrote that much of the audience "reacted with religious fervor as the preacher of lust and love gyrated and teased in an effort to incite a marijuana-soaked dance orgy."

Now that Rick was near the top of the music business. he began to wonder what had been happening during the previous decade to his daughter Tyenza and his son Rick Jr. Their mother, Syville Morgan, had been raising them alone without any contact with Rick.

"I was starting to miss my daughter," Rick wrote in *The Confessions of Rick James*. "I hadn't seen her for years," and he also had never seen his son. "As time went on," he wrote, "I felt more and more guilty that my own kids were poor and struggling." Since he knew nothing about where they were living or how they were doing, he hired a private detective to find them. When the detective told him they were living in a poor neighborhood in the L.A. area, a conscience-stricken Rick visited them there with Levi Ruffin.

"So we go over there," Ruffin said, "and she's got this little small apartment, really tiny, and there's little Ricky and Ty and Mom, nice and clean and neat." Ruffin noted, however, that "they definitely lived in the hood, like Compton kind of shit, deep hood. . . . I met her and she was very cordial. Rick was just asking to get a chance to see the kids. You could see she was mad as shit because she needed money. She was raising two goddamn kids and this son of a bitch is on television, and now he comes around."

Shortly thereafter, Rick asked his brother LeRoi Johnson to provide Syville and the children with funds and relocate them to a house in a better neighborhood. Rick then invited Ty and Rick Jr. to Buffalo for a three-week visit. Rick went to the airport to meet them but was so anxious about seeing them again that when he saw a young girl and a little boy holding hands, he rushed up and hugged them, only to be told they were not his children. Ty and Rick Jr. were on the same plane, however, and Rick finally found them. They continued to visit Rick for the rest of his life, and Ty, a rapper, and Rick Jr., an artist, still live in the L.A. area.

Today Syville heads the House of Syville Couture in L.A. and sings in a Christian rock group called the Rapture. "We sing very edgy gospel," she says.

41

Rick Struggles to Integrate MTV

*American culture has one great theme, race, and one great art form,
pop music, and the two are and will always be inseparable,
will always be the twin helices of our national DNA.*

—David Kirby, in *Crossroad: Artist, Audience, and the Making of American
Music* (2015)

Rick's struggle to force MTV to play videos starring well-known black musicians was one of the most moral actions of his life.

MTV, the first twenty-four-hour all-music television channel, began broadcasting at midnight on August 1, 1981, with a brilliantly selected video by the Buggles, a British new wave band, titled "Video Killed the Radio Star." As the video's title implied, MTV's goal was to supplant radio in the minds and ears of music fans.

Within a short while, MTV became the fastest-growing network in cable television history and was spinning out new musical stars. Owned by the corporate giants Warner Communications and American Express, MTV, after two years on the air, was reaching twelve million homes with videos of popular songs. It was also delivering a dream audience for advertisers: 85 percent of its viewers were between twelve and thirty-four years old.

The problem with MTV from Rick's point of view was that the station wouldn't play his work, or the videos of any black artists or groups that had achieved widespread popularity. Over the years, the network rejected all five videos Rick sent it, including those based on "Super Freak" and "Give It to Me Baby." Other black musicians were also turned away. As veteran video producer Kenneth Matthews told *Vibe* magazine in 1995, MTV only wanted "images that won't threaten their audience: safe, non-threatening images of black men." Matthews called the station "racist."

Rolling Stone reported that of more than 750 videos played on MTV during the channel's first eighteen months, fewer than 24 featured black artists. Adding insult to bigotry, the first purportedly "black" video played on the channel was "Rat Race" by the Specials, a seven-member British ska band that included only two black musicians.

Author J. Randy Taraborrelli wrote that MTV's research and marketing departments seemed to have decided white kids in the suburbs did not like black music and were afraid of black people. Other analysts thought, however, that the nature of television itself accounted for MTV's stance: to skittish whites, hearing black musicians might be one thing, but seeing them would be another. In other words, who was black and who was white hadn't been clear over the radio, but it would be on TV.

The station's only semi-viable defense was that music played on the radio was also somewhat segregated. But that argument ignored the many black crossover artists who were being played on white radio stations. It also overlooked the fact that MTV broadcast thousands more videos per year than any other video broadcasting station, that it was the biggest video broadcaster in the United States in the early 1980s, and that it was growing so fast it would soon dominate the entire music video field. There were many more radio stations than video outlets playing music in America, but no radio station held the dominant position MTV held.

Rick raged against MTV's anti-black policy on numerous occasions for more than two years at public events, in interviews with the press, and on TV and radio. That he was unable to make any headway during that period shows the depth of American racism in the 1980s, and the hold that racism still had on the popular music business.

Soon after MTV rejected the first video Rick submitted to them, and long before they rejected all five he sent, Rick began fighting for video equality not only for himself but for all black musicians. He pointed out to journalists and music critics that if MTV's proclamations that its broadcasts helped musicians sell many more records were true, the station was costing him hundreds of thousands of dollars in record sales. "Fuck MTV," he concluded, calling the channel's policy "a terrible crime" and "racist bullshit, pure and simple." In April 1983 he upped the ante by telling *Newsweek* magazine MTV "probably started out with a requirement of no niggers." Rick called MTV's action regarding his own videos "pitiful" but added that even if MTV started showing his videos, he wouldn't be happy until MTV was "showing a ton of black videos regularly."

He had expected that other black artists would join him in his protest, but very few did. As Rick's brother LeRoi Johnson notes, "The only person out there protesting was Rick . . . not Michael Jackson, not Prince, not the Gap Band, not any of those acts." In fact, one of the only other musicians to publicly join in the criticism was Maurice White of Earth, Wind & Fire, who criticized MTV's policies on *20/20*.

Some black musicians supported Rick privately but were taken in. MTV's only black video jockey, J. J. Jackson, said Miles Davis once approached him, looked him in the eyes, and said, "Tell me, young man, how come MTV doesn't play any black videos?" After noting irrelevantly that the long-dead Jimi Hendrix hadn't made any videos, and that MTV didn't play any videos by the also-long-dead Elvis Presley, Jackson told Davis, "Believe me, if I thought they weren't playing black artists because they were black, there's no way in hell I would be their patsy for that." According to Jackson, Davis "then looked at me for like 20 seconds—man, it felt like a lifetime—and said absolutely nothing." Finally, Davis said, "Very good, young man."

Rick speculated other black musicians were "afraid to offend MTV" because they still hoped the station would play their videos. "I can't believe how stupid they are," Rick said. "MTV may play their videos when hell freezes over, but not before." *Newsweek* called Rick's protests "gallant."

MTV's power in the music industry was so huge at this time, however, that even Rick, not known for his lack of aggressiveness, pointed out that he wasn't "talking about a boycott." A boycott might have seriously upset MTV, and no one, even the fearless Super Freak, wanted to stick a pin that sharp in one of the giant's toes. Still, Rick was hurt by the silence of other black musicians. "I'm mad at them, really mad," he told an AP reporter. "They're going to let me do all the rapping and get into trouble, and then they'll reap the benefits." Some other black artists, including Stevie Wonder, Teddy Pendergrass, Nick Ashford, and Valerie Simpson, did complain to MTV execs in private but refused to criticize the channel in public.

White musicians David Bowie, Bob Seger, and, later, Keith Richards, did support Rick publicly. During an interview by video jockey Mark Goodman on MTV in 1983, Bowie asked Goodman, "Why do you think MTV doesn't play black music?" Goodman, surprised, said, "We try to play music for a particular type of demographic and genre."

"What about all the black kids?" Bowie responded, and Goodman replied, "You got to talk to MTV about that." Of course, Bowie was talking to MTV.

Music companies employing both black and white artists remained silent during Rick's crusade. Even Rick's own record company, Motown, pointed out that its top artists' videos, while not shown on MTV, had been broadcast on the other much smaller TV video outlets.

MTV president Robert Pittman, a white man from Mississippi, aggressively defended himself against charges of racism by Rick and others. He called people who objected to MTV's virtual exclusion of black artists "little Hitlers or people from Eastern European bloc communist countries" and said, "I don't know who the fuck these people are to tell people who they should like."

MTV representatives also noted that they had broadcast a few videos by the relatively little-known African American and Hispanic group the Bus Boys, as well as the black British reggae band Musical Youth, but that those videos never caught on with their audience.

In a revealing conversation with MTV executive Carolyn Baker, a black woman who wanted MTV to air a James Brown video, Pittman said the station's preferred audience "doesn't think that rock 'n' roll came from James Brown. They believe it came from the Beatles." In support of this mistaken belief, MTV aired Phil Collins singing the Supremes' song "You Can't Hurry Love" as well as Hall & Oates, Men at Work, and other white musicians and groups singing songs originally sung by black musicians.

In the end, however, two years after Rick's crusade began, MTV decided it had to yield to the forces of progress once they were applied by another corporation that was big enough to scare it. In 1983, CBS Records complained to MTV executives after they declined to play Michael Jackson's newly released "Billie Jean" video.

Jackson had a big advantage over Rick. Rick's employer, Motown, had only two superstars, Rick and Lionel Richie, both black. But Jackson, after leaving Motown, had become a superstar for CBS Records, which also employed the superstar act Journey, a white and Hispanic band, and the superstar white band REO Speedwagon.

Ron Weisner, one of Jackson's managers, told *Billboard* he took MTV a rough cut of "Billie Jean" and MTV declined to play it. When Weisner told CBS Records head Walter Yetnikoff and CBS head Bill Paley about MTV's rejection, the two executives told MTV, "This video is on by the end of the day or [CBS Records] isn't doing business with MTV anymore," Weisner said. "That was the video that broke the color barrier."

MTV duly played "Billie Jean," and also aired Jackson's next video, "Beat It." They became the most popular videos in MTV history—so popular that when Jackson's next video, "Thriller," was released, Pittman not only aired it but paid $250,000 for the right to air it first. MTV also pre-promoted "Thriller" on-air every time it was going to play, and after every viewing, the channel's ratings spiked dramatically. "We learned a lot about programming," Les Garland, an MTV cofounder, said lamely.

Years afterward, MTV was still trying to come up with acceptable cover stories for its refusal to play Rick's videos. In 2006 Garland argued that Rick's "Super Freak" video was not aired because "its contents were a little over the top for us," and he said the network's "standards and practices" wouldn't allow it because of the content of the visuals. Carolyn Baker added that the "Super Freak" video was rejected "because there were half-naked women in it," and called it "a piece of crap." These arguments are surprising, because while this excellent video implied women might enjoy sex, it showed no flesh you couldn't see at a high school prom in Iowa in 1965 and no sex acts. It did, however, show Rick flirting with a group of women, only two of whom were black, which may have shocked some MTV execs.

After playing Michael Jackson's videos, the channel soon began playing videos by Prince, Whitney Houston, Janet Jackson, and Stevie Wonder, generating massive new revenues for itself and for CBS. In 1985, however, apparently still writhing with pain at the thought of being forced to air black videos, MTV relapsed and reestablished segregation by founding another channel, VH1, which played not only Rick's videos but many other black videos MTV still refused to play.

Rick sort of made it onto MTV itself in 1985 when the channel aired the Eddie Murphy video "Party All the Time," which Rick had produced and in which he appeared. One of its major selling points for MTV execs was that Les Garland actually appeared in the video, listening to Murphy sing. Movie star Murphy sang the song, not Rick, who played his real role in the song, its producer, on the video. Although Garland said Rick had apologized for calling him a racist by that time, Rick's own videos remained relegated to VH1.

Racism in the music business will probably never die completely. In 1998 Rick's managers tried to schedule a performance for him at the Omaha Civic Auditorium. Auditorium managers rejected their application, saying "two other black groups were already booked" for dates shortly before and shortly after the date Rick had requested. Only after Rick protested to Mayor Hal Daub's office was the rejection rescinded.

42

Rick Fantasizes the Mary Jane Girls
into Existence

Oh, something's got me so excited, baby
A feeling I've been holdin' back so long . . .

—"All Night Long," Mary Jane Girls (1983)

The Mary Jane Girls were far and away the most controversial group Rick ever created. They were also the closest to his heart. This made complete sense, because they were women named after a drug, and he was obsessively interested in both. The onstage personalities Rick created for them, and their onstage performances of songs he wrote for them, called forth a wave of condemnation as well as a torrent of congratulations and made their relatively brief career an outstanding one.

Rick had hired female background vocalists in the late 1970s and called them the Colored Girls, after the line, "And the colored girls go 'Doo do doo do doo do do doo'. . ." from the Lou Reed song "Walk on the Wild Side." That group at various times included Levi Ruffin's wife, Jacqueline Ruffin, Lisa Sarna, Tabby Johnson (not related to Rick), Joanne McDuffie (later JoJo McDuffie Funderburg), Teena Marie, and the sisters Maxine and Julia Waters. They're credited for background singing on various albums by Rick and by various groups he produced. However, though they were referred to as the Colored Girls on albums, amongst musicians and themselves they casually adopted the moniker the Mary Jane Girls.

In the early 1980s Rick decided to turn the Mary Jane Girls into a full-fledged group, one that would perform on its own, as opposed to singing behind him onstage. Rick's original idea for the new group sounded much more interesting than the Mary Jane Girls turned out to be. He told *Jet* magazine in September 1983 that he wanted to create "a black female group . . . that could express more reality with relationship to men," explaining that he "wanted black girls who could really speak about love, the pain, money, power, hate, and everything." On another occasion Rick said he wanted the Mary Jane Girls to sing about issues "that are sex-related but not actually about sex, such as honesty, jealousy, and emotional security."

Rick also said he wanted the new group to consist of "female characters that *women* could identify with." Many of his own songs addressed sexual issues, he said, and he was looking for a way to address them from the other side of the gender gap.

Rick planned to write the songs the new group would sing, however. When asked why he thought he could speak for women, he pointed out that Smokey Robinson, the Motown writing team of Holland-Dozier-Holland, and many other songwriters had written songs for females with great success. This was initially derided as old-style thinking: a man arranging for women to express their feelings. "C'mon ladies," the *Washington Post* sneered, "it's the '80s. You don't need a Phil Spector these days to merchandise your talents." (Spector, a record producer, started the girl-group craze in the late 1950s and early '60s.)

When he actually created the Mary Jane Girls, Rick also seemed to be thinking about appealing more to white audiences than to black people, however. He told one interviewer before creating the group that he "might go over better in Montana and Nebraska" with a female group that sang about gender-related issues. In any case, one of the four Mary Jane Girls he selected was white, one was of mixed race, and the other two were light-skinned black women. After all this theorizing about singers who would address issues or illustrate them with their appearance, however, Rick eventually settled on what he had said early on would be a possible alternative to this ambitious plan: three girls in skimpy clothing "doing the punk thing." The only change was that he added a fourth Girl.

Rick selected Joanne McDuffie Funderburg, the former Colored Girls singer, from Buffalo; Candice "Candy" Ghant, a Motown session singer from Detroit and a former member of the girl group SofTouch; Kimberly "Maxi" Wuletich, a white woman from Pittsburgh; and Cheryl "Cheri" Bailey Wells, from New Jersey. Wells, who originally played the Valley girl character in the group, was later replaced by Yvette "Corvette" Marine (now Yvette Barlow), the daughter of disco singer Pattie Brooks. The group reminded the London *Telegraph* reviewer of a female version of the Village People.

Rick claimed that although he loved to smoke marijuana, he hadn't named the Mary Jane Girls after the drug. He said he had "named the group after [Mary Jane] candies, because the girls are as sweet as candy." He was likely lying.

Rick selected the role each girl would play in the group based on his own fantasies about different kinds of women. McDuffie Funderburg was the "powerful woman" fantasy. After all, Rick explained, "she wears braids, like me." She was also known as the "street-savvy, 'round-the-way girl" and said in a 2013 interview for this book that this was her real personality. Wells was the adorable Valley girl fantasy, the cheerleader, the young wild girl who liked to boogie and go to new wave clubs (like her later replacement, Marine). Ghant was the "sophisticated vamp" fantasy, the runway supermodel who wanted Rolls-Royces and diamond rings. Wuletich, the white girl, was "the dominatrix" fantasy, the leather queen. She often wore a badge and a police hat, plus handcuffs dangling from the belt of her leather jacket. She also often carried a whip. "There's a hardness about her personality that I find intriguing," Rick said. That the only white girl in the group played a dominatrix and dressed like a police officer says a lot about Rick's view of race relations in America.

Wuletich may have played a dominatrix, but Rick really dominated the group. Ghant told author Mike Sager that Rick was very strict with the Mary Jane Girls while they were on tour as well as in the studio. They worked with a choreographer five days a week as well as with a vocal teacher. "Whatever it took," Ghant says. "With him there were no hours." McDuffie says the group would sometimes start work in the studio at 2:00 PM and not get out until 4:00 or 5:00 the next morning.

"Rick was like a slave master," Ghant told author Mike Sager for his book *Scary Monsters and Super Freaks*. "We didn't party, we didn't go wild. We weren't supposed to have boyfriends. After the shows it was interviews, pictures and we were escorted to our rooms. And they would take a bed check to make sure you were in there. He was like a boss, a husband, a mother. He was hard on us." She notes, however, that if Rick hurt one of the girls' feelings, "He always gave you a gift to say he was sorry."

McDuffie Funderburg paints a more nuanced picture of Rick. She told the *Los Angeles Times* that while he was in "creative control" of the group, he was flexible and treated the girls fairly. She said, "I don't know anything about writing and producing, but Rick does—he's very knowledgeable in those areas. I like the fact that somebody who knows what they're doing is in control."

After the Mary Jane Girls began performing, the *Washington Post* charged that Rick, "always quick to jump on someone else's trend," had put together the group in imitation of three female groups created by George Clinton and one called Vanity 6 (later renamed Apollonia 6 when frontwoman Vanity left the band), created by Prince. (The three girls were called Vanity 6 because that was the number of breasts among them.)

The *Post* called the Mary Jane Girls "a second-rate version of Vanity 6," and the *Los Angeles Times* sunk so low as to aver that the Mary Jane Girls had failed as imitators, lacking "the focus or seductiveness" of the admittedly very sexy Vanity 6. And indeed, onstage, the Mary Jane Girls just wore revealing costumes, wiggled a lot, and didn't sing all that well, with the exception of McDuffie Funderburg. One critic for the *Washington Post* did note, however, that thanks mostly to what he called Rick's "sweetly sensuous songwriting," the Mary Jane Girls were "considerably less shrill about their sexuality" than Vanity 6.

In several published interviews, Rick furiously rejected the suggestion that he stole the idea for the Mary Jane Girls from Prince. He said he'd come up with the concept of a girl group six years previously but had temporarily shelved it for lack of time. He told one of the Mary Jane Girls that Prince had actually stolen the idea from him when Prince was the opening act on Rick's tour and Rick told him his plans. McDuffie Funderburg indignantly seconds Rick's argument that the group had been Rick's idea first. She says the only similarity between Vanity 6 and the Mary Jane Girls was that both were female groups doing club or dance music.

Rick also claimed the Mary Jane Girls were much more skilled than Vanity 6. "The selling of human bodies is one thing," he said in reference to Vanity 6, and indeed, the *Washington Post* wrote that the Mary Jane Girls "sing better than Prince's stable of undie-clad crooners." McDuffie Funderburg insists the Mary Jane Girls should be compared to "real singers," such as the Pointer Sisters or the Supremes. She's right about herself, at least. Judge Sweet noted in his 1989 opinion that McDuffie Funderburg "was the group's only member with significant singing skills and she had sung most of the lead vocals" on the group's recordings. The judge said she had "furnished the distinctive sound of the Mary Jane Girls" and that "her voice . . . was essential to the 'sound' of the group." A nonjudicial critic added that the other Girls only provided "adequate whispery backup" for McDuffie Funderburg.

The Mary Jane Girls' costumes and sex appeal became additional objects of controversy. While some observers called the group a "lingerie-clad quartet," others criticized them as "sleaze-dressed beauties." A *Philadelphia Inquirer* reviewer charged that in their tiny miniskirts and high heels, "wiggling ostentatiously to every third beat or so, the Girls are little more than an adolescent boy's fantasies come to life." The *Los Angeles Times*, however, suggested the Mary Jane Girls weren't even good at being sexy, opining that their "clumsy blend of 'Valley Girl' humor and bump-and-grind flirtation seemed hopelessly laborious." But English pop music critic and author Sharon Davis praised Rick for giving the Girls "no-nonsense lyrics and bold sexual personalities without being obscene." *Vibe* magazine chimed in, praising the Mary Jane Girls for "flaunting their femininity." There was "no shame in their game," *Vibe* said. "They freely articulate their needs and desires."

Rick was determined to make the Mary Jane Girls' first album a success. As Levi Ruffin remembers it, on Christmas Eve 1982, Rick called him and said, "Look, man, you ready to go to Cali, back to Sausalito, and cut a record?" Levi remembers, "I said 'No problem. How long we gonna be gone, Rick?' He said, 'I want you to pack for a week, maybe a week and a half.'" But that wasn't how it went down, according to Ruffin. "Right after New Year's Eve, me and him, we fly out there with a couple of guys. That was January. March, we were still there. First Mary Jane Girls album was done. Very successful week and a half, right? March we came back home."

In April 1983 Motown released that album, which was self-titled. The *Washington Post* called it "one of the most dubious projects ever released by Motown," saying that "the four women show off their chests and legs on the cover but show little talent on the vinyl inside." By today's standards, the women were dressed with extreme modesty on the album cover.

The album highlighted the fact that the Mary Jane Girls were Rick's fantasy of how women should treat him. The *Washington Post* noted that in every song on the album, the "girls explain how they're going to do it all for their man." Davis, however, called it "a musical landmark" and "a superb release crammed with excitement." Rick was the sole writer, producer, and arranger of all the songs on this and the next album by the group, with the exception of the song "Leather Queen" on the second album—1985's *Only Four You*—which was cowritten by Daniel LeMelle (credited as Danny LeMelle).

Davis also wrote that the Mary Jane Girls "were an extension of Rick's own personality and would record repertoire unsuitable for his own use." This was a credit to Rick's marketing savvy: he knew what he wanted women to say and do in sexual or romantic situations, but since he couldn't say it himself without switching genders, he had the Mary Jane Girls do it for him. The group reflected Rick's marketing savvy in a different way as well: they became so popular that Rick's managers developed a line of action wear in their honor, the Ultimately line, which Rick's brother LeRoi Johnson says earned between $300,000 and $400,000 in 1985.

The Mary Jane Girls' eponymous album rose to number 6 on the *Billboard* top R&B album chart and remained on the chart for forty-seven weeks while rising to number 56 on the *Billboard* top pop album chart. The RIAA certified it as a gold record.

Reviewers disliked the album as a whole, but they loved its best tune, "All Night Long," which the *Los Angeles Times* called "smoldering." *Vibe* congratulated the Mary Jane Girls for recording the song, which, it said, urged women to throw off their inhibitions. Appearing on the top R&B singles chart on July 23, 1983, the song remained there for eighteen weeks, rising to number 11, while rising to number 101 on the pop chart. McDuffie Funderburg was the lead vocalist on the track, as well as on three of the other seven tunes on the album.

"All Night Long" also rose to number 13 on the British charts and remained on that chart for nine weeks, becoming the group's most popular British song. Davis said the Mary Jane Girls delighted the public with their "outrageous stage act" and "warm off-stage manner," a combination calculated to appeal to the English public, and that the group would remain popular internationally as long as Rick "could keep his fantasies alive."

Vibe magazine insisted the Mary Jane Girls "stand as the bridge between the Shirelles and the Supremes and the R&B divas of the 21st Century," noting the Mary Jane Girls' impact on groups such as En Vogue, Destiny's Child, 702, TLC, and the Spice Girls.

43

Rick Romances Linda Blair in Cold Blood

Nothing splendid was ever created in cold blood. Heat is required to
forge anything. Every great accomplishment ·
is the story of a flaming heart.

—Arnold H. Glasgow

At age fourteen in 1973, Linda Blair became a movie star for
playing the possessed child Regan in the hit movie *The Exorcist*.
Nine years later, at twenty-three, the voluptuous Blair, still working in
movies, posed for a topless pictorial in *Oui* magazine. In the accompanying interview, Blair was asked who she thought was the sexiest man in
the world. She answered, "Rick James."

When Rick, who had just returned from his *Throwin' Down* tour,
was shown the interview, he sent her roses, and Blair responded with
a letter saying she wanted to meet him. She flew to New York, where
they began an affair and posed for topless pictures together. Rick was
so taken with Blair that he told *USA Today* he planned to produce and
star in a movie about interracial love, with Blair as the love interest. No
such movie was ever made, however, and Blair eventually flew back to
California.

Around the time Rick started working on his next album, Rick said
in *The Confessions of Rick James*, Blair called to tell him "that she had had

an abortion, and that it had been my child. She said she was in the middle of shooting a movie and was starting to show, and she didn't think I would care anyway.

"She was wrong. I did care deeply. I loved Linda and it hurt me that she would choose to abort our child without even wanting to talk to me about it first. I still look back on her choice with sadness, and wonder about our baby, and how having the child might have changed my life." Rick said he was influenced by Blair's failure to consult with him when he wrote the song "Cold Blooded," which also became the title of his next album.

Blair told an interviewer Rick had written the song as a tribute to her, and asserted that "cold blooded" means "You're hot." In the song itself, in fact, Rick sings, "Girl, I think you're so sexy, sexy, sexy . . . cold blooded," "My point of view / Girl, I think you're hot," and notes that "You look like a movie star." Blair, who was thanked on the album sleeve, refused a request for an interview for this book.

Rick sang about drugs, pimps, his love for black women, and the death of a prostitute in the other songs on the album, collaborating on the tunes with the Temptations, Smokey Robinson, and Billy Dee Williams. He told author David Ritz that the song "U Bring the Freak Out" referred to a "drug that nearly destroyed my mind." He didn't specify the drug, however, and the cheery way he sings this song seems to contradict this explanation. The song rose to number 16 on the R&B singles chart and to number 101 on the pop chart.

Having partnered with the Tempts on his previous album, Rick collaborated with another old-time Motown artist he idolized, Smokey Robinson, on the tune "Ebony Eyes." He told Ritz, "[I wrote the song] because of the negative fan mail I was receiving about my relationships with white women. It was my way of telling black women that I loved them and looked on them as queens." He asked Robinson to accompany him, he said, because "no one sings more adoringly to women." Rick also was attempting to rehabilitate his reputation as a balladeer with "Ebony Eyes," and did well enough to inspire the *Toronto Globe and Mail* to write that the song showed that Rick could "croon with the best of them." In fact, in a turnaround for Rick, several reviewers liked all the ballads on *Cold Blooded*. Barney Hoskyns of the *New Musical Express* wrote that "Ebony Eyes" and "Tell Me (What You Want)" "lift the heart . . . these are the wide, sweeping love testaments Rick was aiming for" in his previous ballads.

With "Ebony Eyes," Rick and Robinson also upped the ante in Rick's battle with MTV by making a video of the song. To Rick's delight, although it was not broadcast on MTV, it did appear on NBC-TV. The video, while technically excellent, is pure schmaltz. The two men, as pilots, leave on a small plane named *Ebony Eyes* during a romantic mist that unfortunately also heralds an oncoming storm. Both "pilots" recall saying good-bye to their African American wives, neither of whom want the men to make the flight.

The plane is then forced down by the storm, and the two men must parachute onto an island with their supplies. Robinson sings a love song to his wife's picture, which he has rescued, and Rick literally burns a torch for his own wife. The two men then change into white suits (which miraculously wash ashore), and Rick fires off two flares that are seen by the wives, who are coincidentally on a rescue mission on a sailboat not far from the island. They soon pick up their husbands. In the video's final scene, Rick is shown back home writing "Ebony Eyes" with Robinson.

In *The Confessions of Rick James*, Rick wrote that while making the video, he and Robinson were "high sunup to sundown." "Ebony Eyes" rose to number 22 on the R&B singles chart and number 43 on the pop chart.

A third song on the other side of the album had a much more jaundiced view of the relationships between men and women. In "P.I.M.P. the S.I.M.P.," Rick tells the story of Mary, one of his female friends' daughter, who became a streetwalker and then died. Rick told an interviewer the girl's pimp was neither arrested nor charged, and that the girl's mother had asked him to warn the world about evil pimps. The message was somewhat confusing, however, because it's not clear in the song or from Rick's comments how the girl died. Nevertheless, the song tells about the pimp recruiting the young woman and living high on her earnings while she stayed in a motel room going insane with only cocaine for comfort. On the album's record sleeve, "P.I.M.P. the S.I.M.P." is dedicated to "Maryanne Fletcher, born 1960–1983 . . . Rest in Peace . . . To the Fletcher Family—it's done."

While Rick may have had strong feelings about the death of his friend's daughter, when he was asked if performing the song would make him "think twice about demeaning women and making them appear as sex slaves," he answered coldly, "I think prostitution should be legal is what I think."

"P.I.M.P. the S.I.M.P." was a rap song. Rick didn't like rap, yet the growing market had forced him to try his hand at it. He employed Grandmaster Flash to rap a verse and a half near the end of the song. Later in 1983 Rick told one interviewer he had begun to see it as "a brighter light" and "an emerging form of poetry."

Cold Blooded was also notable for Rick's extensive use of synthesizers and drum machines. Rick wrote in *The Confessions of Rick James* that he started using synthesizers because musician Quincy Jones told him the audience was becoming so familiar with his sound he ought to change it. He also pointed out he was hardly the first to use synthesizers and noted, "The drum machine has become a new frequency . . . tuned into people's brains."

In any case, the Moog company in Buffalo had given Rick both the synthesizers and the drum machines. Calling them "new musical toys to play with," he put aside some of the material he'd originally written and used them, along with other electronic instruments, to record *Cold Blooded* in the studio he'd built into his home in Buffalo. It was the first time he'd recorded an album in his hometown.

Some reviewers were impressed by the synthesizers, but others could think only of Prince. The *New York Times* pointed out that the album "recalled Prince's synthesizer-driven dance music," and the *Washington Post* complained that the album was "an inept attempt to match Prince's blend of streamlined synthesizers" as well as that singer's "taunting eroticism." As Prince continued to upstage Rick, comments like this became more and more common.

Rick was credited with writing, arranging, and producing all the songs on *Cold Blooded* and was glad to hear, on December 12, 1983, that the album had been certified gold by the RIAA. (In its 1989 suit against Rick, Motown said *Cold Blooded*, which had been released on August 5, 1983, had sold 821,957 copies through mid-1988, slightly more than *Throwin' Down*.) Although Rick was definitely not back in the stratosphere, in terms of number of albums sold he appeared to be headed back in that direction.

Cold Blooded didn't do as well on the pop chart as Rick's previous two albums, however. While it rose to number 16 on the *Billboard* top pop album chart and stayed on the chart for twenty-nine weeks, its chart position was three places below the high point reached by *Throwin' Down* and way below that of *Street Songs*. The album reached the number 1 position on the R&B chart, however, staying in that position for ten weeks and spending an additional twenty-three weeks elsewhere on the chart.

The song "Cold Blooded" didn't do quite as well as the album. It hit number 1 on the R&B chart, stayed there for six weeks, and became a crossover success as well, rising to number 40. Nevertheless, it was Rick's first number 1 single on either the R&B or the pop chart since "Give It to Me Baby" two years before.

In support of the *Cold Blooded* album, Rick, the Stone City Band, and the Mary Jane Girls began what was billed as "the most extravagant tour of the year," lasting from July through December 1983. Rick and crew, with Rick occasionally billed as Slick Rick (five years before the rapper of that name began his career), performed from coast to coast. The tour, while successful, included a very bad moment for Rick. While performing at the New Orleans Astrodome, Rick told author David Ritz, he looked out at the audience and saw "little girls sticking out their tongues at me like snakes. They couldn't have been older than 13. They'd gyrate sexually and even pull up their tops to reveal their small budding breasts. It wasn't that they disgusted me; I disgusted myself . . . I felt deep and shameful guilt. I was corrupting . . . girls young enough to be my own daughters."

Partly in response to this guilt, he said, he increased his drug intake, which caused him to wish he was dead. He lost his desire to write music. He stayed in his room for days just getting high, "hoping the next hit would bring instant death . . . . Finally, [he] lay down on [his] bathroom floor and called on all the Powers That Be to kill [him]." They didn't, but the powers that were at Motown told him it was time to produce his next album. To prepare himself for the task, he visited Studio 54 in Manhattan and invited a seventeen-year-old girl up to his hotel room.

44

Jailbait

I see the girls walk by, dressed in their summer clothes
I have to turn my head until my darkness goes.

—"Paint It Black," Rolling Stones, written by Mick Jagger
and Keith Richards (1966)

The highlight of Rick's next album was his song about his night of love with the seventeen-year-old girl he met on his visit to New York City. He described her as a six-foot-one white woman with long brown hair, whom he called "young and fine and oh, so tender."

The song, "17," became the third-biggest pop music hit of Rick's career, after "You and I" and "Super Freak," although, or because, its lyrics horrified some reviewers. Rick told author David Ritz that just before writing "17" he had purchased a Yamaha DX7 keyboard and "that between the new woman and the new instrument, [he] was highly stimulated."

When Rick sang in "17" that the young woman he spent the night with was "almost" jailbait, he signaled his awareness that in New York State he was not breaking the law but that he would have been committing statutory rape had she been any younger. The *Chicago Metro News* charged that Rick was "a man in his 30s singing about committing statutory rape," and indeed, in twelve American states, an adult having sex with a seventeen-year-old is a criminal act.

The *News* went on to ask the purpose of a song like this. If its purpose was to sell records, it succeeded. The song rose to number 6 on the R&B singles chart and remained on the chart for sixteen weeks. It rose to number 36 on the pop chart and stayed on the chart for three weeks.

Reflections, the album that "17" appeared on, was primarily a greatest hits collection. Released in August 1984, the album wisely concentrated on Rick's most popular songs, which were his dance tunes and his sex singles, and included no ballads. Rick agreed to *Reflections* only after demanding his usual $1 million per album, even though he recorded only three new songs rather than the usual six to eight. Motown grumbled but finally ended up paying Rick what he wanted.

Reflections appeared on the *Billboard* pop chart on August 25, rose to number 41, and stayed on the chart for nineteen weeks. It did better on the R&B chart, hitting number 10 and staying on the chart for twenty-three weeks. The *Philadelphia Inquirer* called it "an outstanding example" of a greatest hits collection. But while it was more popular than Rick's *Garden of Love* album, which wasn't saying much, it didn't go very far beyond that. *Reflections* sold only 284,426 copies, many fewer than *Cold Blooded*.

But Rick's disappointments were larger than the lackluster sales of *Reflections*: both Michael Jackson and Prince had swept past him in album sales. Prince also had dealt a fatal blow to Rick's moviemaking ambitions by releasing his successful autobiographical movie, *Purple Rain*, in 1984. The film won an Academy Award for best music and original song score, and the record of the score won a Grammy Award for best album of an instrumental score written for a motion picture. Rick was still interested in making movies but was worried that a similar movie released by him would be tagged as a "me-too" production. Rick's brother LeRoi Johnson alluded to this when he told Nelson George of *Billboard* magazine that the field of black movies was overcrowded. "We know there have been and will be more black films with music geared for release," he said. "We don't want to get lost in a crowd."

Johnson added that one of the problems with Rick's movie effort was the difficulty of coming up with a decent script: "We're spending a lot of money developing a script we can be happy with," he told George. He added, "Rick knows that it's music that generates the dollars for him and we don't want to get too far away from it."

45

Rick Involves Himself
in a Murderous Family Feud

Of all the famous feuds that have been fought in the mountain country
of the United States, probably no other has equaled
the famous Hatfield and McCoy feud in deadliness,
in duration, and in desperateness of conflict.

—G. Elliott Hatfield

Rick's devotion to his mother, Betty Gladden, who cared
for him and his brother LeRoi after his father abandoned them,
was the underlying motive for his entire life. It made him want to make
himself into something that impressed her, a goal he certainly achieved.
It also made him want to abandon the use of illegal drugs, a goal he
only partly achieved, but not for lack of trying. Unfortunately, it also
involved him, his mother, and two of his brothers in a partly criminal
Upstate New York version of the Hatfield-McCoy feud.

In the early 1980s, single again, Gladden began seeing a Buffalo
resident named Montey Harper. Gladden was in her late fifties and
Harper was in his twenties when the relationship began. After a time,
Gladden broke off the relationship, but Harper wanted to resume it.
Gladden called his attempts to resume the relationship harassment and
complained to Rick and his brother Carmen Sims, then thirty.

Rick and Sims confronted Harper in a Buffalo barroom in June 1984. A barroom fight, which included bottle throwing, resulted. Harper, claiming the two men had beaten him up, charged them with assault.

Harper then approached Gladden once again. He said he would stop bothering her and drop his complaint against Rick and Sims if she paid him $10,000. She agreed, but only paid him $6,400. When he threatened to reinstitute his complaint, Gladden consulted a lawyer, who told her that her payments to Harper could be considered bribery and urged her to see the Erie County district attorney about the matter. The DA granted Gladden immunity in exchange for her testimony in the subsequent prosecution of Harper.

Rick told an interviewer he was "totally freaked" when he learned his mother had paid Harper. "To me, it was not fair and not agreeable for my mother to be paying him for throwing bottles at me," he said. In January 1988 Harper was convicted by a jury of one count of bribe-receiving as a witness, a felony punishable by up to seven years in prison. His conviction, however, was overturned by a higher state court in December 1988, and he served no jail time. The assault charges against Rick and Sims eventually were dropped, but now the Harper-Johnson feud had taken a darker turn.

In April 1985 another of Rick's brothers, William "Head" Johnson, went out looking for Montey Harper but shot Montey's brother Raymond by mistake. The confusion was understandable: it was 2:25 AM, and Raymond, who closely resembled his brother, was driving Montey's car.

Raymond Harper survived, but William Johnson was convicted in April 1988 of attempted murder and sentenced to between six and twelve years in prison, a term he began serving in 1989 in Attica. His sentence was later reduced, and he was released in 1992.

46

Rick and Eddie Murphy "Party All the Time"

I've always had confidence. It came because I have lots of initiative.
I wanted to make something of myself.

—Eddie Murphy

Eddie Murphy was discontent. Although still in his early twenties in 1984, he'd already conquered several worlds. He was a successful television, film, and stage performer, and his comedy albums were best-sellers. He'd been on *Saturday Night Live* from 1980 to 1984, America's theater owners had voted him the nation's second-most-popular box-office attraction, and he'd signed a contract with Paramount to star in five films. He even coproduced his films through his own production company.

But he'd always wanted to sing. He said he'd organized and sung with his own bands in high school, that Elvis Presley was his idol, and if an album of his own singing was successful, he would integrate his comic and singing talents into a new kind of stage show. "I might open with a short standup routine," Murphy said, "sing a song or two, do some impressions, all with a nice hot band playing behind me, and with lights, explosions, all the effects you see at a rock concert," alleging that this approach would "revolutionize standup comedy."

Murphy and Rick had become friends when Rick appeared on *Saturday Night Live* in 1981 while Murphy was a cast member. Later on, Murphy sometimes joined Rick onstage at concerts as a big-haired, sleazy Rick caricature. Rick enjoyed the teasing, and in fact named his poodle Rick Eddie.

Murphy convinced Rick to write and produce the tune "Party All the Time," which Murphy sang on his 1985 album *How Could It Be*. The song was about a woman Murphy had showered with expensive gifts only to discover she then continued to go to parties without him.

In spite of Murphy's thin voice, the song did well. In fact, it did a lot better on the white charts than many discs by veteran black vocalists. Released by Columbia Records and billed as "written, produced, and arranged by Rick James," it reached number 8 on the R&B singles chart and number 2 on the *Billboard* pop singles chart, probably because so many white people had seen Murphy's movies.

Although "Party All the Time" was definitely a hit, Rick got the credit and Murphy got the dis. Wayne Robins of *Newsday* wrote that the only thing distinguishing the record "from any other well-crafted, full-bodied, formulaic James hit is the uncharacteristically high-pitched, melodically correct but pubescent vocal. That's Murphy." The *Washington Post* called the song "thoroughly innocuous."

Murphy completed *How Could It Be* with help from Stevie Wonder as well as from Rick, with Wonder writing, producing, and arranging the song "Everything's Coming Up Roses" and writing the song "Do I." *Newsday*, noting Murphy had performed "cruelly hilarious parodies of Stevie Wonder," thought Wonder might have succeeded in taking revenge against Murphy with the songs he contributed, which the paper disliked. The paper also called Murphy a "polite wimp" as a lyric writer.

The album itself rose to number 17 on the R&B album chart and 26 on the pop album chart, which wasn't bad for a first try. The success of Murphy's comedy albums, to say nothing of his movies, made this otherwise respectable showing look pitiful, however.

Murphy believed that of the sixty million people who had seen his hit movie *Beverly Hills Cop*, at least a million would buy the record. "Unfortunately," he said, "I see now it doesn't work that way. . . . People expect so much from this album. They think it's supposed to be as good as my comedy. They forget I'm new at singing." (He shouldn't have been that disappointed. The album did indeed sell almost a million copies.) Murphy said the lyrics he wrote weren't funny, and weren't meant to be, but that "they [told] how [he felt] about certain things."

Rick appeared in the video for "Party All the Time," although he didn't direct it. In it, Murphy walks into the recording studio control room with MTV executive Les Garland and is greeted by Rick, who has dyed his hair blond. Everyone in the room—including three attractive women—pats Murphy on the back. Murphy then walks into the live room and starts singing, accompanied by members of the Stone City Band.

Soon after Murphy starts singing, everyone in the studio slowly begins to overreact, snapping their fingers, smiling very broadly, bopping along with the music, and generally behaving as if they've never heard so wonderful a song. Rick bops around and smiles so much it looks like the top of his head is going to blow off. Unable to control himself, he then rushes into the live room near the end of the tune to sing the last part of the song with Murphy and embrace him.

This overreacting is so obvious that the video shows Murphy flashing the other people in the studio a look that clearly says "What's wrong with you?" or, perhaps, "Are you trying to insult me with this shit?" A panel of *Los Angeles Times* reviewers rated the video "wretched," with one reviewer giving it an "Oh barf!" rating.

Ironically, "Party All the Time" was the only video that included Rick to be aired on MTV. Murphy had agreed to host the MTV Video Music Awards that year, giving him an edge with the station. Also, since MTV cofounder Garland actually appears in the video MTV execs really had no choice.

Murphy seemed to want to blame some of the criticisms of "Party All the Time" on Rick. He later released a second album of music, *So Happy*, which Rick had nothing to do with; it was more favorably reviewed and did better on the charts than *How Could It Be*. While praising *So Happy* producer Narada Michael Walden in an interview with *USA Today*, Murphy somewhat ungratefully criticized Rick's lifestyle. Comparing

Walden to Rick, Murphy said, "I'd go to Rick's and end up hanging out for two weeks when we were supposed to be doing a record. Narada gets the job done, and quickly." (In 2013, in an interview with *Billboard*, he changed his story, saying that the reason he stayed in Buffalo with Rick for so long was because a snowstorm hit and he was stuck in Buffalo for two weeks. In the same article, he said he learned how to produce music from Rick.)

Music biz history eventually delivered Rick's revenge: "Party All the Time" was Murphy's only hit single.

47

Rick Tries and Fails to Shake Off
the Drug Yoke

Drugs are a waste of time. They destroy your memory and your self-respect and everything that goes along with your self-esteem.

—Kurt Cobain

Rick's dope habit, combined with hot groupie sex, almost ruined his appearance on the TV show *The A-Team* in 1985. Rick told a writer for the *A.V. Club* that his performance on this show was so bad he was embarrassed. Before the taping, Rick said, he'd been up all night with two women, "getting high and having ferocious sex." When he arrived on the set, he said, staffers had to write out big cue cards for him because he couldn't remember his lines. One of Rick's costars, George Peppard, walked off the set in disgust. "Not only was I loaded, but I forgot the shit," Rick told the *A.V. Club*. "I hate it when I don't do a great job on something."

In the same interview, Rick said he tried to atone for the *A-Team* debacle when he subsequently performed on the soap opera *One Life to Live*, reading the script in advance, going to sleep on time, and "kind of redeeming myself." He also said his good behavior in this instance was motivated by the fact that *One Life to Live* was his mother's favorite soap opera.

But Rick's continued drug use prevented him from fighting success-fully against his declining popularity. He realized this, and as his record sales fell, his efforts to free himself from cocaine increased. He tried to avoid drug dealers, but as Rick's accountant Dick Romer notes, "Drug dealers are like leeches when you're Rick James. Everyone wants a piece of you. It's just one big party. As soon as people heard he was coming, the dealers would line up for an opportunity to get their foot in the door."

People not only sold him drugs, they gave them to him. Richard Wesley, a screenwriter who worked with Rick, talks about an actor he refused to name who showed up at the Chateau Marmont in Los Angeles when Rick was staying there. "Rick was sick and exhausted and not at his best," Wesley says. "He needed rest, but this guy showed up, and instead of saying, 'Rick, How you doin'? What's goin' on?' the first thing he did was bust out some cocaine for Rick to snort. That was the last thing Rick needed." Wesley says that the next morning "Rick was worse than he'd been the night before."

By 1985 Rick's habit began nudging him toward death. Shortly before *Reflections* was released, a friend found him unconscious in his Buffalo home around midnight, and an ambulance rushed him to Erie County Medical Center to recover. Before Rick began producing his next album, his accountants and attorneys, alarmed at his now contin-uous drug usage, said they would resign unless he entered a rehab pro-gram. So in March 1985 Rick agreed to enter the drug dependence treat-ment unit at McLean Hospital in Belmont, Massachusetts, for treatment of his cocaine addiction.

According to court records introduced by Motown's attorneys during that company's later suit against him, Rick stated he had been "lackadaisical" and neglectful of his business "while high" during the months preceding his hospital admission. He said he felt responsible for various adverse events and believed these were "signs from God," or forewarnings to change.

After the arrangements had been made with McLean, Johnson called Levi Ruffin to ask him and his wife, Jackie, to help get Rick there. When the Ruffins walked into Rick's room, Ruffin said, "Rick was sick, with [imagined] bugs on his body, and he was scratching them. . . . Jackie saw him, and she cried."

At the last minute, according to Ruffin, Rick decided he didn't want to go. "Me and Jackie went in there and we drug his ass," Ruffin said. "He was kicking and screaming like a little child, not wanting to go to the goddamn drug spot. We got him in the van, he finally calmed down, and we drove him there and we just prayed and hoped that when he came back he would be all right."

Rick was never all right. He repeatedly returned to drugs after pledging fealty to clean living. On one occasion, after McLean, his staffers had arranged a showcase performance by the Mary Jane Girls for record company executives that unfortunately coincided with one of Rick's many stays in the Betty Ford Center. Managers at the treatment facility allowed Rick to attend the performance provided two guards stayed with him to ensure he did no drinking or drugging. On the way to the show, Rick announced to the two busloads of staffers and performers that no one, including himself, would be allowed to ingest any drugs or drink any liquor at the nightclub where the performance was to take place. But an hour into the performance, Rick evaded the two guards and disappeared for the rest of the night. No one had any doubt about what he was doing.

His addiction to drugs would plague him until his death.

48

A Glowing Rick Chases a Woman Along a Beach

> When I got sober, I thought giving up was saying goodbye to all the
> fun and all the sparkle, and it turned out to be just the opposite.
> That's when the sparkle started for me.
>
> —Mary Karr

For a while after McLean, everything went well. Rick had met fellow drug user and musician Steven Tyler of Aerosmith there and managed to graduate from the twenty-eight-day program. As was his habit after temporarily shucking drugs, Rick began to demonstrate his newfound sobriety to the world. He announced his recovery on *Entertainment Tonight*, on *The Tonight Show Starring Johnny Carson* while Joan Rivers was guest-hosting it, on other TV shows, and in several magazine interviews. He then began attending the Full Gospel Tabernacle church in Buffalo and became a born-again Christian. "I now feel serene and at peace," he said, adding he was writing "new material full of the hope and joy that I feel."

"It's funny how sobriety can affect your life," he wrote in *The Confessions of Rick James*. "It's like you turn into this nice person, which is not what I was known for, to say the least."

Rick designed his next album, *Glow*, to reflect his feelings of hope and release, as well as his growing discontent with Motown and his longtime dislike of endless touring. Everything about the album screamed renewal: every song on it was new, it was the first album produced entirely in his new home recording studio, a glowing Rick held a glowing diamond on the album cover, and no guest artists got in the way of the message.

The *London Times* described the title cut "Glow" as "a banal love song that opens up into real joy," a comment that could well have been inspired by the schmaltzy video, which expressed Rick's relief at being free from drugs. In it, we first see Rick, in a dream, pursuing an anonymous woman wearing white along a beautiful beach. He wakes up in his dressing room gulping from a bottle of bourbon. When his manager comes to tell him it's almost time to go onstage, he tells him to get out.

Rick's girlfriend arrives to say she can't stand what he's doing to himself, and that she's leaving. He tells her to get out too, adding that he's Rick James and doesn't need anybody. The girlfriend is played by Rick's favorite video costar, Jere Fields.

Rick then marches onto the stage carrying the bourbon bottle in his hand and falls over drunk. The crowd starts booing, but he gets up, signals for his guitar, and starts playing and singing very competently. He rushes into the audience, retrieves Fields, who was fleeing the auditorium after seeing him fall, and kisses her, to great audience applause. We then return to the dream, and Rick catches up to the woman on the beach, who turns out to be Fields.

"Glow" rose to number 5 on the R&B singles chart. It also rose to number 106 on the pop chart. "Can't Stop," the first song on the album, had been featured in 1984 on the soundtrack of the blockbuster movie *Beverly Hills Cop*, starring Eddie Murphy. After litigation between Motown and Paramount Pictures, the movie's distributor, the bouncy dance tune was removed from the soundtrack album to become the first single on *Glow*. In spite of the litigation, Rick made the inclusion of "Can't Stop" on the record a feel-good moment by dedicating the song to Murphy. "The Creator has blessed you with a special talent that has not changed your heart," he wrote. "You'll always be a part of us." He signed the dedication, "Your friend & brother Rick James."

"Can't Stop" rose to number 10 on the R&B singles chart and stayed on the chart for twelve weeks. It also rose to number 50 on the pop chart. *Billboard* called the tune "ebullient" and noted it showed more pop music influence than some of Rick's past songs.

The *Los Angeles Times* praised Rick's singing style on *Glow*. On previous albums, the paper said, Rick's vocals had been "ferocious," but on this one they were subdued. The *Times* noted approvingly that Rick obviously had decided to "cruise in lower gear" as a vocalist and said his new approach worked. On this album Rick's "subtle, slow-burning vocals" contrasted appealingly with the "rowdy funk rhythms and blistering instrumentals" that accompanied them, the paper said.

The *Omaha World-Herald* also praised Rick for not "cluttering" the album with guest stars, as he had on *Cold Blooded*. Process and the Doo-Rags, a group Rick had created, aided Rick on the title tune, but they were hardly stars. The *Toronto Globe and Mail*, however, complained that too many of the songs on the album were about lonely nights and girls met on the road. The paper took this as a sign that Rick's public persona had eclipsed the importance of his music, but it also could have been evidence that he was weary after many years of touring. The paper also said that on this record, Rick sounded "desperate to impress," possibly a manifestation of his desperation to reverse his declining record sales.

On the LP's inner sleeve, Rick told the story of a young boy who lived in "a land of darkness, where wicked men ruled," then journeyed to "the Kingdom of the Light." He stayed there for ten years, acquired a "glow," and then returned to the dark land to "defeat the evil Dark Wizard King Luto's [sic]." Rick wrote in *The Confessions of Rick James* that he was the "young boy."

Rick's brother LeRoi Johnson says this tale was based on Rick's recently acquired enthusiasm for the writer Khalil Gibran, who wrote in part about darkness, kings, wizards, and searchers after truth. Also, because Rick had become discontented at Motown after having worked there on and off for approximately ten years, it's tempting to see him as the boy who grows to be a man and confronts Motown with his glow.

Rick thought Motown was stealing or "looting" royalties from him, so King "Luto's" might well have referred to Motown president Berry Gordy.

Glow was not only the first album of Rick's on which he may have been denouncing Gordy in code, it was the first album of his career in which he mentioned Syville and their two children. On the album's inner sleeve, Rick thanked Syville, Ty, and Ricky, and told them "I Love You."

In its 1989 suit against Rick, Motown said that three years after its April 1985 release, *Glow* had sold 280,586 copies. That was more than Rick's worst-selling album, *Garden of Love*, but almost four thousand fewer than his previous album, the greatest hits collection *Reflections*. *Glow* rose to number 7 on the *Billboard* R&B album chart and remained on the chart for twenty-nine weeks, but it rose only to number 50 on the *Billboard* pop album chart. The *London Times* may have put its finger on one reason for Rick's declining sales when it noted that although he hadn't lost his touch as a funkster, he was now competing with younger funksters in groups like Midnight Star and the Prince-inspired group the Time.

Unlike *Glow*, another Rick James product was doing very well. The Mary Jane Girls' second album, *Only Four You*, produced by Rick, was also released in 1985. It contained eight tracks, including "Shadow Lover." It sold 542,611 copies, about 100,000 more than the group's first album and almost twice as many as *Glow*, and was certified gold by the RIAA. It rose to number 5 on the *Billboard* top R&B album chart and remained on the chart for forty-seven weeks while rising to number 18 on the top pop album chart and staying there for thirty-eight weeks.

The lyrics for the first tune on the album, "In My House," were the most risqué ever released by Motown, but would now bore most people. Although the song is certainly about sex, it contains nothing explicit. In 1985, however, the tune was among the "Filthy 15" denounced by the Parents Music Resource Center (PMRC), a group led by Tipper Gore, the wife of then-senator Al Gore (later Bill Clinton's vice president and a Democratic presidential candidate). The PMRC's efforts led to the proliferation of "Parental Advisory" stickers that were later applied to some of Rick's CD's.

The PMRC also denounced, with somewhat more reason, Prince's song "Darling Nikki," which contained references to a girl named Nikki "masturbating with a magazine" in a hotel lobby, "Eat Me Alive," by Judas Priest, "Let Me Put My Love into You" by AC/DC, "Animal (Fuck Like a Beast)" by W.A.S.P., and Sheena Easton's gynecological classic "Sugar Walls," which included the lyrics "Blood races to your private spots . . . You can't fight passion when passion is hot / temperatures rise inside my sugar walls." Compared to these, "In My House" should have been G-rated.

Vibe acclaimed "In My House" a "party-starter," and the *Los Angeles Times* called it a "buoyant disco single." Another song on the album, "Wild and Crazy Love," sounded even more than the others like a production of the Rick James of old: it had a funky beat, no real tune, and endless references to sex, such as "I kiss you from your head to toe . . . / I'd make you scream in sheer delight . . . / When you want me, just open up and come on in."

Among Rick's most successful groups, the Mary Jane Girls headlined twenty of their forty concert dates in 1985, the first time any of the groups Rick produced had performed as headliners while still affiliated with him.

49

Rick Lets His Freak Flag Fly

White collar conservative flashin down the street,
Pointing their plastic finger at me.
They're hoping soon, my kind will drop and die
But I'm gonna wave my freak flag high.

—"If 6 Was 9," by Jimi Hendrix (1969)

Although *Glow* **celebrated** Rick's return to sobriety, he remained drug-free for only six months after leaving McLean. He then began producing another album of his own while also producing successful songs and albums for Eddie Murphy, Val Young, Process and the Doo-Rags, the Mary Jane Girls, and the Stone City Band.

By 1985 Rick was earning much more from the songs "Party All the Time," "In My House," and "Seduction"—a Top 20 black single he'd composed for Val Young—than from his own vocal efforts. The Murphy album sold seven hundred thousand copies in 1985, and the Mary Jane Girls sold seven hundred thousand of their own albums that same year.

Rick's own next album, 1986's *The Flag*, was highlighted by a very controversial song: "Funk in America/Silly Little Man." Rick wrote in *The Confessions of Rick James* that he composed the song after being horrified to learn that there were fifteen thousand missiles in the United

States alone. He said the song was aimed at Soviet leader Mikhail Gorbachev and at President Reagan, whom he called the "assholes with the power of the button."

The "Funk in America" portion of the composition was spoken rather than sung, and in it, Rick delivered a somber, pessimistic lecture about a real US policy stating that any enemy daring to launch a nuclear attack on America would be destroyed. Known as the mutually assured destruction (MAD) policy, it includes the mostly unspoken assumption that the United States would also be turned into rubble by the enemy's incoming missiles.

Rick continued denouncing the MAD policy in the "Silly Little Man" portion of the piece, which he sang. It began with the line "Did you read the news, oh boy," an obvious homage to the first line, "I read the news today, oh boy," of the 1967 Beatles song "A Day in the Life."

In "Silly Little Man," Rick told his listeners a variant of the old Cold War joke, "If nuclear war occurs, put your head between your legs and kiss your ass good-bye." (That humor had been based on real US Civil Defense instructions to citizens under nuclear attack to put their head between their legs to avoid head injuries.) In Rick's version, he substituted "boop!" for "ass."

In a more serious vein, at the end of the same cut, Rick added the sound of children playing. This detail was reminiscent of Lyndon Johnson's so-called "daisy" campaign ad, which he'd planned to air during his 1964 presidential race against Barry Goldwater. The ad, which was widely publicized although it was broadcast only as a news item, showed a little girl playing with a flower just before she was vaporized by a nuclear blast. The *Los Angeles Times* complimented Rick for getting serious, if only briefly, with this song.

Some of Rick's critics said that, musically, "Funk in America" was strongly reminiscent of tunes and riffs by Prince and Gil Scott-Heron, including Prince's 1981 song "Ronnie, Talk to Russia," in which the singer urged the president to begin arms control talks with the Soviets. Others said Rick seemed to be imitating Prince when he referred to

President Ronald Reagan as "Ronnie," just as he had in the song "Money Talks" on the *Throwin' Down* album.

Hospital records reveal that when Rick recorded *The Flag*, he was freebasing approximately $7,000 to $8,000 worth of cocaine per week. On one of the songs on the album, "Free to Be Me," Rick actually announced that he was on coke. "I'm up, down, middle of my room," he sang in the first verse. "Someone got excited, someone dropped the spoon / A joke, a smoke, I'm crawling on my knees / I'm feeling paranoia, someone rock it please / A place, a space, any box will do / Just don't let the sun in, please, until I'm through."

There was no actual flag pictured on the cover of *The Flag*. Instead, Rick stands looking straight ahead with his arms folded, posing in front of a rectangular background divided into red and black portions and bordered in green. He wears black pants and a black top with a cross around his neck, his hair is cut short, and a dangling earring hangs from his left ear. He told an interviewer he thought short hair made him look sober. Rick said the flag referred to in the album's title wasn't the US flag, but "the freak flag" instead, and that the freak flag's colors were red, green, and black. The word *freak* often referred to drug users, but red, green, and black were also the colors of Kwanzaa and the Pan-African flag.

Later, however, Rick told Sharon Davis for her book *Motown: The History* that the red, green, and black flag was "a free flag for the people, not just a country." Green represents "Mother Earth, the planet which we are destroying and which we must save. The red stands for passion and/or love and also for blood, which must not be shed. The black is alpha-omega, ying-yang, the beginning and the end."

The Flag may have been Rick's most unoriginal album, and the critics came out in force to denounce it. He was accused of ripping off its basic album jacket design concept, as well as the colors of "the freak flag," from a banner on the cover of Funkadelic's 1978 album *One Nation Under a Groove*. The only apparent similarity between Rick's album cover and the Funkadelic banner, however, was their colors.

On the back of his own album jacket, Rick was standing in front of another red, black, and green rectangle, this time wearing a black headwaiter-type jacket decorated with two vertical rows of three silver buttons and long, white-stringed epaulets. Unlike most headwaiters, however, Rick wasn't wearing a shirt beneath the jacket, revealing a V-shaped view of his middle chest. The cross remained around his neck. He wore studded bracelets on his wrist and held his right hand to his forehead as if saluting an invisible flag. At both the beginning and end of the album, Rick and his background singers urged listeners in song to "Wave your freak flag! Wave your freak flag! Rally round the red, black, and green."

Rick later disputed the accusation that he had stolen the flag idea from Funkadelic by arguing that the flag the album referred to was neither the Funkadelic flag nor the freak flag, but the US flag. He also implied that the US flag was linked to the album because it represented a country whose existence was being endangered by the possibility of nuclear war, the subject he explored in "Funk in America/Silly Little Man."

The Flag had another, more serious problem, however. So far, Rick and Motown had done very well at choosing the singles they traditionally would release early to build public anticipation for an upcoming album. This time, however, the company chose "Sweet and Sexy Thing" for early release because it was a rocking love song that sounded like many of Rick's previous hits—but Rick wanted "Funk in America/Silly Little Man" released first.

All seemed well for a while. Black stations played "Sweet and Sexy Thing" often enough to push it to number 6 on the *Billboard* R&B singles chart by May 1986 and keep it on the chart for fifteen weeks. (The tune didn't make the pop chart.) But this time the record's intended audience didn't react as expected. They listened to it on the radio but by and large refused to buy it. "Sweet and Sexy Thing" became a "turntable hit," a disc that makes it on the air but not at the store. Of 77,100 copies of the single sent to stores for sale, 44,615 were returned, giving "Sweet and Sexy Thing" sales of about thirty-two thousand copies, far from being either sweet or sexy.

Motown then released a second single from *The Flag*, "Forever and a Day," and promoted it to radio stations as a follow-up to "Sweet and Sexy Thing." "Forever and a Day" did even worse, however. Many radio stations refused to play it, and it never charted. According to testimony by Motown executive Alvin "Skip" Miller during the *Motown Record Corporation v. Mary Jane Girls* court case, radio stations said they wouldn't play "Forever and a Day" and other songs on *The Flag* album because the album "wasn't up to the type of quality that Rick James was known for."

Discouraged by the reception given "Sweet and Sexy Thing" and "Forever and a Day," Motown refused to release a third or fourth single from *The Flag* as the label had for all of Rick's—and both of the Mary Jane Girls'—previous albums. In particular, Motown execs refused a direct request from Rick that they release "Funk in America/Silly Little Man." Because that song could have been seen as a denunciation of then–President Ronald Reagan, it might actually have increased the album's sales—especially among black people, who were mostly anti-Reagan.

In a second controversial move, Motown also cut its promotional spending on *The Flag* album to the bone, spending a total of $56,743 on it. That sum was a mere drop in the record bin compared to the $402,816 the company had paid to promote *Glow* just the year before, the $468,498 it had spent on his *Cold Blooded* LP, and the $834,260 it lavished on promoting the Mary Jane Girls' album *Only Four You* in 1985. Rick later argued that the large sums the company poured into promoting those discs were what made them more popular than *The Flag*. The album sold only 94,697 copies from its release date of May 20, 1986, through mid-1988.

People magazine called *The Flag* one of the worst albums released in 1986 and described it as a "half-mast performance that nobody is likely to salute" and an "over-embellished façade" that could not hide the fact that Rick was "creatively becalmed." Rick, of course, disagreed. He wrote in *The Confessions of Rick James* that he needed to "express his views, even if it put [his] career at stake" and that he needed to "compose for [him], not for Motown."

The Flag rose to number 16 on the *Billboard* R&B album chart and stayed on the chart for seventeen weeks, but only managed to reach number 95 on the pop album chart. Motown lost $1,053,711 on the project, and Rick's royalty account with the company soon ran up a deficit of $896,616, partly because he'd demanded and received an advance payment of $1.2 million for the album. He'd always insisted on large advances from Motown, and the company had acceded to his demands because in most cases his albums, once released, made more in royalties for Rick than the company had advanced him.

Not this time. Except for "Funk in America/Silly Little Man," the contents of *The Flag* went mostly unnoticed. The *Los Angeles Times* called the song "Slow and Easy (Interlude)" a "teasingly effective type of love/sex ballad" but went on to say Rick could probably have tossed off the song in his sleep. (They added that the rest of the album "could just be tossed out, period.") The combination of sensual lyrics with sensual music in this song makes it one of Rick's erotic classics, however, and shows how effective he could be using no pornographic lines whatsoever.

As his recording career declined, Rick also expressed discouragement with moviemaking. He continued to talk about doing films but didn't "plan on doing a Sidney Poitier trip." He said, "I only want to do the things I know I can do and make them believable." Nevertheless, he never really dropped the idea. "I'm not really an actor, but I think I could have fun" doing movies, he told an interviewer in 1986.

In a 2002 interview with the *A.V. Club*, Rick blamed his failure to become a moviemaker in the 1980s on drugs. He said, "I was doing so many drugs in those times that there were a lot of things that I was working on that I just kind of displaced." If a project "didn't have much to do with music," he said, "I would get involved with it and then kind of drop it."

50

Rick and Motown Duke It Out in Court

Rick obviously had a hot-and-cold relationship with Motown.

—Chuck Stokes, Rick's second cousin and a Detroit television broadcaster

On September 26, 1986, Rick reentered the McLean rehab facility, telling a doctor there he had returned because his use of cocaine was becoming too "time-consuming" and because when high, he became lackadaisical and "neglectful of his business." Unfortunately, McLean discharged Rick less than a month later, before his treatment was completed, because he had a fight with another patient.

His drug addiction certainly was interfering with his business as a Motown recording artist. Daniel LeMelle notes, "Cocaine helps you as a musician," but only up to a point. He said he quit using coke before Rick did and never used it again after Grace Slick, who had been the lead singer of the Great Society and Jefferson Airplane in the 1960s and Jefferson Starship and Starship in the 1970s and 1980s, suggested he stop.

"You've already seen what you need to see," LeMelle says Slick told him. "You know what [getting high] sounds like, you know what it looks like. You have heard different notes in rainfall. . . . Whenever you need to recreate it you can, but come out of that room or you'll be lost in it." LeMelle says the conversation with Slick "was like she'd hit me in the head with a baseball bat." In the long run, drugs and alcohol are depressants, and, Levi Ruffin says, "It seemed like the more money that Rick got, the less happy he was. When Rick and me were broke, we had fun. When we got more and more income—we called it 'nigger rich'—he had everything he was dreaming about. Cars, bitches, go anywhere you want when you want, but the more he did, the less happy he got."

Rick agreed with a vengeance. "My world was crumbling right in front of me and I didn't give a fuck," he wrote in *The Confessions of Rick James*. "I was even angry with God. I felt He had deserted me. . . . Why when I was so low wasn't He there to help me out? . . . I felt there was no hope, only death."

At one sold-out concert in Dallas during the 1980s, before an audience of eighteen thousand people, dope's hold on Rick was obvious. According to Ruffin, Rick was getting ready to perform when he fell over, without even trying to catch himself, and hit his head on the stage. "People thought this was part of the show, but when they realized it wasn't, they started booing," Ruffin says.

In 1986, while Rick was getting high in his bedroom, his Stone City Band was recording albums in the basement, supposedly under his direction. They waited and waited for Rick, but he never came downstairs. Finally, they gave up, disbanded, and left his house for the last time. As Rick told *Behind the Music* years later, "They had to make a living. They couldn't depend on me."

That same year, a woman named Gina Perry said Rick beat her in Buffalo after accusing her of stealing a $15,000 diamond ring from him. Rick's attorney in that case, William Gersten, admitted Rick had slapped Perry at his Buffalo ranch but argued Rick had struck her after she "went nuts" and began slapping him and screaming when he demanded to see if she had put the ring in her purse. Perry sued for $2 million and the jury awarded her $25,000. This scenario, featuring a cocaine-using Rick attacking a woman he believed had stolen something from him in his own home, would reoccur at a much greater cost to him a few years later.

In February 1987 Rick told *Jet* magazine he had become a "born-again Christian" in reaction to his drug problem. "God has saved me from overdosing," Rick said. On March 2, however, when Rick appeared for a deposition related to a legal proceeding, Motown attorney Marc Gottridge wrote in a a later affidavit that Rick's "eyes were glazed over, he was unable to sit upright in his chair, and he appeared not to comprehend what was going on." One of Rick's attorneys said Rick's condition was "the worst he had seen in some time." At about 1:00 AM the next morning, Rick entered BryLin Hospital, a private psychiatric and drug abuse treatment facility in Buffalo, for "depression with associated cocaine dependency." He checked himself out the next day, however, against medical advice.

Rick told an Associated Press reporter in 1988 that his cocaine habit was costing him $10,000 to $15,000 per week, but he wasn't really aware how much he was spending. He began doing drugs twenty-four seven, stayed awake for days at a time, and had aluminum foil mounted on the windows of his house to keep out the daylight. He began waking up with several strange women in his bed, uncertain whether it was day or night. Basically a hermit, he rarely left his house and rarely mixed with people unless they came to his house to get high. He had virtually no new song ideas and wrote less and less music.

Even when Rick did go out in public, it was easy for him to keep doping himself. He told an interviewer, "I could walk on the street and smoke a joint and do cocaine in a restaurant . . . and people would say, 'That's cool, that's Rick James.'" Although he had been arrested for marijuana possession as a youth, there's no indication he was ever arrested as an adult for consuming mountains of Peruvian marching powder.

By his account, he used most of his waking hours to "snort all of Peru and drink all the cognac" he could imbibe. Then he'd pop sleeping pills at night. He said this cycle continued for about a month, until he began falling into fifteen-hour periods of coma-like sleep at home. And his addiction kept growing. "I didn't really care about making albums anymore," he told one interviewer. "I started to get very complacent."

Rick's complacency weakened his bonds with Motown. His 1986 admission to McLean Hospital's drug treatment program had occurred while he was trying to supervise the recording of a third Mary Jane Girls album for the company, and the album—which was never released— was one of the many issues dividing Rick and Motown. That album, *Sweet Conversations*, resulted in only one very short conversation.

Rick sent a rough cassette of some of its tunes to Motown in August 1986. Motown executive Lee Young Jr. said "the Motown employees who heard the cassette told Rick they thought it was unsatisfactory" via telephone and "[Rick] hung up." Motown employees heard no potential hit tunes on the album, and the company filed suit against the Mary Jane Girls for turning in master recordings that were "not suitable for manufacturing commercially saleable records." Both sides knew most of the fault was in Rick's continued drug use rather than in the Mary Jane Girls' performances.

These issues became the basis of the federal court case known as *Motown Record Corporation v. Mary Jane Girls.* As the progress of the case revealed, both Rick and Motown wanted to end their relationship, but on dramatically different terms. The case consisted of two clashing lawsuits, one filed by Motown in 1986 and one by Rick in 1987, followed by numerous claims and counterclaims. It was tried and decided in the United States District Court for the Southern District of New York in Manhattan over a four-year period.

According to the written decision issued by the presiding judge, Robert W. Sweet, in 1989, Motown's major issue was that Rick didn't adhere to deadlines, and the company "no longer had confidence in [Rick's] capacities to perform his contracts." Meanwhile, Rick "complained that he wasn't receiving adequate promotional support."

In a larger sense, however, the two suits were the culmination of longtime mutual dissatisfaction. During the course of the case, Judge Sweet argued, somewhat surprisingly, that Rick's drug use may not have been all that bad for him as a recording artist or a record producer during the early part of his Motown career. "Given the reportedly widespread drug use in the music industry," Sweet wrote in his 1989 decision, "it is not unlikely that some of this generation's more successful albums were recorded by persons under the influence of drugs. Indeed, Rick James's own history of drug use makes it conceivable that he achieved some of his earlier successes while using drugs."

Drugs were not the only issue in the case, however. Judge Sweet noted that the parties' differences over specific issues were sharpened by Rick's "outspoken comments, his need for funds, his belief in his own

efforts, and his suspicion that Motown was not treating him in the fashion which he merited based upon his work."

Rick's brother LeRoi Johnson says he agreed with the judge that one
reason Rick was unpopular at Motown was that he would "go into the
[Motown] offices and insult people, loud-talk them." Rick "wasn't a diplo-
matic person. He would say, 'Either do it this way or I have no use for you.'"

In a 1979 interview with *Jet* magazine, Motown president Berry
Gordy had hinted at this problem while still expressing warmth toward
Rick: "He thinks he knows everything there is to know, and we argue."

Rick's former road manager Rick Abel expressed the same opinion,
although he may have overstated it. During an interview for this book
in 2013, Abel said he'd just finished reading *The Rise and Fall of the
Third Reich* by William Shirer and said to himself after he read it, "Adolf
Hitler is Rick James with immense power and immense evil behind him.
Nothing could be right unless it came from his lips. Nobody could control him. Nobody could tell Rick, 'Great idea, let's try taking it in this
direction.' He thought that his ideas were first and last the best things
that ever came to light."

There was also speculation that Rick was unpopular at Motown simply because he was too sexy for the still somewhat staid company. "The
sexually graphic themes of his music conflicted with the company's conservative approach," one AP interviewer wrote. In the 2013 Broadway
production of Berry Gordy's *Motown: The Musical*, an onstage history of
the company, the actor playing Rick, Eric LaJuan Summers, spent much
of his brief time onstage sticking his tongue in and out of his mouth like
a frog in heat.

Rick put the issue in a different way to the interviewer, charging
Motown with "never totally understanding what I was trying to do."
The company "just didn't allow me to have the freedom I needed to
really make the kind of records and do the kinds of things in the industry
I wanted to do."

In his autobiography, *To Be Loved*, published in 1994, five years after
the suit was decided, Gordy was very complimentary about Rick: "Rick
did it all—singer, musician, writer, arranger, producer. Watching him

work in the studio was amazing. He was innovative, and could come up with some of the greatest rhythms and vocal arrangements in his head, on the spot." But the Motown president also wrote that Rick was "outrageous . . . cocky and wild" and coined "phrases that I had never heard before." His "live shows were so daring they shocked me."

Rick argued that his ties to Motown had never been that strong in the first place. "I'm not a cat who came up with Berry Gordy" in the music business, he said in an interview with *New Musical Express*. "If Motown ever fucks me around, then I want the fucking money and I'm out. I've told Berry that."

Motown may have felt the same way about Rick. As part of its suit, Motown's attorneys introduced into evidence Rick's album sales through mid-1988. The numbers revealed that Rick's next-to-last album for the company, *Glow*, sold only one-tenth as many copies as his first, *Come Get It*, and only one-twenty-fifth as many as his biggest Motown album, *Street Songs*.

In Motown's nine-page initial complaint, filed in September 1986, the company specifically charged that Mary Jane Girls Inc. had not delivered an acceptable third album by July of that year as required by its 1983 contract. Mary Jane Girls Inc. was the company that managed Rick; LeRoi Johnson was its president. Motown therefore asked the court to require the Mary Jane Girls to provide their services directly to Motown, rather than through Rick's company. Motown also demanded unspecified monetary damages of more than $10,000.

In a fifty-page countercomplaint filed in January 1987, Rick and his lawyers accused Motown of numerous contractual violations, including "failing to use reasonable efforts to promote and sell *The Flag* in a manner consistent with Motown's other top-line artists." Rick also said Motown had failed to pay him and Mary Jane Girls Inc. $10 million in royalties due them in numerous different accounting categories, and demanded the company release him and Mary Jane Girls Inc. from all their Motown contracts.

During the four-year duration of the case, Rick moved back to Los Angeles, rented a Hollywood Hills home formerly owned by Mickey Rooney, and spent most of his time there, producing nothing and staying high on drugs. His downward trajectory became public at Hollywood's China Club, later the setting for two of the skits about Rick on Dave Chappelle's TV show. While drunk, Rick clambered onto the stage with Herbie Hancock to perform, then climbed onto a speaker in front of the stage to dance, and finally fell backward into the space between the stage and the speaker. The fall must have been spectacular; witnesses said "people were screaming and running in all directions," and the rest of the concert was canceled. Rick had broken four ribs and spent the next three weeks recovering at Cedars-Sinai Medical Center.

While Rick and Motown were dueling in court, his comments about Motown were completely negative. This was hardly surprising, considering the bitterness involved and the length of the struggle. "I have no good feelings—none!" he said about Motown. "Just because you've been married doesn't mean you're in love." He referred to Motown as Notown or Lowtown. (Due to professional pride, he failed to refer to the company as Hotown, which others have delighted in doing.) When he was asked to comment on rumors that Gordy might sell the company, he remarked, "All bad things must come to an end." Gordy sold Motown in 1988 to a joint venture of MCA Inc. and Boston Ventures.

Rick's put-downs of Motown ignored the ten years he had spent profitably with the company, and the fact that while he was there he had become a superstar. The only charitable remark he would make about Motown was that it had given him the opportunity to work with Stevie Wonder and the Temptations, and that he had found Teena Marie there.

Over the course of the more than three years of dueling suits, hundreds of pages of legal briefs and deposition transcripts changed hands and numerous interim rulings were handed down. A twelve-day court trial then took place in June and July 1989, including testimony from thirteen witnesses and several hundred exhibits. On December 6, 1989, Judge Robert W. Sweet, in a thirty-eight-page decision, decided in favor of Motown in seven of ten legal areas.

Regarding Rick's charge that Motown had been legally required to do more than it did to promote *The Flag*, the judge noted that Rick "was indisputably a top Motown artist" and that "Motown's promotional efforts on *The Flag* paled in comparison" to the company's similar expenditures on Rick's three preceding albums, and in comparison to what the company had spent to promote its other top artist of the era, Lionel Richie.

Judge Sweet ruled, however, that the contract allowed Motown to consider the prior sales of the artists involved when it decided what to spend on promotion. In this context, he noted that *one* of Richie's albums had sold fifteen million copies, twice the combined sales of all of Rick's Motown albums. Rick, "as an artist, may have been in the same league as [Stevie] Wonder and Richie, but his record sales did not share the same status." While Rick's contract with Motown required the company to use "reasonable efforts" to promote Rick's albums, it didn't say the company needed to make its "best efforts" to do so. And after the public had rejected two singles released early to publicize *The Flag*, radio stations had refused to play them. That, Judge Sweet ruled, showed Motown had been correct to spend relatively little on promoting the album.

But two big things did go in Rick's favor. For one, the judge decided the various contracts between Rick and Motown no longer carried any legal weight, which was one of the outcomes Rick had sought. The judge also said Motown owed Rick a minimum of $365,000 in unpaid royalties, adding that the total amount of money it owed the singer "will, regrettably, require a further hearing." He went on to suggest the parties involved confer informally and reach an agreement on the final sum.

They did. According to Johnson, who was not only Rick's brother but one of the attorneys representing Rick in the case, after conferring, Rick's attorneys demanded $7 million from Motown. Motown refused, and said it would appeal a ruling forcing them to pay this amount. Instead, the company offered an immediate $2.5 million, which Rick accepted. As a result, Judge Sweet dismissed both suits on October 30, 1990.

For Rick, the suit, although long and arduous, had freed him from Motown and dumped an avalanche of money in his lap. Now, all he needed was a new girlfriend.

51

Rick Meets the Love of His Life

*We're all a little weird. And life is a little weird. And when we find
someone whose weirdness is compatible with ours, we join
up with them and fall into mutually satisfying
weirdness—and call it love—true love.*

—Robert Fulghum

round 1987 in Los Angeles, Rick met Tanya Hijazi, a
seventeen-year-old white woman, the same age as his daughter Ty
at the time. He found Tanya very attractive and was impressed when she
traveled to Buffalo to visit him a short time later. (At that time he was
shuttling back and forth between Buffalo and L.A.)

Tanya, who had brown hair and hazel eyes and was five foot nine,
had been born on June 24, 1970. Judging by how Rick's usually sober
attorneys describe her, it's surprising Rick could think about anything
else after their first encounter. One of those lawyers, Les Greenbaum,
calls Tanya "breathtakingly beautiful." Attorney Robert Sheahen, who
met Tanya in 1991, describes her as "everything you could possibly
want, personally and sexually explosive." Sheahen says he could see how
she had beguiled Rick, adding that Tanya was "as free a spirit as you
would ever want to see" and that "she would have experimented with
anything."

Talking about Tanya in *The Confessions of Rick James*, Rick wrote, "I felt I had found someone who wasn't jaded by Hollywood and I wanted to keep it that way." He was upset later on when Tanya "began changing drastically. Her clothes, hair and mannerism were becoming 'Hollywood'—pretentious and fake." But he remained mesmerized by her because "[he] knew deep down she wasn't like that at all."

From the early 1990s on, although Rick was occasionally involved with other women, Tanya was the main woman in his life.

52

Rick Makes Loosey Feel Wonderful

They call me Loosey, 'cause I'm so loose
I make all the right moves, when I seduce.

—"Loosey's Rap," performed by Rick James and Roxanne Shanté,
written by Rick James (1988)

Rick signed with Warner Brothers in July 1987 and moved to that company while his suit against Motown was continuing.

Born from what Rick saw as his dual escapes—from Motown and, he innocently believed, from drug and alcohol addiction—his next album, 1988's *Wonderful*, reflected what he thought his life had become. Rick told an AP interviewer he was "really excited" about finally getting a chance to do a non-Motown album and that those who listened to his next LP would hear "a joy in the album that I haven't had for years." Part of the joy was the result of his recent conversion to born-again Christianity, which had been inspired by a born-again girlfriend from his recent past.

Although Motown had paid him $1 million per album, he said he was flattered that Warner agreed to pay him $800,000 for *Wonderful*. He also was pleased that Warner would release his albums on their Reprise subsidiary label, on which they'd released Jimi Hendrix's records. There was a problem, though. Rick wanted to make an album of Christian songs for Warner Brothers, but that company wanted an old-style punk-funk Rick James album instead. After weighing his newfound born-again Christianity against his love of money, Rick caved to the lure of lucre.

Once he had made that decision, he remembered one of his tried-and-true ways of making money from an album was singing about sex. He also knew the popularity of rappers had been growing and that women were as popular as ever. He decided, therefore to collaborate with nineteen-year-old Roxanne Shanté, the first female rapper to make a record, to produce what turned out to be the most popular song on the album, "Loosey's Rap."

This song brings to full fruition the use of the word "freaky" to mean "fuckable." Rick introduces Loosey as a "freaky thing" with long legs and juicy lips. Then Loosey, after identifying herself as a "super freak," raps about how great she is at sex and seduction and asks a listener "How would you like for me to freak you?"

After listening to this song, a *Los Angeles Times* reviewer called Shanté "tougher than a truckload of leather-wearing Mary Jane Girls" and touted her "B-girl boasting, which she sounds fully capable of backing up." A *Dallas Morning News* reviewer accurately described the song as a "lean, scorchy and hypnotic tune with a dead-on bass line and a hip Roxanne rap."

Although Shanté made the track sizzle, she didn't appear in the inevitable video for the song, probably because she was less attractive than the lanky supermodel types who dominated the video striding around in their undergarments. While certainly sexy, the models probably disappointed some of Rick's male fans by wearing lingerie that mostly protected their modesty. They also barely touched each other or a fully dressed Rick and mimicked no sex acts whatsoever, making the video resemble a soft-porn fashion shoot.

In at least two cutaway scenes while Rick was singing, various supermodels, all but two white, got their hair done and applied bright red lipstick while a tiger on a leash growled nearby. One model wore an American Revolutionary era soldier's uniform with the jacket open to reveal her black bra. Two of the models, one wearing a dress and the other a negligee, appeared to be trying to wash their hair in a shower stall. They started squirting each other with a hand-held shower attachment, and ended up shooting mouthfuls of water at each other. One of them was kneeling while the other was standing, causing frissons of delight among thousands of imaginative viewers. MTV, always in character, refused to play the video, but, amazingly, it aired on *Playboy's Hot Rocks*, a Playboy Channel show.

"Loosey's Rap," Rick's first single release on Reprise, hit number 1 on the *Billboard* R&B singles chart and stayed on the chart for sixteen weeks, becoming Rick's first number 1 hit on that chart since "Cold Blooded" five years before. Showing how accustomed Rick had become to being nearer the middle of the heap than the top, he expressed amazement that "Loosey's Rap" did so well. "That was a very strange thing for me," he told J. D. Considine of the *Baltimore Sun*. "I never thought it was going to be a number one record; I really didn't."

Motown was shocked and dismayed. After years as No-Hit Rick at Motown, Rick had scored a number one record on the R&B chart with his first release for another firm.

Because two of Rick's three favorite things were sex and money, it was appropriate that the other outstanding song on *Wonderful* was called "So Tight." Most listeners thought "So Tight" had a sexual connotation, but they were wrong. The song was about money, and referred to the tight budgets of ghetto dwellers. Rick made that eminently clear beginning with the song's first verse: "You got no money in your pocket / No shoes on your feet / Every place that you go / You can't afford to eat." The song was also about Rick's opinion of Motown's financial treatment of its artists. He made this clear when, in thanking people on the inside album sleeve, he told Motown, "Don't Be *So Tight!*" apparently referring to the millions in royalties he believed the company owed him.

After recording "So Tight," Rick said he wasn't going to record any more songs with topical themes, because listeners already knew what their problems were, and the songs weren't going to solve those problems. Rick may have been disappointed because his earlier protest songs, "Funk in America/Silly Little Man" on *The Flag*, and "Ghetto Life" and

"Mr. Policeman" on *Street Songs*, hadn't made any discernable impact on the world.

Another song on *Wonderful*, "In the Girls' Room," really did refer to lesbian sex acts but didn't go into any detail. The song was actually a cry for justice for a boy caught watching some sexually playful girls through a locker room peephole. The *Dallas Morning News* called the song "loutish" and "sexist" and pointed out that "In the Girls' Room" was about a peeping tom, and Rick excused this conduct with the line "Boys will be boys, no need to get annoyed / He was just having fun and got busted."

"Sexual Luv Affair," on this album, on the other hand, did live up to its title somewhat, with the *L.A. Times* calling it a "torcher." They somewhat paradoxically complimented the song's "angelic, 1950s-sounding three-part harmony."

Rick had great expectations for his new LP. "It's just a very happy album," Rick told an AP interviewer, adding, "Now is my time. Everything I've done up to this point is just a warm up." His publicist said *Wonderful* has "gotta be *wonderful* news for anyone who loves music that shakes the soul, their booty and their preconceptions." But was it?

Besides being his first non-Motown album in years, *Wonderful* was a big change for Rick in several other ways. Although the music was still recognizably punk funk, with the *Cleveland Plain Dealer* describing its sound as "soulful, new-wave," Rick had thrown heavy smatterings of rap and acid rock into the mix, making the record sound, in part, like a Prince imitation. Rick acknowledged this in a way when he made the basic color of the cover purple.

Rick also had drastically changed his look on the album cover to make himself look more like Prince—or like Louis XIV, depending on your point of view. He'd replaced his shoulder-length braids with a full curly hairstyle, and changed out of his gladiator garb and other deliberately shocking outfits and into a floral-print suit consisting of a three-quarter-length red-lined floral jacket, long flowered pants, and a flowered hat. Rick wore this look on both sides of *Wonderful*'s jacket, signifying in part that his new album was going to be a mellow trip. Although Rick wore a twelve-step antidrug, antialcohol emblem around his neck along with his usual cross, LeRoi Johnson attributed his brother's new costume to "too many drugs."

Reaction to the album ranged from negative to lukewarm. *People* magazine denounced it for its "stale grooves and clamorous instrumentation." The *Dallas Morning News*, hearing traces of LL Cool J, Keith Sweat, and Prince on the album, quipped about Rick, "If you can't beat them, incorporate them," and pilloried Rick for going so far as to emulate Prince's strange spelling. Quoting Rick's thank-you to Teena Marie from the album's liner notes—"Ur a soulful bird that rests in my heart 4ever"—the paper asked, "How much more work does it take to spell out 'you are' and 'for?'"

When Rick heard he was being accused of imitating Prince, he responded with a spectacular triangle shot aimed at his critics, Motown, and Prince. "I was wearing ruffles and frills before Prince," he told an interviewer. "Rick was Rick long before Prince came along." He then explained the reason he was dressed like a butterfly on the album cover: "I was trapped in a cocoon at Motown, but at last I'm free."

He also said he was glad to be working at Warner Brothers, calling it "even more exciting" than Motown. Citing its star vocalists by name, including Al B. Sure!, Club Nouveau, Morris Day, and Prince, he added, "There's room for all of us to work together."

Some fans and reviewers were just glad to have Rick back, no matter whom he might be imitating. As one reviewer said, in Rick's world "the party is always just beginning and freaky fun is just around the corner." Rick proclaimed, in fact, that "Good old funk" was back.

"People got to have it in their lives," he told author Mike Sager. "There's too much thick shit out there . . . too many rappers out there talking about death and Mac-10's [machine gun pistols] and all that shit. What happened to the fun, man? What happened to the funk?"

Released on June 28, 1988, *Wonderful* only made it to number 148 on the pop album chart, but after appearing on *Billboard's* R&B album chart on July 23, 1988, it stayed on that chart for nineteen weeks, peaking at number 12.

This was nice, but unfortunately, according to Warner Bros., the album sold only 195,978 copies through December 31, 1988, making it the third-worst-selling album in Rick's career. It lost the company more than half a million dollars, just about the amount Warner Brothers had spent promoting the album. Rick attributed the failure of *Wonderful* to a relapse into his old habits. He said, "[I was] spending my time getting high and having women running in and out. . . . It was very decadent. Everybody was smoking crack." Competition from other artists, including Bobby Brown and New Kids on the Block, was another problem.

The real significance of *Wonderful* in Rick's career was the release of "Loosey's Rap." But although it became a hit, it didn't seem to make Rick any happier than he had been previously. Mike Tyson, the former heavyweight boxing champion, wrote in his 2013 book, *Undisputed Truth*, that he was sitting outside a hotel on Sunset Boulevard in Los Angeles in 1988, after *Wonderful* had dropped. With him was seventeen-year-old actor Alfonso Ribeiro, who played the character Carlton Banks on the NBC sitcom *The Fresh Prince of Bel-Air*. Rick drove up, looked at Ribeiro, said "Aren't you an actor?" and then hit him before Ribeiro could say anything. "Gimme that fucking beer," Rick then said. He then grabbed Ribeiro's beer and drank it.

Despite Rick's newfound freedom (and financial windfall) from Motown, his downward spiral was continuing.

53

Rick Kicks Out

The chains of habit are too weak to be felt until
they are too strong to be broken.

—Samuel Johnson

Kicking the habit is what Rick, by now once again doing drugs almost full-time, should again have tried to do. But he didn't. Instead, in 1989 he recorded an album titled *Kickin'* for Warner Bros. *Kickin'* is slang for *Great!* but the word also could refer to kicking the dope habit, kicking out angrily against repeated failure, or, for that matter, kicking the bucket. The company did its own kickin' by refusing to release the album in the United States, due in part to what it said were "concerns over production quality."

Like his *Great White Cane* album, *Kickin'* was distributed during Rick's lifetime mostly in the form of promotional copies. In the case of *Kickin'*, however, those promotional copies were released only in the United Kingdom.

Rick's estate released a remastered CD of *Kickin'* in 2014 that displayed on its cover a sullen, overweight Rick in a loose black outfit and large black beret, smoking a cigarette. The songs were all pretty good examples of Rick's punk-funk style, and the album sounds as good as his other albums in terms of production quality. It should have been released years earlier. One of the songs on the album, "Get Wit It," featured the line "Stuck-up little Jew girl" about a woman who wouldn't yield to Rick's charms. Except for this offensive line, this song was one of Rick's better ones from the record.

Rick tried once again in 1989 to buttress his recording career at Warner Brothers by performing on that company's album *Rock, Rhythm & Blues*, producer Richard Perry's attempt to remake great rock 'n' roll and R&B tunes of the past. (Perry had jump-started the stalled careers of Ringo Starr, the Pointer Sisters, and others during the 1970s.) Rick sang a medley on the album consisting of "This Magic Moment," first recorded in 1960 by Ben E. King and the Drifters, and the pop classic "Dance with Me."

Rick, wearing a 1950s Elvis nightclub outfit and hairstyle, did a great job of recalling that era's music. The *Record* newspaper of Bergen County, New Jersey, was absolutely correct in noting that Rick had "never sounded so smooth or so soulful." On the video, which seemed to have been blurred on purpose to signify a bygone musical era, Rick tossed his mic from hand to hand and was backed by a musical combo, a male singing group, and a female singing group resembling the Supremes. Girlish screams issued from the audience.

Most reviewers denounced the album and Rick's part in it. The Austin *American-Statesman* called Rick's treatment of the two songs "lush, lovely and utterly passionless" and said his performance pushed the entire album toward "sugar-coated banality."

Record buyers appeared to agree. The album sold so badly that, in the words of one reviewer, it put a nail in the coffin of Rick's career. But the best was yet to come.

54

Please Hammer, Help Him!

The chart's legit.
Either work hard or you might as well quit

—"U Can't Touch This," by MC Hammer, Rick James,
and Alonzo Miller (1990)

Although Rick had occasionally made favorable gestures in rap's direction, he was no fan of the form, and really didn't want rappers to sample his work. In fact, Rick had often said how much he disliked rap. "Some groups that rap really have substance, but a lot of them are just rapping a lot of nonsense," he told an interviewer in 1985. "That stuff is here today, gone tomorrow."

Rick refused to allow sampling of his songs for years, partly because he found the very practice of sampling depressing. "The government took music out of the schools, and kids have no way to learn an instrument or theory and harmony," he told the *A. V. Club*, "so they have to resort to sampling. If music were taught in schools, kids would learn how to create on their own." The success of the Motown Record Corporation in Detroit, many believe, was based in part on the extensive music education program offered in the 1950s and '60s in the Detroit public schools. Once that program ended, music in Detroit and elsewhere suffered.

A master stage performer himself, Rick also put down the rappers for what he saw as their poor performance skills. "The majority of them don't have an idea of what it is to entertain a crowd," he told the *Washington Post*. "Holding on to your [anatomy], walking back and forth with your baseball hat turned backwards, throwing your hands up. . . . That ain't [expletive] entertainment." Rick said what he most disliked about rappers was their constant use of the *n*-word and put-downs of women. As he told the *A.V. Club*, "I'm so down on that word that I had trouble relating to it. . . . I don't like the derogativeness [*sic*] of what a lot of [rap] says and the demeaning fact of how it puts the race." Much rap "seems to be all about how women are hoes and bitches. Number one, my mother's not a ho, and not no bitch, and she never was. And I'm sure a lot of [rappers] don't want to hear their mamas and sisters called hoes and bitches."

As sampling's popularity kept growing, however, Johnson finally proposed that Rick sample his own work, thereby "beating the rappers at their own game." Rick refused, so Johnson, noting the potential revenue involved, argued that in that case, "we should get the rappers to use our music." Rick said he didn't want to get involved but that Johnson could do it.

Johnson then called MC Hammer to suggest he sample Rick's work, Hammer accepted the idea wholeheartedly, and used the very recognizable bass line from "Super Freak" in his song "U Can't Touch This." This was not only a great compliment to Rick and Motown but also briefly revived Rick's career.

A sample of a few seconds of the instrumental portion of "Super Freak," repeated over and over, was the entire musical score of "U Can't Touch This," except for a couple of interventions by a background chorus and a brief bridge. (Hammer's contributions were the rap lyrics that dominated the song and the hip-hop dancing on the song's video version.)

Stone City Band member Levi Ruffin said that one day in 1990 a friend called him and asked him if he'd heard it. "I said no, so I put on the radio and I said, 'goddamn, that's us! [meaning the Stone City Band playing the bass line from 'Super Freak'],' and my friend said, 'No, that's

Hammer!'" Ruffin says. "Rick didn't know Hammer was going to take the whole damn hook, the whole fucking thing."

Rick was shocked when he heard "U Can't Touch This." "What the hell is going on here?" he asked Johnson, and protested in public. Johnson reminded Rick that he had agreed to let his music be marketed to rappers, but Rick decided to keep the feud going in public to increase sales of his own records, which it did. He even told people he had filed a lawsuit against Hammer that had been settled out of court.

"When the first check [for royalties for using the "Super Freak" bass line] came in, Rick was very happy," Johnson says. Rick also obtained cowriting credit on Hammer's version of the song for himself and Alonzo Miller, the cowriter of "Super Freak." Hammer's name was on the song, and his revenues were also high, so Hammer was happy too.

Ruffin claims Rick eventually made $800,000 every three months from "U Can't Touch This" and that during this period Rick made more money from rappers, mostly Hammer, than he did from the sales of his own records. Still, Rick never really admired rap or rappers. Although he called being sampled "a very high form of compliment," he always expressed annoyance at rarely being credited by the samplers. "Yes, it's their rap," he told *Billboard*. "But it's our fucking music. If [the samplers] think their rap is what's really getting it over, try playing it without our shit." Various reviewers, taking their cue from Rick, accused Hammer of "borrowing," "stealing," or "pirating" the "Super Freak" bass line.

Realizing that keeping the controversy going would sell more records, Hammer struck back at Rick by comparing Rick unfavorably to the Chi-Lites, whose 1971 song "Have You Seen Her" Hammer had also sampled. "I've seen [the Chi-Lites] in several situations and they made a point to contact me and say thank you for reviving their career," he said pointedly.

As rumors continued to leak out that there was no actual dispute between Rick and Hammer, the two staged a public "reconciliation" in Buffalo in October 1990. Wearing his bolero hat and his gaucho outfit, Rick shook hands with Hammer backstage at Buffalo Memorial Auditorium. The two men smiled warmly at each other and exchanged compliments. They then went out and jammed onstage in front of fifteen thousand fans, who greeted them with massive applause.

Rick complimented Hammer on his use of the song, saying it was good "because he didn't degrade black people in it and didn't get off anything that was demeaning."

Hammer told Rick, "Whenever I think about doing a new song, first thing I do is look at your stuff. . . . Good stuff lasts a long time. It's like fine wine. Gets better with the years." Hammer insisted he'd been a fan of Rick's "from the first record [he] heard."

"U Can't Touch This" rose to number 8 on the *Billboard* pop Top 40 chart and remained on the chart for thirteen weeks, becoming, in the words of one reviewer, "a crowd-thumping anthem heard in every sports arena in the country." The tune also rose to number 1 on the R&B chart and stayed in that position for one week. For their 1989 and 1990 NBA championship victories, the Detroit Pistons informally adopted it as their anthem.

"U Can't Touch This" was the most popular single on the MC Hammer album *Please Hammer, Don't Hurt 'Em*. That album rose to number 1 on the *Billboard* top pop albums chart and stayed on the chart for 108 weeks. It also rose to number 1 on the top R&B albums chart, where it stayed for twenty-nine weeks. Certified by the RIAA as having sold ten million copies, it became one of the biggest sellers in hip-hop history and the fifth-bestselling rap album of all time.

The resurrection of part of "Super Freak" via Hammer, which occurred while Rick was in a down cycle in 1990, benefited Rick by reminding everyone how good the original was. There were more obvious benefits for "U Can't Touch This" too. When DJs heard Hammer had sampled "Super Freak," they were motivated to yank Hammer's rendition out of the pile of newly released discs and air it immediately. Some DJs went so far as to blend "Super Freak" and "U Can't Touch This" into what one reviewer called a "strange duet."

Hammer, Rick, and Miller shared the Best Rhythm & Blues Song Grammy Award for "U Can't Touch This" in 1990, Rick's only Grammy. Hammer won the Best Rap Solo Performance Grammy as well.

Two Grammy Awards couldn't protect "U Can't Touch This" from some scathing criticism, however. The *New York Times* called it "less a song than a noisy sonic toy whose music is only marginally more sophisticated than the sound effects of Nintendo." Another reviewer said Hammer merely "motor-mouthed a lot of inane lyrics" on top of "Super Freak."

But there were continued benefits for Rick. Encouraged by Hammer's success with "Super Freak," Will Smith, who had started as a rapper named the Fresh Prince before becoming a TV and movie star, used some samples of Rick's other music on his 1991 tune "I'm All That." Numerous other rappers have sampled Rick in the ensuing decades as well.

55

Trouble

I abuse drugs, not women.

—Rick James, 1993

Rick's life was a struggle between his good impulses and his horrendous ones. His larcenous impulses dominated the 1960s and '70s. His creative impulses triumphed during the '80s. During the '90s, however, he surrendered to crack and the devil.

In 1989 Rick learned his mother was dying of cancer and reacted to the news by abandoning any semblance of control over his drug use. At this stage of what became a long, gruesome journey, he was still a famous rock star, still attracted endless female attention, and still had lots of money. He used the money and fame to ensure an endless supply of dope for himself and anyone who wanted to smoke it with him. As *Vibe* magazine reported, he "became a recluse, seldom emerging from a trash-strewn bedroom filled with smoke from around-the-clock freebasing." Although by this time he lived in a rented Hollywood Hills home previously owned by Mickey Rooney that featured an enormous rose garden, he told the *Vibe* interviewer he never saw the roses until police dragged him out of the house months after he'd moved in.

Death was his goal. He told one interviewer he surrounded himself with "the lowest, most depraved people" he could find, including people he knew were out to get him. "I didn't give a fuck," he said. Pretty soon, he found himself sitting all day and all night naked in a room with Tanya—and a revolving cast of other women—smoking crack.

He smoked it continuously, comparing the experience to "looking Satan in the face," or sometimes to "sucking on the devil's dick." The last time he saw his mother before she went into a coma was when she visited him at his house and told him he was either going to go to jail or die right there.

Worse was yet to come. Among those who joined Rick and Tanya in smoking dope in July 1991 was Frances Alley, age twenty-four. After she joined them at Rick's house, the couple offered to put her up for a few days. Soon afterward, both Rick and Tanya were arrested. What happened between their offer of lodging and their arrest was revealed in pieces at their arraignment, their preliminary hearing, their trial, and in interviews Rick gave later.

Alley was a blonde white woman with a southern accent who called herself Courtney. Author Mike Sager, in his book *Scary Monsters and Super Freaks*, wrote that Alley had recently dropped out of a drug rehab program near her home outside Atlanta, had arrived in Los Angeles from Georgia only a few weeks before the incident, and had worked for one of those weeks in an L.A. massage parlor.

According to Alley's lawyer, she had moved to L.A. to pursue a movie career. But the *Buffalo News* soon revealed she was wanted in Augusta, Georgia, for failing to appear on a charge that she had tried to buy crack at a Holiday Inn there. She also had been found in contempt of court in Richmond County, Georgia, for violating probation on two other charges: battery, for allegedly beating another woman, and falsely claiming in 1989 that she was a kidnap victim. Rick's lawyer said that before Alley met Rick she'd "been scrounging the streets for drugs."

Rick told Sager he liked Alley because he'd never met a woman who could smoke as much crack as he could. Alley said she'd had sex with Rick at his house on two occasions, and then joined Rick, Tanya, and several others in using cocaine almost nonstop for a week.

Things began to turn bad on July 16, 1991, Alley said. She had been asleep for more than twenty-four hours when Rick called her into his bedroom, she said, and accused her of stealing an eight ball of coke: 3.5 grams, worth about $200 then.

The idea that someone would steal something from him while a guest in his house was something Rick could not stomach. Rick wrote in *The Confessions of Rick James* that once, when he thought a male guest in his house had stolen some drugs from him, he put a long, sharp knife against the man's neck. "I put it so hard against his neck I could see blood," he wrote. "I told him if he ever laid his hands on my drugs, I'd cut his fucking heart out, and I meant it. Seeing his fear gave me a sense of power I had not experienced before." Now, according to Alley, Rick told her to strip, ordered her to sit on a chair, and had Tanya tie her to it with two neckties, one from Dior, the other from Barneys. Using the neckties, Tanya lashed Alley's arms behind her back and tied her legs to the legs of the chair. Then, Alley said, Rick slapped her across the face with the butt of a small gun. (Rick's only previously known attack on a woman occurred in 1986 after he'd accused that woman, Gina Perry, of stealing another small object from him, a diamond ring, in his own house.)

Dousing Alley with rubbing alcohol on her waist, stomach, and legs, Rick continued to smoke a coke pipe, and after each hit, Alley said, he placed the hot pipe on her legs or stomach, leaving small circular burns. She said Rick then ordered Tanya to use a Bic cigarette lighter to heat up a butcher knife, and ran the knife along Alley's legs, knees, abdomen, and stomach, causing about twenty severe burns.

Alley testified that although Rick "burned [her] right there in [her] abdomen right above the pubic line," he didn't burn her vagina. She added, however, that "he told me I better hurry up and tell him the truth or I was not going to use my vagina again."

While Rick was torturing her, Tanya stroked and held her hand. Later, Alley said, Rick forced her to have oral sex with Tanya while Rick also had sex with Tanya. "It was like a 'Super Freak' sandwich with

Tanya in the middle," Alley said, a reference to the line in "Super Freak" in which Rick sang, "Three's not a crowd to her."

Alley also said that after the three-way sex, Tanya urinated on her, greatly irritating her burns. A person involved in the case who asked not to be identified said this was meant to be a "golden shower," that is, a means of sexual gratification through urination for either Rick or Tanya or both. It also could have been merely a way to humiliate Alley.

On the witness stand, Alley raised the legs of her pants to show the judge her partly healed scars. Prosecutors displayed photos of her that were taken at the hospital that showed large burns over much of her lower body. Alley told the court that while she was being tortured, she was thinking, "What have I done to deserve to die this way?" She also said she was hoping her family would be able to find her body.

Alley said Rick's torture was intended to teach her a lesson: that she was not to steal from him again, especially in his own house. After torturing her for forty-five minutes, however, he finally untied her, saying no one could have endured that much torture and still lie about not stealing his cocaine.

Rick and Tanya scoffed and laughed as Alley testified, likely because, as Alley told the court, after the torture was over the three of them took more cocaine and "partied into the next day." She didn't seek medical treatment until she noticed the burns on her legs and abdomen were blistering and swelling. After getting help at the Cedars-Sinai Medical Center in L.A., where hospital workers—not Alley—notified the police, she then returned to Rick's house twice over the next four days. "I was afraid to go back and afraid not to go back," she said.

Tanya's attorney, Leonard Levine, pointed out that Alley had told the L.A. police she had returned to Rick's house because she needed somewhere to stay. Levine noted that this was not how someone who had allegedly escaped from a hellhole of drugs, sexual assault, and violence usually acted. He called Alley a drug addict who was seeking publicity and money via a civil suit against Rick.

He buttressed his argument with the fact that one day after the end of the preliminary hearing on the criminal case against Rick and Tanya,

Alley filed a $15 million lawsuit against Rick for emotional and physical damage. That suit, however, was eventually dismissed because Alley drifted away and failed to keep in touch with another of her attorneys, Joseph Shemaria. A second suit was filed in Alley's name in July 1992, but Alley said she did not know it had been filed. It was apparently never adjudicated.

One of Rick's attorneys, Robert Sheahen, says Alley's behavior was due to what he called a "celebrity Velcro" complex. "She had no life at all," he said. "She'd rather go back to being burned with Rick James's crack pipe than go back to nothing." Rick apologized to Alley when she came back, blamed his behavior on cocaine, and gave her a check for $320.

Rick's brother LeRoi Johnson says he didn't believe any of Alley's allegations against Rick and said they need to be understood in the context of a typical rich crackhead's environment. When you're as rich as Rick, Johnson says, "all you have to do is keep ordering, keep ordering, keep ordering" instead of having to sober up and go outside. With this environment in mind, Johnson says he believed Alley and another of Rick's later alleged victims had burned themselves. "They were so high they were burning each other as they passed the pipe around, trying to catch little fragments of ash coming out of the pipe and burning each other in the process," Johnson says.

On August 2, 1991, L.A. Police officers arrested Rick, then forty-three, and Tanya, twenty-one, at Rick's home. Rick and Tanya were charged with assault with a deadly weapon, torture, aggravated mayhem, false imprisonment, and forcible oral copulation. Rick was also charged with making terrorist threats and furnishing cocaine. They denied everything.

The charges shocked the general public and certainly alarmed Rick, who saw himself facing a potential life sentence. He called Eddie Murphy on Murphy's private telephone line to ask him for help, but Murphy wouldn't even take the call.

The charges were less shocking, however, to those who had listened closely to Rick's music. As one writer said, much of it broadcast "a streetwise sexual bravura," mixing drugs, sex, and violence. Very aware of this, Rick hemmed and hawed when asked how the accusations would affect his career. "I don't know. I've always been seen as a bad boy," he told *USA Today*. But as the *Los Angeles Times* noted later, the crimes Rick was accused of "outdid the debauchery of his songs."

In addition to revealing lurid details about sex and drug use among rich crackheads, the first stage of the trial became a debate about Rick's actual wealth. Rick was held on $1 million bail (and Tanya on $500,000), and when Sheahen protested, the judge said he thought $1 million was low for someone that rich. Sheahen then told the judge that Rick's house couldn't be used as a basis for bail, because Rick didn't own it and was renting it for $6,000 a month (a tremendous amount at the time, and not a small amount these days). He went on to say Rick actually had very little money because he was a big spender who lived off his advances.

At least one person thought Rick was rich enough to be worth stealing from, however. Jeffrey Matusak, thirty, who had been hired to help move Rick's furniture and possessions out of his rented house while Rick was in jail, was charged with stealing $25,000 worth of jewels and Rolex watches from the singer. He was jailed and, later that fall after pleading guilty to grand theft, sentenced to nine months imprisonment.

Rick, who was held in jail throughout the long bail dispute, hated being there, and couldn't help showing it. At one point, after Myron L. Jenkins, a deputy district attorney, had unsuccessfully sought to have Rick and Tanya held without bail, Rick glared at him as he walked out of the courtroom and told him, meaningfully and audibly, "Take care, Myron." After several hearings, however, Sheahen managed to convince the judge to lower Rick's bail from $1 million to $500,000, and Tanya's from $500,000 to $200,000, allowing the couple their freedom after weeks in the slammer.

That was the good news. The bad news was that the judge, while noting the inconsistencies in Alley's testimony, said that testimony from Rick's maid, Dinorah Zumbado, that she saw Tanya crying and observed a knife being heated convinced him a trial was necessary. An arraignment was scheduled for September 25 for Rick and Tanya.

After his release, Rick was contrite enough to admit to an interviewer, "I am an addict," and he called the three weeks he had served in jail "OK" because they "gave me three weeks of sobriety." Johnson said later that he had resisted the idea of raising bail for his brother until Rick had been in jail long enough to break his habit. Rick may have been drug-free for those weeks, but once out, he soon reverted to form. As he later said of addiction, "It always calls you, it always beckons you, it's always at your ear."

Four days before the scheduled arraignment, on September 21, 1991, Rick's mother, the major motivating force in his life, died of stomach cancer at age seventy-three. The arraignment was postponed until Rick's return from the funeral.

Rick's mother had been his best friend. "I loved her more than anything," he told reporters, and he kept a framed photograph of her next to his bed. He said he was particularly devastated by her death because he felt he should have spent more time with her and tried to understand "more about what she was going through raising all those kids and being a black woman alone." He told one interviewer her passing "was a stunning, terrible, terrible experience. . . . My mother's gone, man, that's the only thing that meant something to me. That's what kept me surviving, that's what kept me strong, that's what kept me in the business, to show her, prove to her . . ."

On her deathbed, Rick's mother had asked him to stop taking drugs. He was honest enough this time not to pledge reform. "It's hard beating addiction, but I'm going to do my best," he said.

While on release, on May 8, 1992, Rick joined Young M.C., Tone Loc, the Beach Boys, and Gerardo for a videotaped recording session of the song "City of Fallen Angels." Considering Rick had recently been charged with assault, the song was oddly appropriate. It was dedicated to Reginald Denny, a white truck driver who had been pulled from his truck and beaten during the recent Los Angeles riots.

Soon after that recording session, on May 24, 1992, Tanya gave birth to Rick's third child, a boy, Tazman James Johnson, also known as Taz. Rick's friend Peter Kelly said Tazman's name was inspired by Rick's interest in and occasional practice of rituals linked with devil worship. (The name Tazman is a reference to the Tasmanian devil, a small but aggressive animal that lives in the Australian state of Tasmania, and the aboriginal myths that have clustered around that animal.) Kelly remembers seeing a drawing of a star within a circle hanging on the wall over Rick's bed around the time Tazman was born, and indeed, a downward pointing pentacle, which could be described as a star in a circle, is a symbol of Satanism. Various rock stars have proclaimed themselves Satanists over the years, but Rick never did, and there's no indication that either Rick or Tanya were ever serious Satanists. But Rick, like many who feel themselves lost, flirted with various religions over the decades. "I had revolted against my Catholic upbringing since my youth and had turned to other religions and the occult in my search for some meaning in life," he wrote in *The Confessions of Rick James.*

Soon after Tazman's birth, Rick, Tanya, and Tazman moved in with Tanya's mother, Susanne Shapiro, in the L.A. suburb of Agoura Hills. The baby would stay with Tanya's mother for years because the state would take Rick and Tanya away from him.

56

Rick and Tanya Strike Again

And as for what's next for Rick James and his exciting and diversified
career, there's really no telling. He's always been a few steps ahead
of the trends (when he's not too busy setting trends himself),
and there's every indication that he will continue to be
an explosive and dominant force in pop music . . .

—Motown Press Release, 1985

Considering Rick and Tanya's denials, along with Alley's
background and her close-to-inexplicable return to the alleged torture house, the case against Rick and Tanya looked weak. But as both
sides were preparing for trial, Rick and Tanya were accused of torturing
another young woman while they were out on bail.

Their alleged second victim was Mary Elizabeth Sauger, thirty-four,
of West Hollywood. A brown-haired white woman who worked as a
secretary at a small film company, Sauger had experience in the music
business. She said she had known Rick for six years. Rick asked her to
meet with him and Tanya on November 2, 1992, at a hotel room at the
St. James's Club and Hotel, later the Sunset Tower Hotel, on Sunset
Boulevard in West Hollywood. (Although Rick and Tanya had separated after being arrested in an effort to stay off drugs, they kept rejoin-
ing each other at various sites.) Rick told Sauger he wanted to talk to her

about working for a record label he wanted to establish and call Mamma Records.

Sauger met with the couple on the eleventh floor of the hotel late one evening. The three of them drank wine and Sauger took one hit of cocaine, she said.

Rick and Tanya then began arguing, Sauger said, so she left and entered an elevator to go to the lobby. Somehow she ended up back on the eleventh floor, however, where Tanya persuaded her to stay. Tanya disappeared for a minute, then returned wearing only panties. After that, according to Sauger, the conversation rolled around to relationships that often develop when performers go on tour, how the wives and girlfriends of performers often are harassed by other musicians, and about Sauger possibly accompanying Rick on a future tour. Tanya suddenly became angry with Sauger and began slapping her repeatedly, Sauger said.

Rick's version was that "Mary and Tanya started to get in a fight about being on the road. Mary said Tanya was too jealous and would never be able to tolerate the groupies and the sex," he wrote in *The Confessions of Rick James*. "The next thing I knew the two of them were in a catfight and Mary was kicking Tanya in the stomach."

Then Rick got involved. "Tanya had gotten pregnant again," he said, "so when I saw Mary kick her like that I flipped out and pushed her away from Tanya. [He said Tanya later miscarried their child.] Mary swung at me and I punched her in the eye. We started punching each other and I slugged her good a few times."

He continued, "Afterwards, Mary looked like a punch drunk prize fighter, her eyes bruised blue and swollen nearly shut and her lip split in three places. . . . There was blood spattered on the walls and carpet."

Sauger sobbed through most of the two hours on the stand it took her to tell her version of the incident. "I couldn't breathe," she said. "I thought that was it." She also said Rick and Tanya seemed to be "getting their kicks out of beating someone."

Rick then walked her out of the room they were in, Sauger said, and down the stairs to another room on the eighth floor. She speculated they may have made this move because of complaints by other guests at the hotel about the noise Rick and Tanya were making by beating her. Later, Sauger said, Tanya gave her cab fare home. Assuming Sauger's testimony was correct, Rick, in true Super Freak style—in which there are no limits on outrageous behavior—had added immensely to his problems by repeating a crime with which he'd already been charged while out on bail awaiting trial on the first charge.

Although Sauger said her left eye was swollen closed and her right eye was nearly so after the alleged beating, Rick said she stayed with him and Tanya for two days after the fight, smoking their crack. When she finally went for treatment at a hospital, doctors notified police. Sauger consulted an attorney, and charges were filed against Rick and Tanya. Prosecutors convinced the judge to allow them to consolidate the allegations from both Alley and Sauger and try Rick and Tanya for both sets of offenses simultaneously.

Just before Rick's criminal trial began, Sauger filed a civil suit against Rick, Tanya, and the St. James's Club and Hotel for assault, battery, false imprisonment, and intentional and negligent infliction of emotional distress. She eventually sought a total of $30 million from Rick in both lawsuits.

LeRoi Johnson believes the lawsuits by Alley and Sauger were motivated by greed and by Rick's wealth. "Robbers rob banks because that's where the money is," he says. And, in fact, Sauger testified on the stand that she had wanted the criminal proceedings dropped because all she cared about was her civil litigation against Rick. Rick's old pal, Deputy District Attorney Myron Jenkins, refused Sauger's request because of the similar charges by Alley. He also insisted that Sauger testify.

When the police went to arrest Rick and Tanya on the new charges, they found them gone. Having panicked and fled, they were declared fugitives, but surrendered after a few days.

They were then charged with assault on Sauger with deadly weapons (Rick's fists), causing great bodily injury, false imprisonment, and sale or transportation of cocaine. Rick was also charged with kidnapping. Facing maximum sentences of more than fourteen years on these new charges, they were returned to jail.

Anthony Brooklier, who had replaced Sheahen as Rick's attorney, told an interviewer he had spoken with hotel security guards about Sauger's accusation and that "many of the facts [were] disputed."

Brooklier, who, the *Los Angeles Times* has noted, cultivated the appearance of a mob consigliere, was the son of Dominic Brooklier, a former Los Angeles Mafia boss. As a boy, one of Anthony Brooklier's playmates was Aladena "Jimmy the Weasel" Fratianno, a Mafia hit man who killed at least five people. In 1986 Anthony Brooklier defended Robert "Fat Bobby" Paduano, whom the California state attorney general described as a Mafia associate, and succeeded in winning Paduano's acquittal on stock-swindling charges. (Brooklier died of an apparent suicide in 2016.)

Before the trial began, however, Tanya decided to call it quits.

57

Tanya Pleads Guilty

> There's no problem so awful that you can't add
> some guilt to it and make it even worse.
>
> —*Calvin and Hobbes*

On August 11, 1993, with one-year-old Taz to care for, Tanya pled guilty to assaulting Sauger and accepted a four-year prison term rather than risk a much longer sentence, or even life, in the slammer.

In return, prosecutors dismissed ten other charges against her on the grounds that she also had been a victim of physical abuse—by Rick—in the assault on Alley. (Alley had alleged that Rick had burned Tanya as well.) Sympathetic observers attributed Tanya's guilty plea to her desire to be out of prison as soon as possible in order to take care of Taz. That certainly was her major motive. But that doesn't necessarily mean she'd pled guilty to acts she hadn't committed. Both Alley and Sauger had claimed Tanya had participated in their abuse.

On September 21, 1993, the judge in Rick and Tanya's assault case, Michael R. Hoff, sentenced Tanya to four years in prison, as expected, and agreed to her request that she not report to prison until she and Rick could be married in court on the day Rick was sentenced.

Love and possible marriage aside, Tanya's move left Rick alone facing fifteen felony counts.

Her decision to cop a plea looked smart on the first day of his trial, when deputy district attorney Andrew Flier, in his opening statement, called Rick a "sadistic animal" and showed the jury photos of Sauger's swollen, blackened eyes and Alley's burned legs and burned lower body. Shortly after charging that Rick "burned [Alley] for no reason whatsoever," Flier somewhat contradictorily noted that Rick had accused Alley of stealing his narcotics, and for Rick "that is a good enough reason to torture someone."

In response, one of Rick's attorneys, Mark Werksman, noted that the prosecution had no eyewitnesses, no fingerprints, no blood samples, and no other scientific evidence. With the physical evidence inconclusive, Werksman said, the case would boil down to "he said v. she said." Undermining whatever "she" was going to say, Werksman then denounced Alley and Sauger as "parasitic groupies" and said their testimony would be "incredible," presumably meaning it would be unbelievable.

Werksman also argued that Rick was vulnerable to false claims of brutality just because he was a good guy who frequently opened up his home for wild sex-and-drug orgies. He said the case against Rick was not really a case about torture, mayhem, threats, forced oral sex, or copulation, because those charges were based on lies, but was really "about sex, drugs, and rock 'n' roll." Considering the hundreds of thousands of people for whom these three were one and the same, this was the most trenchant comment issued during the course of the trial.

While he was being denounced in the courtroom, Rick played it cool—perhaps too cool. He often wore his bright red double-breasted coat with the three embroidered golden rings on each cuff, his black shirt and short red tie with black dots, his hoop earrings, and his snakeskin-and-leather red-and-black cowboy boots. He yawned at times and rested his head in his hands. At one point, during Sauger's later testimony, he dozed off and began snoring audibly. Werksman tried to explain Rick's behavior by saying his client had bronchitis, and that, along with the pressure of the trial, made it difficult for him to sleep at night. It occurred to many in the courtroom, however, that at what could be seen as the pivotal event of Rick's life, he was still using crack.

58

The Prosecutors Summon Their Star Witness

Accomplished artists cannot be equated to people
simply because they happen to be people.

—Pola Negri

That the case pivoted on Rick's drug use became even clearer when a woman named Michelle Allen, called to the stand by the prosecution, testified that in December 1991 she had delivered 2.2 pounds of cocaine to him. She said she was to be paid $16,000, and while she, Rick, and Tanya waited for his bodyguards to fetch the purchase money, they smoked cocaine and had sex throughout the night and early morning.

But when she finally asked where the money was, she said, Rick became belligerent and abusive, and grabbed her and threw her to the ground, causing her to land on her right wrist and break her arm. "He said I should just be glad that I'm partying with Rick James," Allen said.

Allen had been brought to court from prison, where she was serving a seven-year term on theft charges. Werksman described her to the jury as a "15-time-loser" who was trying to reduce her latest sentence by testifying against Rick. (Allen had used at least fifteen aliases, six dates of birth, and eight Social Security numbers at various times.) She had first been arrested in 1979 and had been convicted of offenses involving theft, burglary, and fraud, in addition to drugs. The *Los Angeles Times* later called Allen "a self-described 'Hollywood party girl' with a rap sheet as long as her legs."

Allen's story was semi-believable, except that she insisted for some reason that both Rick and Tanya had confessed to her about the two assaults for which Rick was now being tried. She said Rick had told her on at least three occasions while she, Rick, and Tanya smoked coke that he had sexually assaulted and tortured a woman, presumably Alley, in his Hollywood Hills home, and she quoted Rick as saying, "The bitch deserved it. She had it coming."

Even more unbelievably, Allen said that after Rick and Tanya were arrested and jailed for allegedly assaulting Sauger, and Allen was arrested separately on theft charges, she and Tanya were placed in the same cell, where Tanya confessed to Allen that she had assaulted both Alley and Sauger.

A source close to the case characterized Allen as a jailhouse informer. Rick's attorney in the Alley case, Sheahen, said in an interview for this book in 2014 that such informers had come into disrepute in Los Angeles a few years after this trial, because they often would "get hold of" a police report about a case and then say that a defendant had confessed to them what the police report charged them with doing. New cases that relied on such informers were set aside around 1999, Sheahen says.

Allen denied that prosecutors had promised her a sentence reduction for testifying against Rick, claiming her only goal was to stop Rick from hurting other women. "How many women have to be hurt before something gets done here?" she told the trial jury of ten men and two women.

Rick, during his three hours on the stand, denied all the accusations against him. Quietly sobbing, he said his mother's final illness and her eventual death had contributed to his downward spiral of sex and drugs. He said he smoked cocaine more heavily in 1991 because he had learned of his mother's cancer. "I didn't care about living. I wanted to die," he told an interviewer later. But, he added, he had never fallen so low as to brutalize women.

At one point during his testimony, Rick blamed the standard misinterpretation of the lyrics of his biggest hit for biasing the public against him. Because the title of that hit was "Super Freak," the public, including members of the jury, thought he actually was the super freak being described, thus biasing them against him. He pointed out that the song was not about him but about a certain sort of women, who were, in fact, exactly the women who were attracted to him as a result of the song: "very kinky girl[s] . . . the type you don't bring home to mother."

While testifying on the stand, Rick was dressed relatively conservatively in a tan double-breasted suit with a white shirt buttoned at the collar. He wore his hair slicked back into a ponytail, a conservative style for him, and sported only one gold hoop earring. None of this impressed Flier, the prosecutor, who said outside the courtroom that Rick was a perjurer who fabricated stories. "He has a justification for every fact that goes against him," Flier said.

Rick denied he'd assaulted Alley, saying that after he'd given her $300 to $400 to buy groceries, she'd returned a day and a half later with dirty bandages wrapped around burns on her legs. She said she'd been injured riding a motorcycle and would treat the wounds herself with medication from a drugstore, Rick said, but he told her that her burns needed more than ointment and suggested she go to the hospital.

Asked about the allegation that he had forced Alley to have sex with Tanya, Rick replied, looking jurors right in the eyes, "I never had to force a woman to do anything." After the trial, he told reporters, "I abuse drugs, not women."

While testifying, Rick smiled affectionately at Tazman, then fifteen months old, who was sitting in the courtroom on Tanya's mother's lap. Tanya was not present.

Rick did say under cross-examination that Tanya had struck Sauger with a champagne bucket, a comment on the Hollywood lifestyle if ever there was one. Saying Tanya struck Sauger while he himself did not was ungentlemanly, but since Tanya already had pled guilty, many would consider it allowable.

Years later, when asked about Sauger, Rick told the *Buffalo News*, "I had been in a fight with a girl, yes." He elaborated on this account somewhat later in an interview with the *New York Daily News*. "I had been up for two weeks smoking cocaine, and this woman kicked my old lady [Tanya] in the stomach when she was pregnant," he said of the scene at the center of the 1992 case. Tanya was carrying what would have been her second child with Rick, and later miscarried. "So I punched her [Sauger] in the fucking eye," Rick told the *Daily News*, "and yeah, I jumped on her." Tanya refused several requests for an interview for this book.

59

Guilty . . . Sort Of

Rick's virility is buttressed by his equally gentle,
humorous and sensitive demeanor.

—Motown Records Press Release, 1980s.

Attempting to curry favor with the jury during his trial, Rick
had testified that if acquitted, he would make a new album and
launch a concert tour that would have an antidrug theme. On September 17, 1993, the day the verdict was announced, he came to court carrying Tazman in his arms. He wasn't acquitted, but the result was much better than many of his supporters expected.

Although the horrendous and detailed allegations that Rick had tortured Alley were the emotional basis of the entire trial and underlay most of the four days of jury deliberation, he was acquitted of all torture charges, but just barely. Eleven jurors voted him guilty of torture, but the one no vote was enough to prevent his conviction on those charges.

That was a major break for Rick, because the torture charges had carried a potential life sentence. Due to the jury deadlock, he also was declared innocent of aggravated mayhem, assault with a deadly weapon, making terrorist threats, and forced oral copulation. After the verdict, a juror told reporters it was difficult to determine the credibility of witnesses because every witness had been high when the alleged crimes occurred.

Rick had been found not guilty of the most publicized and the most shocking allegation against him, that he had tied a naked young woman, Alley, to a chair and used a hot cocaine pipe and a heated knife to burn and torture her.

He was convicted, however, of supplying Alley with cocaine. In the rock 'n' roll culture, in Hollywood in general at that time, and among many other American subcultures, the idea that Rick or anyone else could be put through a lengthy and expensive trial, and actually convicted, for *giving* cocaine to another confessed cocaine user older than eighteen was laughable. If Rick had been found guilty only of this offense, the fact that the charges had been leveled against him in the first place would have been the shocking part of this story, and in all probability, his resulting jail term would have been a short one.

Unfortunately for Rick, however, he was also convicted of assaulting and imprisoning Sauger. His repetition of a crime similar to his alleged assault and imprisonment of Alley had done him in: attacking Sauger had put him in the way of a fairly long jail sentence. As a result of his conviction on three charges, Rick faced up to eight years and eight months in prison.

There was more bad news: In December 1994, adding monetary pain to Rick's upcoming imprisonment, Sauger was awarded more than $2 million in damages, including more than $200,000 in lost future earnings. She told the jury in her civil suit that she had been unable to work since the incident occurred in 1992, due in part to what she said were recurring headaches and long-term constant throbbing in one eye.

60

Shocking New Allegations

"When the Whip Comes Down"

—Title of a 1978 song by Mick Jagger and Keith Richards

Sauger's civil court win paled in comparison to what seemed to be about to happen next. In a sentencing memo prosecutors gave to the judge, they said they had obtained a videotape that showed Rick having apparently consensual group sex with a young woman, as well as a lot of narcotics being consumed. According to prosecutors, the tape showed Rick "striking the female repeatedly and graphically with a belt. Blood is observable." And at one point on the tape, according to prosecutors, Rick was allegedly shown saying, "Maybe I should hire myself out as a professional woman beater." Fortunately for Rick, the alleged videotape was three years old, putting the alleged crimes it showed beyond the statute of limitations.

But Rick hadn't been sentenced yet on the Alley and Sauger charges for which he had been convicted, and the prosecutors said they were ready to show the videotape in court to illustrate what they said was Rick's "propensity for violence and sadomasochism." The prosecutors also said in the memo that they had been sent an audiotape in which a former girlfriend of Rick's claimed she had been abused during a different sex-and-drugs session.

The prosecutors were also more than ready to file for a retrial on the numerous charges for which Rick had not been convicted. They were expected to do so because the jury had voted 11–1 for conviction on those charges, and L.A. prosecutors usually retried when a jury voted any higher than 9–3 for conviction.

Rick's doom seemed sealed. A judge who saw a movie of Rick beating a woman and boasting about it would be very likely to hand down the maximum sentence, or risk a major public outcry. Even worse would be a new trial with refiled charges. Decades in prison loomed in Rick's future.

61

The Prosecutors Accuse an Investigator

A preacher was talkin', a sermon he gave, Said every man's
conscience is vile and depraved.

—"Man in the Long Black Coat," by Bob Dylan (1989)

Before this new evidence could be introduced in court and
before Rick was scheduled for sentencing, it was revealed that an
investigator in the district attorney's office had supplied heroin to, and
had sex with, Michelle Allen, the prosecution's star witness, before she
testified against Rick. Sometime later, Craig Gunnette, the accused
investigator, confessed that he actually did give Allen heroin in a private
attorney visiting room, stuffing it between court papers. Gunnette also
bought Allen cigarettes, toiletries, Xanax, and a TV.

Stunned by these revelations, on January 7, 1994, the prosecutors
agreed to a moderate sentence of only five years and four months for
Rick, and he was allowed to begin that sentence, after a short stay in
county jail, with a drug treatment program at the California Rehabilitation Center in Norco. During the 1930s, the center had been the
Lake Norconian Club, a gathering spot for bigwigs and celebrities. It
had a red-tiled roof and pink walls and was surrounded by perfectly
manicured rosebushes. As Rick later reported, the inmates there lived
in dorms rather than cells and spent their days playing basketball and

baseball and attending anti-addiction classes. They called the facility Camp Snoopy.

This relatively favorable move was nothing compared to what happened next: the judge ruled that if Rick successfully completed the eight-and-a-half-month rehab program, he would not be required to serve the jail term. Considering the hideous nature of some of the crimes with which Rick had been charged, some observers saw less than nine months in rehab as an unbelievably light sentence. The judge himself called it a gift. However, the experts who evaluated Rick after his arrest had agreed that he probably wouldn't have hurt either Alley or Sauger if he hadn't been high on cocaine.

Defense attorney Werksman called the sentence "decent, human and phenomenal." Rick showed his pleasure by flashing a V sign to family members and supporters, and also to the photographers gathered in the jury box for his sentencing. Rick's brother LeRoi Johnson exulted to reporters, "Rick will get another shot at life."

The sentence was certainly "decent and humane," but was it really "phenomenal"? Rick had been protesting all along, and would continue to say, that he had been singled out for arrest and prosecution only because he was a well-known black man. He made this point most succinctly by referring to what happened to Michael Jackson in 2003, after allegations of sexual misconduct with young boys had been made against the gloved one. "As soon as you get famous and black, [prosecutors] go after you," Rick said. Jackson was indicted on charges of child molestation in 2003 and acquitted on all counts in 2005.

LeRoi Johnson points out that in 1997 a famous white man was convicted and sentenced for an offense much like Rick's. Sportscaster Marv Albert was accused of throwing a woman on a bed, biting her, and forcing her to perform oral sex after an argument in his hotel room. Albert's DNA was found to match material in the woman's bite marks, as well as semen in her underwear. A second woman then came forward and said Albert had bitten her on two different occasions in 1993 and 1994.

After Albert pled guilty to misdemeanor assault and battery, he was given a twelve-month suspended sentence. In real-life terms, that means Albert got nothing and Rick got eight and a half months of confinement. Many would argue, however, that Rick's crimes exceeded Albert's in duration and ferocity.

62

Rick and Tanya Attempt to Marry

It is a truth universally acknowledged, that a single man in possession
of a good fortune, must be in want of a wife.

—Jane Austen, *Pride and Prejudice*

Rick asked to be allowed to marry Tanya before he was sentenced
on the grounds that he and Tanya wished to give Tazman "the
legitimacy of married parents."

But the judge in the case, Michael R. Hoff, reacting to Rick's con-
victions on three counts, ruled him a danger to the community and
ordered that he be jailed immediately after the verdict was announced.
The judge did leave open the possibility that the couple could be married
in court when Rick returned there for his sentencing. He declined to
perform the ceremony himself, though, on the grounds that it would be
"a farce to wish them well" immediately after sentencing Rick to prison.

Rick and Tanya then made plans for a minister to marry them after
Rick was sentenced, and procured a marriage license and rings. Tanya's
mother brought wedding clothes to court for Rick, consisting of a black
shirt, black tie, black pants, a white jacket, and a black pair of western-
style boots. On the hoped-for wedding day, however, Rick and Tanya
weren't even allowed to see each other, much less marry. The supervisor of
court bailiffs, citing safety concerns, said his deputies would not allow the

couple to tie the knot there unless the deputies were specifically ordered to do so by the judge, and the judge said he would not issue that order.

Judge Hoff did give Tanya a wedding present of sorts that day: because she and Rick had committed their crimes jointly, he cut Tanya's sentence in half in order to conform it more closely to Rick's.

As Rick left the courtroom, Hoff's bailiff tossed aside a bouquet of colored plastic flowers she had on her desk. "I don't think we'll be needing these," she said.

The couple's matrimonial future didn't look good: the two were first going to be held in county jail, where weddings were not allowed, and then sent to different facilities, which would make arranging a wedding very difficult. And with both of them incarcerated, conjugal visits would not be allowed even if they were married, officials said.

In addition to all that, before Rick entered the quiet rehab center located on the premises of the former country club, he was required to inhabit a cell in the Los Angeles County jail for five months. Louise Continelli, a reporter for the *Buffalo News*, wrote that the cell was not much larger than a loudspeaker from one of Rick's concerts, and that he was locked inside it twenty-three and a half hours per day. Flung "from the limelight into the slime-light," he saw no sunlight, apart from visits to court. Continelli also reported that Rick's trademark Jheri curl had been cut off and he had gained "a solid 20 lbs." from starchy jail food and no exercise. Unfortunately for his future appearance, he never lost the weight he gained in jail.

Rick had prominent people he could complain to, however, because he had been placed in an isolated wing of the jail reserved for high-profile cases, including child molesters and parent killers. This placement was allegedly for the prisoners' protection from other inmates. Among Rick's new acquaintances were Lyle and Erik Menendez, who had been accused of the shotgun murder of their parents. Lyle Menendez and Rick became so friendly they wrote a couple songs together.

Rick complained to one interviewer that some of his other "rich so-called good friends," including Eddie Murphy and Arsenio Hall, could have offered to help him after he was accused, but "all they did was run."

According to Rick, "They didn't want to have their little careers tainted with the fact that they knew me, when everyone in the world knows they knew me anyway."

The prison guards joined Murphy and Hall in showing little compassion for Rick or the other inmates. The Northridge earthquake, a major quake that struck Los Angeles on January 17, 1994, shook his cell early that morning, shaking Rick out of his bed and causing him to drop to his knees to pray. He noticed that rather than save the inmates, the guards just left. "The place could have caved in for all they cared," he said. "They don't care whether we live or die."

Rick told one interviewer that being in jail would be good for him, because it would give him a chance to rest, eat three meals a day, get healthy and stop doing drugs. Rick could see, he said, "that I can love again, that I can love me again. I'm not a has-been and I'm not a nobody. I'm not a cold-blooded maniacal killer and I'm not a black Marquis de Sade. What I am is James Johnson, also known as Rick James, who happened to let his life run amok because of a fucking pipe and a rock of cocaine."

Ironically the time in jail, and then in the rehab center, seemed to be helping Rick's career. Although he was now forty-five, somewhat old for a rock star, the massive publicity surrounding his trial had rekindled interest in his music. His tunes were getting more radio airplay and had found an unexpected home on *Beavis and Butt-Head*.

Other rock musicians also were paying him more attention. H-Bomb Ferguson credited Rick for the purple wig he wore on the cover of his new album, *Wiggin' Out*. A new album by the Lemonheads, called *Come on Feel the Lemonheads*, featured two versions of the same song: "Style," sung just by the Lemonheads, and "Rick James Style," which was slower and darker and featured Rick on vocals. Rick, prior to his incarceration, had joined Lemonheads front man and fellow former addict Evan Dando in singing this song, which included the lyrics, "Don't wanna get stoned / Don't wanna get stoned / But I don't wanna not get stoned." Critics, noting the Doors-like psychedelic atmosphere created by "Rick James Style," called that song the most powerful cut on the album.

63

Rick Busts Out!

Rick stands tall despite the nadir his life has sunk to.

—*Buffalo News*, 1994

In the spring of 1994, Motown Records responded to the new interest in Rick that his trial had inspired by releasing a new double CD of his music that included some of his greatest hits, as well as four new tunes he had recorded while out on bail.

Unable to resist reusing a title it had used before but was now much more relevant, Motown titled the new collection *Bustin' Out: The Best of Rick James*, a twenty-seven-track, two-disc set not to be confused with his album *Bustin' Out of L Seven*, which had been released on vinyl in 1979.

On the new album, in "Serious Love (Spend the Night)," a new love song with a strong beat, Rick rhapsodizes about the women of Los Angeles, New York, Atlanta, Chicago, and Detroit, in that order. In "Divine Love (So Fine)" he pays tribute to what he calls "the rebirth of Slick Rick" and to some of his former albums, songs, and associates, including *Throwin' Down*, "Fire and Desire," the Mary Jane Girls, Teena Marie, the Stone City Band, "Super Freak," "Mr. Policeman," and *Street Songs*. And in "Down By Law," which amounts to a musical version of his recent arrests, Rick assumes a Rastafarian identity and sings about "living alone in a room," "making money and making jokes," and how a policeman then appears and takes him to jail because he has been a "bad boy." Ganja is also prominently mentioned.

The *Buffalo News*, expressing both appreciation for Rick's work and sympathy for its hometown boy behind bars, asserted that in this collection "Rick stands tall despite the nadir his life has sunk to. The sense of freedom, of life lived for the pleasure of living, comes through." The paper said Rick had played the role society assigns to all artists by "portraying in his music all the vibes he picked up . . . from the streets of Buffalo's East Side to the glitzy glamour of a rock star's milieu." *Entertainment Weekly*, praising Rick's "vibrant body of work," awarded the album an A-minus, but it failed to chart.

Although Rick actually had an inmate number at the rehab center, N63609, things were so loosey-goosey at that medium-security facility that in June 1994 he was allowed to participate by telephone in the release party for the new album. That event took place at Tatou, a trendy Los Angeles nightspot. As Queen Latifah, the Mary Jane Girls, and, of all people, Milton Berle, gorged themselves on pricey hors d'oeuvres washed down with champagne, Rick told everyone over the speakerphone that he felt sad (presumably because he was in rehab and not there). The *Buffalo News* reported that his voice sounded stronger on the phone, as well as in his new songs, than it had in years.

In rehab, Rick became an antidrug crusader via his interviews with reporters, as he always did during drug-free intervals in his life. "If I can change one person's heart to put the pipe down and put the cocaine down and put the drugs down, then I'm more successful than when I was telling 'em to smoke mary jane," he told the *Buffalo News*. He lamented the pro-drug music he had previously recorded that others were now producing. "Parents are letting their kids listen to this stuff, saying it's only music, but this music is going to govern their lifestyle," he said. "God knows, I know I directed a lot of people" toward drug use.

Rick pledged to stay away from bars, other "slippery places," and from anyone who uses drugs, and to go to Narcotics Anonymous meetings. Sounding like his former nemesis, President Ronald Reagan, Rick even asserted he wouldn't drink wine because that would lead to marijuana, which would then lead to harder drugs.

Everyone who knew Rick took all this with several barrels of salt. Later, he admitted that after each of four stays in non-mandated rehab during his life, he had stayed drug-free for only three or four months before returning to Coke City.

64

Rick Takes the Train to Folsom Prison

I hear the train a comin', it's rolling round the bend.
And I ain't seen the sun shine since I don't know when.
I'm stuck in Folsom prison, and time keeps draggin' on.

—"Folsom Prison Blues," by Johnny Cash (1957)

Rick was looking forward to the short stay at the rehab center that his sentence had called for. After five months of both rehabilitation and evaluation in the Norco program, however, he was told he would be removed from rehab and sent to prison instead. Norco warden Jean E. Anderson ruled that those who demonstrate "violence-prone tendencies or who have been convicted of violent crime" were not suitable for the entire eight-and-a-half-month-course of treatment. Since under his sentence Rick was required to complete the course of treatment to avoid his jail term, and was now not going to be allowed to do so, he would now be required to serve the jail term to which he had been sentenced.

Rick's attorney Werksman protested, arguing that Rick "ran afoul of the law solely because of his drug abuse" and pointed out that the victims of Rick's crimes were people who had chosen to do drugs with him. Saying Rick had "done very well in the [rehab] program," he called prison officials "prejudiced" against Rick because of his image and his fame. "They rejected the Super Freak," Werksman said. "They never bothered to learn about the real Rick James." The lawyer's argument was buttressed by experts who had evaluated Rick while he was in county jail and said he would have benefited from the state's drug program.

But nothing could be done. Rick's dream of a short stay in rehab followed by freedom was over, and on July 18, 1994, he was sent to Folsom State Prison in Northern California to serve out the remainder of his five-year, four-month prison term. Judge Hoff told Rick to console himself with the thought that he was "lucky" he wasn't going to prison for a dozen years—or life. The judge rubbed it in by telling Rick he "could thank the D.A.'s investigator [who had provided Michele Allen with cocaine] for his continued luck."

Rick became Folsom inmate #J29237. As one wit commented, Folsom was well named because it housed some of the country's most "foulsome" killers, including Edmund Kemper, who had cut off his mother's head and gunned down his grandparents.

Rick's cell, which he shared with a large prisoner named Darryl Brown, measured less than five feet by ten feet, smaller than the shoe closet at his former home in Buffalo, where he had kept one hundred pairs of shoes. There wasn't enough room for its two inmates to stand up at the same time, and its toilet facilities consisted of a commode with no seat. Rick certainly noticed how uncomfortable the cell was. He also told friends later that he missed little things that nonprisoners take for granted, "like eating when you want to, or just getting up from where you're sitting and simply going somewhere."

Rick was shocked at being sentenced to Folsom and initially depressed to find himself there. "I was in hell," he told one interviewer for MTV. He discovered that some Folsom inmates were fans, however, a fact that may have cheered him up a bit. Their presence "was nice, because there were other inmates there who wanted to get a rep for doing Rick James," he told a reporter for the *Philadelphia Inquirer*. Later he said he'd been afraid "that [he] would have to fight the inmates for [his] manhood, but they treated [him] with respect and love." He said he charmed the female correction officers by singing "Ebony Eyes" to them, fended off the male

COs by reminding them he was rich and had a cousin in Congress, and was protected by the many inmates who loved his music.

On his first post-prison album, 1997's *Urban Rapsody*, Rick thanked several of the inmates who protected him. He also later told interviewers that many inmates thanked him for producing music that helped them get through their time in jail.

Although drug use was rampant in Folsom, prison seemed to solve that problem for him, at least while he was there. "I could easily have done drugs in prison," he said after he was released. "Everybody was doing them." The guards "turned their backs when the inmates shot up," because "as long as they were doing drugs, they were medicated. . . . But Folsom scared me straight. I didn't want to spend the rest of my life there."

Rick talked to so many journalists during his sojourn at Folsom that he soon joined murderer Charles Manson as one of California's two most interviewed inmates. The state's Youth and Adult Correctional Agency became so annoyed by comments from Manson, Rick, and other people behind bars that it urged banning prisoner interviews entirely. In addition to reporters, Rick had other visitors: although Tanya and Rick couldn't see each other while both were jailed, Tanya's mother took their son, Taz, only one-and-a-half years old when they were both incarcerated, to see each of his parents every month.

In spite of such perks, Rick still thought prison was terrible. He dedicated the song "Somebody's Watching You" on *Urban Rapsody* to several prison guards whom he accused of overt racism. In an interview with the *L.A. Times*, Rick claimed "redneck correction officers were after me," and that they had put him in the hole (solitary confinement) for two weeks. He said those same guards also prevented him from using Folsom's music facility, which included recording gear. They were "racists who didn't want me to do anything that would bring joy," he said. "They wanted to take away my joy. And they did."

In an interview for this book, however, former Stone City Band member Daniel LeMelle calls jail "good for Rick," because "it scared the daylights out of him." Rick apparently agreed: "It was in prison that I finally made a conscious effort to stay sober and grow up," he said. And although he couldn't use the music facility, Rick was allowed to play an old acoustic guitar in his cell and compose songs by humming them into a small tape recorder a female prison employee known as Mom slipped him. He also managed to land the relatively cushy job of prison librarian.

But it couldn't have been that cushy: LeMelle says Rick called him every ten days during his two-year stay in Folsom.

65

Rick Tries Again

When the prison doors are opened, the real dragon will fly out.

—Ho Chi Minh

Tanya served only fifteen months before her release on December 4, 1994, but Rick was imprisoned for two years and twenty-three days of his five-year, four-month prison sentence.

He was released on parole on August 21, 1996, the same day he was voted into the Buffalo Music Hall of Fame. One of those voted in with him was songwriter Jack Yellen, who, appropriately enough, had written the song "Happy Days are Here Again."

On his way out of jail, Rick told reporters he planned "to be a father and continue to funk" and said he wanted to try to get a bit closer to his family. One way Rick hoped to do so was by marrying Tanya. Plans called for the wedding to take place at a friend's house in Santa Rosa in Northern California during the third week of August. A crowd of family members and friends, including members of the Mary Jane Girls, began to gather for the occasion.

At the last minute, however, the ceremony had to be postponed because Tanya had been arrested nearby on August 19 on suspicion of shoplifting a thirty-nine-dollar pair of boots. She also was accused of violating her probation by leaving Los Angeles without permission, and was returned to Los Angeles County jail for six months.

Meanwhile, Rick tried to reenter the business of making music. He made appointments with the presidents of three or four record companies, who "were enthusiastic when we met, but then nothing happened," he told the *New York Daily News* at the time. He claimed the executives didn't want to get involved with him because they were worried about his mental stability, or that he would go back to abusing drugs. He also complained that the charges that had put him in jail several years before had made him look like "the black Marquis de Sade."

In truth, however, because this was the recording business and not the bible sales industry, artists frequently got into trouble for violating drug and other laws but kept on working. In 1997, the year after Rick was released from jail, Wilson Pickett was arrested for cocaine possession and Snoop Dogg pled guilty to a weapons charge. The record company executives' real worry about Rick was that he might have lost his voice, or his talent, during his relatively long stint in prison. Therefore, they'd asked him to do demo records before they'd sign him, injuring Rick in his most vulnerable spot: his pride. Referring to the millions of dollars some of these same execs had made from his career, Rick said, "All these people who never asked me [to do demos] before when I was keeping the lights on for them, now they want to know what I sound like?" Refusing to comply with their requests, he suggested the execs listen to one of the millions of records he said he'd sold if they wanted to hear a "demo."

Meanwhile, Rick took some time to adjust to life on the outside. One reporter noticed him in the Foundation Room, the VIP area of the Hollywood House of Blues, sipping mineral water and a little champagne while quietly watching others, behavior that would have seemed unthinkably repressed a few years earlier. Prison also seemed to have cured Rick of major drug use, at least for a while. He joined Narcotics Anonymous and told numerous reporters that his imprisonment had been "a blessing in disguise" because it shocked him into quitting drugs. "Otherwise I probably would have been dead by now," he said. He said he was tired of his pre-prison behavior, which, he said, consisted of "hid-ing in the morning, being paranoid, running around out of my mind, and calling drug dealers all night." His ability to remain drug-free was undoubtedly aided by the requirement that he take a drug test every week for his first two years out of prison.

After serving his time, Rick, by then forty-eight, had started feeling his age. Proposing as his first post-prison project an album of tunes he said he had written while inside, he said he wanted to perform less-energetic music. "I'm getting too old, man . . . to be dancing around singing 'Super Freak,'" he told the *Philadelphia Inquirer*. "I want to do something where I can sit back and chill."

After several months of freedom, Rick joined a weekly jam session at the China Club in West Los Angeles. His trademark braids were instantly recognizable and he stuck his tongue out as provocatively as before. He dissed the rappers who had made themselves rich with his best song lines by dropping a line of MC Hammer's "U Can't Touch This" into the middle of "Super Freak." One observer noted that Rick was still working it, punching the air with virtually every beat. His twenty-pound prison weight gain was evident, however. He told interviewers he planned to slow down, especially compared to the 1980s, when he seemed to be producing endless albums for his protégés and himself.

66

Organized Crime Makes Rick a Post-Prison Star

Well I'm sitting here thinkin' just how sharp I am
Well I'm sitting here thinkin' just how sharp I am
I'm an under assistant West Coast promo man

—"The Under Assistant West Coast Promotion Man," by the Rolling
Stones, written by "Nanker Phelge" (1965)

Rick claimed he had written three to four hundred new songs during his three years in prison and initially wanted to record an album consisting of all the acoustic, angry, and introspective ballads he had written while sitting in his cell. But he dropped the idea, telling *USA Today* he did so partly because he wasn't sure how his fans would react to such a sudden shift in tone, instrumentation, and story line. After all, many of his earlier tunes had been happy ones about sex and romance.

He also said he didn't want to record tunes that would make people say "poor Rick." That was probably wise. In the end, only five songs Rick wrote in prison made it onto 1997's *Urban Rapsody*. What might not have been as smart, in terms of Rick's image, was teaming up with another controversial music biz figure, Joseph Isgro, to produce that album. It's easy to see what Rick and Isgro saw in each other, however, aside from talents of different sorts: Isgro's reputation was in some ways worse than Rick's. Isgro also had been a long-term prison inmate (and may soon repeat that experience).

A former employee of Decca and Paramount Records, Isgro had been hired by Motown as regional director of promotion in 1976 and left a few years later as executive vice president of promotion. Teena Marie was among the Motown artists whose records he handled.

In 1979 Isgro became an independent promotion man. Recording firms hired such individuals to convince DJs to play music the companies released. In the early 1980s, the US government launched a major investigation into payola (a music-industry term for bribing radio stations to play certain records). And in 1987, federal prosecutors indicted Isgro and two codefendants for numerous alleged crimes, some of which were linked to their promotional activities. The charges included racketeering, mail fraud, money laundering, obstruction of justice, filing false tax returns, and clandestine distribution of cash and drugs.

Specifically, the government accused Isgro and two others of furnishing cash and cocaine to radio station program directors in return for airplay. Executives at four radio stations testified that Isgro or his associates had bribed them. Due to prosecutorial misconduct, however—the same phenomenon that would aid Rick four years later—a federal judge dismissed the case in 1990.

Isgro went on to serve as executive producer of the 1992 movie *Hoffa* about the Teamsters Union leader who also had been involved with organized crime figures and may have been murdered by them. Jack Nicholson starred in the film, which received an Oscar nomination. In March 2000, however, three years after the release of *Urban Rapsody*, Isgro was arrested for loan-sharking and identified as a member of the Gambino crime family. He was accused of lending money at interest rates of up to 5 percent a week, and of sending thugs to beat up borrowers who failed to pay. After pleading guilty to extortion and to running a loan-sharking business in Beverly Hills, Isgro served fifty months in federal prison.

In 2014 Manhattan district attorney Cyrus R. Vance Jr. charged Isgro with helping to run a sports bookie ring for the Gambino crime family in 2009. Isgro pled not guilty to gambling, conspiracy, and money laundering charges in state supreme court in Manhattan, and the case against him is pending.

When Rick and Isgro made *Urban Rapsody*, they claimed that they weren't interested in exploiting Rick's sordid past. They both knew, however, that fans would be interested in watching a performer who'd been accused of so many fascinating crimes and convicted of some of them. They also thought a new album could take advantage of the publicity occasioned by Rick's sensational trial, prison term, and widely publicized release.

Songs Rick had recorded earlier in his career were still being played, easily recognizable samples of his work were being incorporated into the latest rap songs, and Motown's reissues of Rick's classics on *Bustin' Out: The Best of Rick James* were still getting air time. "To see kids 16 years old saying they listen to Rick James or Teena Marie or the Mary Jane Girls really touches me," Rick told *USA Today* while working on his new album. At forty-nine, Rick was older than most rock stars, but his enforced silence over the previous several years meant that all that most of his fans remembered about his music were his greatest hits of years before. Here was his chance for a new beginning.

Rick also had a money problem that Isgro could help with. Rick had declared bankruptcy in 1995, while he was serving time in Folsom, and didn't emerge from bankruptcy until 1999, two years after *Urban Rapsody* was released. Rick's signature on the insert in the *Urban* CD shows part of his motivation for making the album: the *s* in *James* is capitalized, and two vertical lines are drawn through it. In *The Confessions of Rick James*, Rick didn't mention Isgro, writing only, "I basically paid for [*Urban Rapsody*] myself with the help of a friend of mine." Another friend of Rick's said Rick was scared of Isgro.

In 1997 Isgro revived his former record label, Private I, with Mercury Records as the distributor, as the launching pad for *Urban Rapsody*. It was Rick's first album in nine years. His contract gave him ownership of his master recordings and a larger royalty percentage than he'd been earning at Motown. Things were starting to improve for Rick, and he was getting a foothold in life outside the penitentiary.

67

Rick Revels in an Urban Rapsody

I was born to funk and roll in the Big Time.

—"Big Time," by Rick James (1980)

After saying for years that he wanted to experiment with music and still sell records, Rick felt his time had come. He told the *San Francisco Chronicle* he wanted the new album, which was released on CD, to appeal to both fifteen-year-old hip-hoppers and forty- to fifty-year-olds.

Although Rick had never been a rap fan, there was quite a bit of rap on *Urban Rapsody*, much of it by rappers he invited to join him in recording the album, including Neb Luv of Da 5 Footaz, Rappin' 4-Tay, Lil' Cease, and Snoop Dogg. He said he'd begun to appreciate the genre in prison when younger inmates turned him on to Snoop, also a former jailbird, and that he was into rappers who played their own instruments, like Snoop and Scarface. Rick also sought and received assistance from R&B singers Bobby Womack and Charlie Wilson, former leader of the Gap Band.

Telling interviewers he hoped his new album would bridge the gap between old-school music and hip-hop, Rick added Womack's singing to Snoop's rapping on one of the tunes on *Urban Rapsody*, "Player's Way." Neb Luv rapped on "It's Time" and "Favorite Flava," and was praised by one critic for her "seductive performance." Rappin' 4-Tay, who performed on the album's title tune, was, like Rick, a former prison inmate. A criminal record was the preferred rap image, of course, and Rick was positioning himself and his new album wisely.

Because he had criticized rappers as nonmusicians for years, some saw *Urban Rapsody* as Rick's semi-surrender to the rap community. *New Times* magazine and others accused him of selling out. Rick's answer to the criticism certainly did nothing to refute that accusation. He said he hadn't wanted rappers touching his music, "but then when [he] saw what kind of money [he] was making from them, [he] said 'Never mind.'" He was undoubtedly thinking mainly of MC Hammer and "U Can't Touch This."

Somewhat touchingly, Rick dedicated *Urban Rapsody* in part to his "Homeys" in Folsom: "Alfred (Bubba) Johnson, Rodney Napier, Rob Bunns, Leonard (Mousy) Fulgram, Payne (N.Y.), Marion Miller, Garry (Red) Eccher, Dewayne (Rahim) Richardson, Country, Freddie Jackson and Loapy."

Rick also dedicated the album to "all U punk-ass C.O.'s [Correction Officers] who tried to keep me down," telling them that "if you ever need a job, you can always wash the tires on my Rolls Royce . . . !"

"Somebody's Watching You" starts out with re-created news reports about Rick being released and goes on to describe his prison experience. One reviewer called it "an honest, introspective look at Rick's incarceration and its aftermath." The *Washington Post* called the lyrics angry and paranoid, however. Referring to the Folsom correction officers, Rick sang, "Look at all the little piggies standing in a row, waiting in the shadows for a brother just to blow [lose control]."

Rick also hoped to attract some of his old fans to *Urban Rapsody* by including some old-style porn numbers on the new album, such as "Player's Way," "So Soft So Wet" and "Back in You Again."

"Player's Way," the song on which Womack and Snoop join Rick, features a pimp and one of his employees pledging their mutual love. This song alone fully justifies the parental warning on the sticker affixed to the album cover—it actually makes prostitution and pimping sound romantic.

"So Soft So Wet" was Rick's obvious attempt to catch up with Prince in the porno sweepstakes. Prince's first album, *For You*, had contained the song "Soft and Wet," referring to an excited vagina, which Rick's song referred to as well. Although Rick initially asks his female partner in "So Soft So Wet" to "open wide" and later refers to their "bodies joined together like the rain and stormy weather," the two songs are quite different musically.

Rick claimed "So Soft So Wet" was inspired not by Prince but by Tanya, who, Rick said, had sent him some "outrageous" photos while he was in jail. As he wrote in the album's liner notes, his time in jail with no sex "was a bitch," and with a "fine ass lady waiting for [him] when [he] got out," all he had were his fantasies. He said he decided to write his feelings about these photos into this song, saying it described a dream about being between Tanya's "soft and creamy thighs." Although Rick wrote that he wrote the song because he didn't want "2 jack off," he called the tune a "musical ejaculation." Beginning with a woman's sexually excited groans, the tune moves on to Rick's deeply masculine tones as he sings lines like "yeah, funk me, baby, funk me yeah."

"Back in You Again," which Rick recorded with the rapper Lil' Cease, was another sexy number about Tanya and was recorded specifically for the popular film *Money Talks*, which starred Chris Tucker and Charlie Sheen. "Favorite Flava" is dedicated to performing cunnilingus on black women. Among the lines in this song are "Can I taste you for a while?" "I like to lick you like a lollipop," and "Say I can play in your sweet milky way?" Rick said he initially wanted rapper and actress Yo-Yo to rap on "Favorite Flava," but she was busy. She may have been "busy" because she advocates female empowerment and dislikes sexism. Rick then asked Neb Luv, who, he said, rushed to work with him because he was her family's favorite artist.

"Turn It Out" includes lines such as "I got a real down girl and she's on my side / You ought to see her dance with her legs butt wide / Yeah, she doesn't mind if you look, stop, and stare / She doesn't give a damn and she just don't care." These lines were followed by the chorus, "I love to see her turn it out." It's clear that what she was "turning out" was her vagina. When *Billboard* reviewed "Turn It Out," it called

Rick "a renegade funkster back in serious action" and said "this wholly accessible jam" showed Rick at his absolute best. The song includes the oft-repeated opening and closing line, "Sex-me funk-me music, that's what I adore."

In the video of "Turn It Out," Rick sings the song backed by several male musicians, two sexy female background singers who flip their hair and wink at appropriate moments, and one female dancer, who, while admittedly wearing leather pants and a top, illustrates the lyrics from a distance by spreading her legs as wide as possible and dancing and undulating for the camera. She then crawls toward the camera miming a tiger, appropriately hissing and clawing, before regaining her feet and dancing while the camera lovingly shoots her from her knees up from about three feet away.

In the song itself, Rick avers that "for three long years I couldn't get a piece, no, couldn't wait to hit it when I got released." After noting that the dancing girl is now on his side, he clarifies what he means by "on his side" when he sings that she's "right lay horizontal with me deep inside."

One overall assessment was that *Urban Rapsody* showed Rick bravely struggling for new direction and meaning. Some publications said he had found both, but others, like the *Philadelphia Inquirer*, insisted Rick "didn't quite capture the tautness of hip-hop" and called his efforts to sound contemporary "near-painful." The paper said *Urban Rapsody* contained overwrought lyrics, refrains that were too simple, and bald attempts at gangsta hip. On the other hand, *Vibe* magazine called *Urban Rapsody* the third-most-important album of Rick's career after *Come Get It!* and *Super Freak*.

USA Today said *Urban* was a "thumping '90s update" of Rick's signature sound, rated it his best album since 1983's *Cold Blooded*, and awarded it three and a half stars out of four. And the *New York Times* called the album "brutally honest and autobiographical," and praised Rick's "irresistible craftsmanship and spark."

In an ideal world, "Back in You Again" and the whole *Urban Rapsody* album would have benefited from publicity about Rick once again being off dope. As he told the *New York Times* in January 1998, "We would never have done this interview years ago. Back then, I'd be in my room for an hour. Then I'd come out, spend a couple of minutes with you, and go back to my room and smoke cocaine again. You'd be here the whole night and you'd say, 'We didn't talk much, but we saw the smoke, the redness in his eyes and the freaks running around buck naked.'"

Rick hadn't returned to that point yet, but according to former Stone City Band member Daniel LeMelle, Rick was high on cocaine when he recorded "Back in You Again" in 1997. The song wasn't recorded until the day it was due to be delivered to the *Money Talks* execs, and, according to LeMelle, before Rick would come downstairs to the recording studio, "he wanted to hit the [coke] pipe again" and "was wasting time looking for a rock [of cocaine]." Impatient with Rick's seemingly endless coke-caused delays, LeMelle stormed out, although Rick made it to the studio later that day and recorded the song.

As if he were acknowledging the recommencement of his worst habit, Rick sang in "Good Ol Days" about how great life had been at the top until "the devil handed [him] a glass pipe." He was accompanied by McDuffie Funderberg and Charlie Wilson.

To promote *Urban Rapsody* Rick reactivated six of the original Stone City Band members to form a new Stone City Band, recruited McDuffie Funderberg from the Mary Jane Girls as one of three backup singers and Teena Marie as a co-performer, and began a twenty-five-city tour in Santa Ana, California, in late September 1997.

From a publicity perspective, the *Urban Rapsody* tour, Rick's first in nine years, was brilliantly planned. It was awkward from a geographic perspective, however, because the conditions of his parole required him to return to California three times a week. California is the nation's most populous state, but even Rick couldn't draw a large enough crowd to do three concerts a week in the same state for very long. That meant the tour devolved into a series of trips that rarely lasted more than two days. Rick rationalized that this was fine, saying two days a week was a long enough workweek for him. Prison definitely seemed to have mellowed him.

The preview concert at the House of Blues in Los Angeles featured Rick in a white suit, McDuffie Funderberg as a backup singer as well as a solo performer, and Snoop Dogg and Bobby Womack joining Rick on the "Player's Way" encore. Rick was worried the concert would flop, but it sold out. Numerous celebrities, including Eddie Murphy, turned up to herald Rick's reentrance into the business. According to Rick's handlers, the second scheduled concert, at Chicago's New Regal Theater, also sold out, but at least two of the planned following appearances bombed.

One that should have been a big success, a performance planned for early December 1997 in Rick's hometown of Buffalo, was canceled after fewer than one thousand fans bought tickets for the three-thousand-seat venue. And when he offered to visit his dropout alma mater, Bennett High School, the school administration told him to stay away.

The quality of Rick's appearances on the tour became erratic. Before a concert at the DAR Constitution Hall in Washington, DC, in early 1998, he gathered the Stone City Band into his dressing room for a prayer led by McDuffie Funderburg. But the *Washington Post* reported that when Rick and the band performed "You and I," the band roared through the tune "while Rick struggled vocally to keep up." The paper's reviewer also said that when Rick and McDuffie Funderberg sang "Fire and Desire," Rick "paid scant attention to the lyrics" and "nearly parodied himself with constant references to drugs and sex." Rick saved the concert, however, by singing his biggest hits, "Give It to Me" and "Super Freak," while the audience danced in the aisles, the paper reported.

The same review described this DC crowd as "forty-something black businessmen, reformed hippies, college students, and loyal funkologists." Rick sometimes wore an all-black ensemble, including a long captain's coat and dark shades, which was his costume on the cover of the *Urban Rapsody* CD. Despite his chubbiness, however, he also sometimes donned a jumpsuit, and as one critic put it, "double-chinned super freaks in too-tight jumpsuits tend to invite ridicule." On the other hand, many of his fans also were probably somewhat heavier than they had been at his pre-prison concerts years earlier.

When Rick played Tramps in Manhattan in 1998, the *New York Times* reported that even though he hadn't been a major star since the early 1980s, all he had to do was cue the bass riff of "You and I" or

"Bustin' Out" and the audience would sing along, shouting verses as well as choruses. Every so often, Rick would even stop the band and the fans would keep the songs going. The reviewer pointed out that the songs had been dance music and makeout music in the days before crack and AIDS, probably making listeners in the late 1990s nostalgic for an era of pleasure without risks.

Rick's voice was coarser at this concert than it had been previously, and a bad hip limited his onstage moves. But in some ways he hadn't changed. "His onstage subject was lust," Jon Pareles of the *New York Times* said, "first exuberant and then in slow motion." At one point, Rick asked the audience if he could take his time with the songs and then stretched them out by offering detailed instruction in foreplay, while chiding young people for rushing things in the bedroom.

Although he hadn't been out of jail for very long when the tour began, Rick backed away from the disgust with songs that glorified drugs he'd expressed soon after leaving prison and continued to perform his drug-oriented hits like "Mary Jane." This time, however, neither he nor the band members backing him would smoke joints onstage, he told one interviewer. (Although he didn't mention it, Rick enforced this measure to avoid violating his parole.)

Anticipating criticism for once again singing drug songs, he said critics of those tunes just shouldn't attend his concerts or listen to his music. "So what, I was a cocaine addict," he said. "So was the mayor [Marion Barry] of Washington, D.C. What are all these people, saints? I'm the only cocaine addict ever?"

He told one interviewer that if *Urban Rapsody* wasn't a successful album, then he'd just make another. "I'm grateful to be back where I belong, making the music and expressing the rhythm of my heart."

Although the critical reaction to the album was generally favorable, *Urban Rapsody* was not very popular. It rose to number 31 on the *Billboard* R&B albums chart and remained on the chart for ten weeks. On the *Billboard* pop albums chart, *Urban Rapsody* rose only to number 170.

Rick would soon record another album, but now it was time to shore up his social life.

68

Rick and Tanya Finally Marry . . .
and Then Divorce

The very word "star" summons up images of remoteness, of loneliness.

—Michael Newton

Rick finally wed Tanya on December 21, 1997. By this time, their relationship was eleven years old, Tanya was twenty-seven, and their son, Tazman, was five. In a way, the prison system had forced them into wedlock: because they were both convicted felons, they weren't allowed to live together without being married if either was on parole, which Rick still was.

Nevertheless, Rick definitely wanted to marry Tanya. While in prison, he said, "[She's] made me happier than any woman I've ever been with. This crisis has brought us closer together. She has stood by my side through all of this madness." He went on to call himself and Tanya "two co-dependent people."

After the small ceremony, attended only by family and friends, the couple and Taz moved into a Spanish-style home in the Woodland Hills neighborhood of Los Angeles, which they shared with Rick's daughter Tyenza, then twenty-seven, and Ty's daughter, Jasmine, who was eight. Rick's other son, Rick Jr., then twenty-four, an artist, lived elsewhere in L.A.

Rick wrote in *The Confessions of Rick James* he was thinking at the wedding that "I hope I can change and I hope she's changed. I hope I can handle this. I hope I can do it the way God would like to see me do it. We would have to work hard to get over our past lives, to forget about the drugs and the sex and raise our son happily. After all the years and the drama, I would finally be a good father and a happily married man."

Rick's friends said he tried to get close to his kids but didn't really know how, and he'd alternate between buying them everything they wanted and screaming at them if they did something wrong.

Rick James Jr. told *Vibe* magazine that one day Rick Sr. told LeRoi Johnson to take Rick Jr. shopping and "get me whatever I wanted." Rick Sr. "told me that day, 'I'm your father, and I want you to let everybody know.'" He and Johnson "took a whole lot of pictures . . . went shopping, got a whole lot of clothes. I came back to the hood, and it . . . was like I was an instant ghetto superstar." On other occasions, however, Rick Jr. would visit his father in California and, in Levi Ruffin's words, "Rick would holler at him and spank him for acting like a kid."

Ty, Rick's daughter, also had problems with her father, Ruffin says. "I remember one time Ty came to me crying. She wanted to go back and play with her daddy in her bedroom, but Rick had freaks [Rick's sex partners or fellow dope users] in there. Ty came out crying . . . 'What's wrong with my daddy?'"

Nevertheless, there were good times as well, according to Ty. "I was Daddy's girl," she told *Ebony* magazine in 2011. "I would roll [marijuana] joints for him—like 20 a day. He said he didn't want me sneaking to do stuff." Ty added that "it was cool hanging out" with Rick. "That's what I miss most. We would party together."

But Rick wasn't able to make a success of his marriage with Tanya any more than he had with Kelly. Although Tanya told *People* magazine that when she needed Rick he was there for her, she also called him "a really self-centered narcissist."

Some of this narcissism seemed to be in play in the fall of 1998 when Rick appeared on TV's *Judge Joe Brown* show to sue fellow musician Geronne Turner for a guitar and amplifier Turner had borrowed from him and never returned. Turner's defense was that the guitar and amp had been stolen from his car. During the televised trial, Rick, despite his constant reiteration over the years of his lack of prejudice against gays, revealed what may have been an additional motivation for the suit when he testified that Turner, while the two men were drinking in a Los Angeles club, had placed his hand on Rick's rear end.

Although Rick testified that Turner's hand had lingered there for some forty to sixty seconds, Turner said it was an accident. "Now hello!" Rick told the judge. "A forty-second accident. . . . That's a no-no." The judge didn't mention this alleged touching in his decision but did rule that Turner owed Rick $4,600 for the lost guitar and amps. Perhaps feeling embarrassed by the somewhat anti-gay nature of the proceedings, Rick shook hands with Turner and hugged him after the show. "He's a great . . . guy and I love him," Rick told the show's interviewer. "If I was a homosexual, he'd be my wife."

At any rate, by mid-1999, Rick had separated from his real wife, Tanya, and Tanya had moved out with Tazman. Rick told *Rolling Stone* that he didn't see Tazman as much as he liked. "That's the hard part," he said.

By March 2002 the couple was in the midst of a divorce. Under its terms, Rick was required to pay Tanya $4,500 per month in child support, plus $8,000 per year for Taz's private school tuition, out of his $53,000-per-month income.

69

The Super Freak Becomes a Senior Freak

Just trying to be Rick James almost killed me.

—Rick James, 1994

In 1998 Rick's rock 'n' roll years finally caught up with him. That February, one of his hips was replaced to repair the damage he had done to it by jumping around onstage. Because Rick was only fifty, not everyone took the surgical procedure that seriously. The *Buffalo News* wrote new "Super Freak" lyrics for the occasion: "He's a very creaky guy / The kind you don't dance with at Mother's / He can never lift you in his arms / Once you get him off his feet."

Then, months later, in early November, one of Rick's brothers, William Johnson, died in Atlanta from leukemia at age forty-four. Rick, who was performing in Denver as part of his *Urban Rapsody* tour, flew from Denver to Buffalo for Johnson's funeral and then returned immediately to Denver to continue the tour.

Shortly after returning to the concert stage, Rick felt something pop in his neck during a head-banging rendition of "Super Freak" after he'd been performing for two hours. He began to experience pain and numbness, but when his fans yelled for an encore, he complied.

Rick said later that when he was finally able to leave the stage, he felt his left side tighten and his shoulders and his right side go numb.

Doctors told him he had ruptured a blood vessel in his neck and advised him to return home to Los Angeles. After he did so, he was unable to walk, his speech was slurred, and he was taken to L.A.'s Cedars-Sinai Medical Center.

Rick thought he was about to die. Tanya said he asked her to put out a press release to tell the fans he loved them, and also started calling people he hadn't talked to in years because of disagreements. "He was taking care of his business, getting his house in order," she said.

Rick's doctors said he was unlikely to die immediately but that he'd had a stroke. When Rick realized he was going to live, he told *Billboard* magazine, "I won't slow down, but I will have to watch the way I shake my head." He also said he would give up alcohol and cigarettes.

Partly because only one in four American stroke victims are younger than sixty-five, Rick's doctors suspected his problems were the result of "rock 'n' roll neck," the result of repeated head-banging onstage. A spokesman insisted the stroke was not drug- or alcohol-related. After an angiogram showed the stroke was the result of blood clotting in two broken neck arteries, doctors operated on Rick to repair those arteries. They told Rick he would need a lengthy period of recuperation and rehabilitation before he could walk again, forcing him to cancel several upcoming concerts.

Rick was somewhat encouraged by the fact that his voice, the core of his livelihood, recovered relatively quickly. While undergoing rehabilitation, however, he discovered that because the two arteries he had broken were near the medulla, the part of the brain that controls leg movement, he couldn't walk and was constantly dizzy. Many people called him to express their sympathies, including Stevie Wonder, Roberta Flack, and Bobby Womack. Entertainers Martin Lawrence, Johnnie Taylor, and Johnny "Guitar" Watson sent flowers. Many well-known entertainers also visited him during his recovery, including Eddie Murphy, Cuba Gooding Jr., George Clinton, Jermaine Jackson, and Berry Gordy.

In an attempt to keep the stroke in perspective, Rick asked that neither cards nor flowers be sent to him and asked instead that donations be made to the Leukaemia Foundation in the name of his recently deceased brother, William Johnson.

With a dozen concert dates remaining on the tour, there was talk that Teena Marie, who had been costarring with Rick, would continue as the headliner, with Rick making an onstage appearance in a chair to sing a duet with her. In the end, however, it was decided to end the tour.

Rick was released from the hospital on December 11, 1998, more than a month after being admitted. Doctors said they expected him to be 80 percent recovered within six months but that he would need strenuous daily physical therapy through the next year.

Even so, Rick's outlook soon improved. He said he hoped to be able to walk normally within a few weeks, that he'd do anything to bring that about, and that he'd dropped cigarettes, coffee, and fatty foods. He also expressed faith in his recovery, saying, "God has taken me through too many changes to drop me off in the middle of the street." God, Rick said, was giving him a message to get his life in order.

When he was interviewed at his L.A. home after his release from the hospital, Rick's braids cascaded over his pillow and he kept his sunglasses on, saying he needed them because he was plagued by double vision. That was an improvement, he said, because just after his stroke he was seeing four or five people where others saw only one. Whenever he tried to stand up, he'd fall over to the right. "I'm like a kid," he said.

Steve Jones of *USA Today*, interviewing Rick as late as 2002, noticed the stroke was still hindering his speech and mobility. He had gained so much weight he began to suffer from sleep apnea. Soon, he was also diagnosed with diabetes, and his drug-damaged heart began causing him so many problems that a pacemaker was inserted in his chest.

Nevertheless, feeling energetic for a while, Rick told various interviewers he had plans for what he called a "double funk" album. Later, feeling less energetic, he revived his earlier idea of producing an acoustic guitar album. He told *Rolling Stone* he admired Neil Young and Stephen Stills's acoustic accomplishments because "they didn't need . . . to go out and play. They just strap on the acoustic, sit down and sing their songs" without bounding around onstage. Sittin' and singin' looked good to the now aged Rick James, but in terms of productivity and fame, he was a long way from death.

In fact, Rick's raunchy lifestyle and pornographic approach to life, combined with his somewhat sickly state, made him a perfect fit for the bawdy cartoon show *South Park*. His animated image appeared on that show in 1998 when Chef, voiced by R&B singer Isaac Hayes, became embroiled in a legal stew. The show's child characters organized a benefit concert, Chef Aid, to pay Chef's legal bills. At the concert, the animated Rick character performed a tune, sung by the real Rick, that also appeared on the CD *Chef Aid: The South Park Album*, released later that year. Considering the title of the Chef/Hayes track on the CD was "Chocolate Salty Balls," the title of Rick's contribution, "Love Gravy," probably didn't shock many of the show's viewers, but the song includes such lines as "Would you like another helping of my gravy? . . . / Don't let it get in your eyes, though," and features Rick singing, "I'm gonna climb into your cockpit / Gonna get those rockets firing / Blast you into orbit / And burn out all your wiring." Accompanying Rick on the song was the real Ike Turner, who, like Rick, was a heavy cocaine user and also had been accused of abusing women, including his wife, Tina.

The next year, 1999, Rick played a role in the Eddie Murphy movie *Life*. In spite of all the sparring between the two men, when Murphy visited Rick in the hospital, Murphy mentioned the film he was working on, which starred him and Martin Lawrence, and Rick took the opportunity to tell Murphy, "[You] better have a role for me." In response, possibly feeling sorry for his old sidekick, Murphy gave Rick the role of Spanky, a part originally intended for actor Louis Gossett Jr. It became the only time Rick ever appeared in a movie.

The film premiered on February 5, 1999. A few months earlier, when Rick was still recovering from his stroke, he said one of his first goals was to recover sufficiently to attend the premiere. "I don't want to go and see it in a wheelchair," he said. "I want to at least be able to use my cane." His wish came true.

In his sole, three-minute scene near the beginning of the movie, Rick docs a good job portraying a Harlem bootlegger and nightclub owner who menaces Murphy and Lawrence. Oddly for a comedy, the film tells the story of two men convicted of a murder they didn't commit who spend sixty-five years in prison as a result. The humor comes from their odd-couple relationship and their interactions with the other prisoners.

Rick, a former inmate, could have helped to bring some realism to this film, but the prison depicted was far from realistic. It was portrayed as a camp-like compound without fences where the guards shoot to kill if a prisoner tries to escape but tolerate conjugal visits, open homosexuality, hookers, booze, baseball games, talent shows, barbecues, and endless horsing around.

Most reviewers urged capital punishment for the film. "Spend 65 years in jail with Eddie Murphy and Martin Lawrence, and you'll understand why they call it the pokey," *USA Today* wrote, adding that "as the years crawl by and Murphy's character concocts his latest escape ploy, those in the audience may beat him to it." The *New York Daily News* called the film "two hours of hard labor" and said the producers "threw away the key to comedy." Interestingly enough, considering Rick's, and to some extent, Murphy's background, one montage within the film spans twenty-eight years by mixing the characters' fates and important historical milestones in what amounts to a music video.

Rick garnered a couple favorable comments, however. *Variety* said he looked "very dapper" in the film, called the movie's supporting players "extremely well cast," and said they "delivered with flying colors." The *Daily News* described Rick as "smooth but deadly" in his role, and called the casting of the movie "more inventive than the story."

Rick discovered, however, that he disliked acting. Murphy, Rick said, "had to pull me through it." In the same interview, he said, "I see why actors get so much money. It's long hours where you don't do anything but linger around the set" and called moviemaking "a long and tiresome ordeal."

70

Comeback

*I'm always making a comeback but nobody ever tells
me where I've been.*

—Billie Holiday

By May 2002, Rick decided to make a new recording that would
incorporate rock, jazz, and funk, creating what he called "a potpourri
of different styles and sounds." With his album sales shrinking with each
new effort, however, he had only one real choice if he wanted to keep his
name before the public: rerelease his greatest hit. That happened when
Motown (now Universal Motown) put out a new double-CD deluxe
edition of his 1981 album *Street Songs*, complete with a recording of a
1981 live show in which he performed "Super Freak" onstage. Rick and
the Stone City Band celebrated the event with a concert at B. B. King
Blues Club & Grill in New York City.

While planning a tour in support of the deluxe CD, Rick, by then
fifty-four, said the trip would be his last. "I don't want to be singing
'Super Freak' when I'm 60," he said. One reason was that although he
had recovered from the stroke enough to perform onstage, Rick's range
of motion was limited. "I move around, but I have to be careful," he
said. "My equilibrium isn't so good."

Nevertheless, Rick and Chaka Khan appeared at the Greek Theatre in Los Angeles on May 10, 2002, in support of the deluxe edition of *Street Songs*. During the preshow publicity buildup, Rick did an excellent job of positioning the twenty-one-year-old song for a new generation. He told the *Los Angeles Times*, "Super Freak came during a time when all people wanted to do was party, get dressed up and go to the disco, and right now people want to revert back to that simpler time. For an hour and a half . . . you don't have to hear about the Taliban, and racism, and economics, and George Bush, and all that. It's therapeutic."

To some, however, Rick wasn't as impressive a performer in his later years as he had been in his youth. Tony Nolasco, who had helped Rick create his first album, *Come Get It!*, remembered seeing him performing at the Miami House of Blues late in Rick's life. "He was overweight and sweating. His big time was obviously over."

Shortly after Rick's release from prison, Rick Abel, Rick's former crew member, heard him on a radio show and was surprised to hear that his voice "was not like Rick's voice at all. It was real deep, like it was ruined." Curious, Abel attended a party at a Hollywood club when he knew Rick would be present. "I had heard all the stories of how fucked up he was, just in horrible shape, so I wanted to go and see if he remembered who I was. He comes in with his entourage, he's a lot heavier than he ever was, they go upstairs, it's a special party room upstairs where all the dignitaries were, so I follow him up there, he's standing near the bar, and . . . they're all clamoring around him."

Abel says he walked up to Rick and tapped him on the shoulder, and Rick turned around. "His face was all bloated and mottled, and his eyes couldn't focus on anything . . . it was like I was looking at someone with full-blown Alzheimer's. There was just no recognition whatsoever."

After a minute, Rick whispered "Red Tex" (Abel had red hair). "He kind of smiled and mumbled a couple of words I couldn't understand," Abel says. "I could see that this wasn't going to go very far, so I said, 'Well, good seeing you, Rick,' and he said 'Yeah,' and that was it."

Rick also made plans to keep himself in the public eye. Tanya said that even after the two began divorce proceedings in 2002, he was talking to her about moving back in with him so they could star in a TV show together. His idea was that even though they'd remain divorced, they'd produce a reality show, full of drama and conflict, about her staying at home while he kept sneaking out of the house, presumably to see other women. In 2002 he told an interviewer for the *A.V. Club* that he was "concentrating on a lot of different things, movies and musicals. . . . I'm writing a musical."

Then Rick's past seemed to be returning in yet another way. In November 2002 a twenty-six-year-old woman accused Rick of sexually assaulting her at his San Fernando Valley home. Rick called her a liar motivated by greed, Los Angeles Police executed a search warrant at the house where the alleged assault took place, and no arrest was ever made. "I just feel that sometimes I'm in a fishbowl," Rick said. "Sometimes the wrong people enter into your space, and they're money-hungry and they're greedy."

Rick appeared to have eliminated the lifestyle that had caused him major problems in the past, i.e., living 24/7 in a house filled with stoned people he didn't know. He seemed to be gesturing to people who had meant a lot to him in his life.

Meanwhile, Rick's father, seriously ill in his late seventies, attempted to reconcile with his son, but Rick avoided doing so. James A. Johnson Sr. died in Buffalo on June 26, 2003.

Legendary baseball pitcher Satchel Paige once said, "Don't look back. Something might be gaining on you." Rick, continuing to look forward, said he was working on an unspecified project with actor/comedian Jamie Foxx and was writing music for a thirty-song double CD. The CD would be the product of a new record label he had established, Ma Records, and would be distributed by Sony/RED. That Rick was still working on this showed the depth of his persistence. Although he had been calling it Mamma Records then, this label was the same idea he and Tanya had been discussing with Mary Sauger on that violent night that had sent both Rick and Tanya to prison. The planned thirty-song double CD became an eleven-song single CD, *Deeper Still*, which was not released until 2007.

Looking backward and forward simultaneously, Rick said he was negotiating a movie and book deal about his life. He also announced that he and Teena Marie would embark on their first tour together in twenty years, which they would call the You and I reunion tour. (In a sense, he was replacing his memories of Kelly with the presence of Teena.) To the amazement of many, this tour actually took place. Rick derived immense satisfaction from the fact that Morris Day and the Time, a former side group for his old rival Prince, joined them on the road.

It startled some fans that Rick still had the energy to go on tour, a ritual so tiring that he'd been talking about never doing it again as early as 1981. Referring to his 1998 stroke, however, Rick said, "God sat me down to pay attention. Then he told me to get back up and hit the stage, and I'm enjoying it."

Rick, Teena, and Morris Day and the Time all performed in fall 2003 at the Show Place Arena in Washington, DC. On October 3 they sold out their appearance at the Arie Crown Theater in Chicago. They then made ten additional appearances in 2003, and continued touring in 2004.

Rick stayed on the road until two months before his death. When he and Teena brought their act to DAR Constitution Hall in Washington, DC, in late May 2004, the *Washington Post* noted that the aging pair crept gingerly down a set of stairs to center stage at geriatric speed, but the *Post* reviewer, after giving this less-than-impressive entrance some thought, decided to blame it on Teena. His review said she was wearing a leather bustier with a large sparkly belt buckle "that made her look like the world's sexiest Teletubby." (Teena had also gained weight over the years.)

The paper wasn't easy on Rick, either, noting that when the couple sang "I'm a Sucker for Your Love," Rick's "rasp was sadly suggestive of a really good karaoke version" of himself. The *Post* also said Rick had come to resemble the actress S. Epatha Merkerson. Merkerson wasn't a bad-looking cast member of the TV show *Law and Order*, but Rick probably didn't appreciate the alleged resemblance.

Nevertheless, Rick's personality remained strong. Levi Ruffin said Rick was "trying to get the old band together" just before his death. Rehearsals were to start in September 2004.

Ruffin was still angry with Rick for allegedly cheating him out of money when Rick and the band were touring during Rick's halcyon days. "I told him, 'Rick, I don't trust you no more. He said, 'Levi, man, I understand. I'm going to make it up, man. I'm sorry, man.'" Ruffin said he wanted whatever money he made on the road held in escrow. Rick agreed.

That Rick could still convince people he'd once cheated to tour with him again says a lot about his personal appeal and the emotions he generated in others. Asked why he never sued Rick for the money he said he was owed, Ruffin replied, "I should have, and I would have won. But he was my friend. I loved him."

The tour never took place; what did occur was much bigger.

71

"I'm Rick James, Bitch!"

*I'm one of the baddest motherfuckers of all time, one of the best
singers and one of the best-looking motherfuckers
you've ever seen. Hold my drink, bitch.*

—Dave Chappelle as Rick on *Chappelle's Show*

Rick's slow march toward a dignified death was interrupted by
a TV dinner. Neal Brennan, cocreator of Dave Chappelle's Comedy Central TV program, *Chappelle's Show*, was dining in 2003 with one
of the show's cast members, Charlie Murphy. Charlie, Eddie Murphy's
younger brother, had known Rick for years.

In the course of the conversation, Murphy told Brennan several
stories about Rick at his cocaine-fueled peak, when Rick continually
announced his own greatness in public places, sucker-punched Charlie
and others, and behaved disgustingly toward women. By the end of the
dinner, the two men had come up with two phrases that would make
Rick semi-immortal: "I'm Rick James, bitch!" and "What did the five
fingers say to the face? Slap!" The skits also connected Rick to the phrase
"Show me your tits!" and the nickname "Daaaarkness!"

On the basis of these phrases and Murphy's own experiences with
Rick, the team of Brennan, Murphy, and Chappelle put together three
skits under the title "Charlie Murphy's True Hollywood Stories." The

skits were broadcast during *Chappelle's Show*'s second season in 2003 and 2004, and became instant classics.

Describing these episodes as "darkly humorous," the Associated Press said the skits portrayed Rick as "violent and arrogant" and a "menacing celebrity Lothario." That may be, but millions of viewers found them hilarious.

All three skits both played and referred to Rick's music. In the first, Murphy tells the audience he was so starstruck by Rick that when he first saw the singer, he could actually see his aura. Chappelle, playing Rick and sporting shoulder-length beaded braids, then appears with a sleazy smile and an orange aura surrounding his face and upper body while Rick's song "Give It to Me, Baby," plays in the background.

The scene quickly shifts to a nightclub, where Rick licks the entire side of a woman's face and tells her, "I'm Rick James, bitch. Enjoy yourself." (Many viewers would interpret this as a reference to Rick's professed enjoyment of cunnilingus.) Later in the skit, still in the nightclub, Rick hits Murphy on the forehead with a ring imprinted with the word UNITY, the theme of his *Cold Blooded* album, leaving an imprint of the word in the Murphy character's forehead for about a week. The underlying joke, of course, is that a call for unity among black people had resulted in a fistfight among black men. Rick then says to himself, "That was cold-blooded," another reference to the album.

Murphy visits Rick's hotel room to seek revenge, while the bass line of "Super Freak" plays in the background. Murphy kicks Rick up onto the top of a bureau, shattering its mirror, and Rick calls security. After Murphy tells the two security guards to back off or he'll throw Rick out the window, the two men agree to a truce. Rick then orders the two statuesque women who've been lying on his bed in their underwear to have sex with Murphy. (The sex is not shown.)

The second skit begins with Rick's character visiting Eddie Murphy's house while both brothers are there, and grinding his dirty cowboy boots into Eddie's brand-new white suede couch. The angry brothers beat Rick's legs so badly they no longer function. Rick's character then crawls out of the scene still shouting defiance, his now-useless legs trailing behind him. What makes the skit funny is the Rick character's continuing verbal abuse of the Murphy brothers while they pummel him. Adding to the humor, after this skit, the real Rick, in a video insert, insists that he would never have done anything like that, would never do anything like that . . . and then recalls that yes, he did in fact do exactly that.

The third skit takes place in the China Club, where in real life Rick often appeared. Rick's character does a gross "Chinaman" imitation and asks two women to "Show me your tits!" which they do. He also refers to Murphy as "daaaarkness" because of the Murphy brothers' relatively dark skin compared to Rick's own. When Charlie Murphy approaches him, Rick's character asks him, "What did the five fingers say to the face?" then slaps him. Murphy waits for a few moments, then reapproaches the unsuspecting Rick at the bar and slugs him. Rick's drug-addled character then complains that it was "weeks ago" that he slapped Murphy, and is flabbergasted when Murphy tells him the incident had just occurred.

Amazingly, Rick not only consented to the showing of these videos, he supported them personally by appearing at least once in each skit via a video insert, uttering such phrases as "Cocaine is a hell of a drug" and "I must be losing my mind."

"Cocaine is a hell of a drug" soon joined "I'm Rick James, bitch!" and "What did the five fingers say to the face? Slap!" as the major memories many people now have of Rick. The three magic phrases also launched thousands of T-shirts and have become the words most associated with Rick's legend.

Chappelle's Show soon became Comedy Central's biggest draw, averaging more than three million viewers, twice as many as the channel's *Daily Show* with Jon Stewart. In 2008, *Vibe* magazine ranked *Chappelle's Show* the fifteenth-most-important TV show of the previous fifteen years. If that ranking seems low, viewers should remember that its competitors included heavyweights such as *The Sopranos* and *The Wire*.

Just as Rick's worst habits had returned to haunt him, however, Rick's worst line returned to haunt Chappelle. When Chappelle visited Disney World with his family, people approached him and screamed

"I'm Rick James, bitch!" in front of his kids. Soon, adults, kids, and old people began doing it everywhere.

In April 2004, while Chappelle was performing a stand-up show in Sacramento, California, members of the audience continuously interrupted his performance by shouting "I'm Rick James, bitch!" Chappelle first tried counterattacking. "If you were Rick James, you'd have a better seat," he told one pesky fan. When the shouting continued, Chappelle walked off the stage. In May 2005 Chappelle's friends said he "freaked" at the enormity of his success and checked into a mental hospital. Chappelle denied that he'd gone to a hospital but said he had sought psychiatric treatment in South Africa.

That same year, a former employee of the Mississippi State Department of Mental Health named Rick James, who was running for city council in Hattiesburg, complained that hundreds of dollars worth of his campaign signs had been defaced with the phrase "I'm Rick James, bitch."

In August 2013, an electronic road sign in Columbus, Ohio, that the city's Department of Public Safety had programmed to tell motorists to drive safely was hacked into to display the words "I'm Rick James, bitch."

In fact, "I'm Rick James, bitch" is still being repeated as part of a series of popular drinking games among the members of the millennial generation, with losers required to repeat the now-famous phrase. Some believe that as long as people drink, Rick James will be immortal.

Several writers have pointed out that the *Chappelle's Show* skits were unfair to Rick, with writer Jonathan Lethem charging that they emphasized Rick's image as a clownish, amoral grotesque. Richard Wesley, Rick's former scriptwriter, says he was so disturbed when he first saw the skits on TV that he got up and left the room. He was "terribly upset" by the physical deterioration that the real Rick displayed in his videotaped interviews but also thought it was unfair that the skits emphasized the Rick "who was really lost in cocaine" rather than "Rick when Rick was sober." Wesley adds that the skits satirized a period in Rick's life when it was apparent that stardom was slipping away from him, and showed Rick as someone desperately trying to hold on to fleeting fame.

They certainly ignored his record as a brilliant musician who struggled to produce a hit for at least sixteen years, created thirteen albums and numerous singles, and produced several other musical groups who would not have existed without his assistance.

Charlie Murphy disagreed, however. Interviewed by *Paste* magazine in 2015, he maintained that the skits "reinvigorated" Rick's career. "I feel good about that," Murphy said, "because Rick didn't live too long after that. He'd been through some hard times and some real sad stuff, and that put the light back in his eyes. . . . He was reenergized and he didn't go sad."

72

Rick Works to Publicize the Phrases That Would Outlive Him

Cocaine is a hell of a drug!

—Rick James on *Chappelle's Show*

Charlie Murphy was right. The skits not only reenergized Rick, they inspired him to launch a campaign to make the phrases the show had introduced to the public even more popular.

He took the opportunity to market his "Cocaine is a hell of a drug" phase on June 1, 2004, when the American Society of Composers, Authors and Publishers (ASCAP) honored him with its Rhythm & Soul Heritage Award at that organization's Seventeenth Annual Rhythm & Soul Music Awards. The ceremony was held at the Beverly Hilton Hotel in Beverly Hills, with Motown Record Corporation founder Berry Gordy presenting the prize to Rick.

During his acceptance speech, Rick, despite his earlier angry shout-outs at Gordy, spoke gratefully about the former Motown president as a "mentor and father figure who said, 'Give the kid a shot. I believe in him.'"

When Gordy handed him the glass statuette, Rick looked pensive and then remarked, "Years ago, I would have used this for something totally different," meaning that he would have sniffed cocaine off its smooth glass surface. He then added, to audience laughter and applause, "Cocaine is a hell of a drug."

Later that month, he took the opportunity to publicize another of his phrases at the televised Black Entertainment Television (BET) Awards ceremony, which was held on June 29 at Los Angeles's Kodak Theater on Hollywood Boulevard.

This appearance would have been merely a footnote in Rick's life had Rick not pretended to have had an argument backstage with a female BET staffer who allegedly didn't recognize him and tried to stop him from going onstage. He had argued with Teena Marie the night before and perhaps that argument had given him the idea for his next move. When he appeared onstage, he appeared to be sputtering with anger and yelled out, "For the girl backstage, let me make it publicly clear, never mind who you thought I was, I'm Rick James, bitch."

The audience laughed and clapped, many of them and the show's 5.6 million television viewers being fans of *Chappelle's Show*. But his use of the phrase at the BET ceremony, on a noncomedy show, also resonated badly with many others because of Rick's sex-soaked songs, the sex-torture charges that had been brought against him, and his prison sentence for imprisoning and assaulting a woman. Even people who didn't know much about Rick had never heard anything like this semi-profane outburst during a televised award show.

For millions of people today, this phrase is all they know about Rick James, and, in fact, it may have captured a large part of Rick's underlying personality. His daughter Ty told a TV interviewer the phrase summed up what he wanted everyone to know about him before he died: "That's me," she said he told her, and he was partly right. Born into a shaky family structure in a shaky environment, he had spent his entire life fighting, stealing, lying, and creating in order to make it to the top, and no one was going to prevent him from crowing about his success.

Rick continued to build his musical legacy. The same month as the BET Awards, he recorded a cameo appearance on a track produced by rapper Kanye West, and soon thereafter declared that funk was "alive and well. There's a resurgence. We're all older, but we're still here."

73

Deeper Still

Rick once said to me, "No one can start over and make
a brand-new start, but you can always start
right now and make a brand-new ending."

—Actor Darius McCrary

Rick's last major act in life was to record the remarkable album *Deeper Still*. Its contents clearly show that he was seeking musical change. He recorded the album in 2004, the year he died, but it wasn't released until 2007.

The press release announcing the album took "the old Rick is back" approach, saying that "Just when you thought the dance floors were safe comes a tidal wave of funk from the super freak himself." Reviewers unanimously disagreed with this analysis, saying Rick had graduated from his past and produced a work of high achievement.

Various reviewers said *Deeper Still* was so different from Rick's previous albums that it could be called his White Album, a reference to the album officially titled *The Beatles* (referred to as the "White Album" because of its otherwise blank white sleeve). The Fab Four had prepared themselves to record that 1968 album by immersing themselves in a Transcendental Meditation course in India. The *New York Times* reviewer thought Rick's songs on *Deeper Still* were so similar to those on the White Album that he said Rick "was also a hippie," and *Billboard* commented that Rick seemed to be "channeling an introspective muse."

The White Album had been a double album, and likewise Rick originally wanted to record an album that would have contained many more of the songs he had written in prison than it eventually did. When *Deeper Still* was released, however, it was a single CD containing eleven tunes.

It's easy to imagine what a Rick intent on his usual filthy vibe would have done with this album's title song earlier in his life. However, only one of the eleven songs on the album, "Funk Wit Me," qualifies as Rick's old-style semiporn, although "Do You Wanna Play" rises only somewhat above that level. In spite of their suspicious titles, the songs "Taste," "Stroke," "Stop It," and "Deeper Still" are porn free, as are the remaining songs on the album. Such restraint by Rick, coupled with his unusual inclusion of the song "Guinnevere," which he didn't write and is the tale of a woman who wanted to be set free, signals that *Deeper Still* contained his final thoughts about his life, plus his death wish set to music. The album's title song includes lyrics such as "My soul is satisfied, Because I'm with you / And you I won't deny or ever quit you," Rick appeared to be promising to be a faithful, loyal, and loving person, a much different person than he'd been toward anyone but some of his blood relatives for most of his life. The *Buffalo News* said Rick was "pledging *fidelity* and vowing to start his life over."

Sexy Spanish-language vocals by singer Ivonne Contreras graced this song, but *Billboard* opined that "nothing about the song is street-wise or gritty in the least, which is unfortunate since being street-wise and gritty was what had made Rick a star." But it wasn't what Rick was trying to be on this album. *Billboard* dubbed "Guinnevere" a "soulfully intriguing" take on David Crosby's 1969 folk song of the same name, which was popularized by Crosby, Stills and Nash. The *New York Times* said Rick had "altered the hippie solemnity of the song, grounding it in an exaggerated but quite beautiful lothario croon," fleshing out Guinnevere, and making her seem "more like someone you don't bring home to mother," an obvious reference to "Super Freak." The *Times*'s comment seemed off base, however, because in this album, Rick seemed to be ignoring his previous hits.

Billboard called the bouncy, autobiographical "Taste" a candid reflection on Rick's sex, drug, and legal problems. The *Buffalo News* liked it for its "velvety sensuality" and the "relaxed jubilation of its melody." "Taste" is part of Rick's effort to produce his autobiography in song, but it's far from complete. Although he tells people not to ask him questions about his life because it's all in his songs, none of the songs, including this one, mention his betrayals of others for the sake of money, dope, or fame.

On the other hand, he hints at them early on in this song, when he refers to himself as "born a beast set out to feast at an early age," reminding some religious listeners of the two beasts described in the biblical Book of Revelation. He also denies once again all the abuse and related charges that eventually sent him to Folsom. And he ends the song with a stunning cosmic bang by singing an only slightly altered version of the words that by the time this song was released were already engraved on his tombstone: "Had it all baby . . . done it all . . . seen it all. I still see, it's all about love, and God is love baby."

The "stroke" Rick refers to in "Stroke" could be his actual 1998 stroke or his prison sentence. The song's an upper, though. Rick says mildly he's not mad about the bad things that happened to him, discloses he plans to go back to singing and songwriting, and admits he's lived his life "on shaky ground." By the end of the song he also appears to be using "stroke" to mean the beat of the music, as in "Get on up . . . on the stroke" but that phrase could also mean "keep going even while bad things are happening to you." *Billboard* seemed to agree when it opined that "Stroke" was a song about Rick's self-realization after two years behind bars and showed that he was determined to mount yet another comeback.

Rick reverts to form, however, in "Do You Wanna Play," a treacly love song that includes such lines as "Girl, you're sweeter than a lollipop / just as sweet on the bottom as you are on the top" and "I wanna be the only man that you come for" as well as "the easier I do it girl the more you blow." On "Funk Wit Me," which bears no resemblance to Rick's earlier tune "Dance Wit' Me," an unidentified but sexy female voice accompanies Rick as he makes it totally clear that "funk me" has joined "freak me" as a synonym for "fuck me." *Billboard* noted that Rick displayed what the magazine called his "signature carnal/romantic side" on both these songs.

In the song "Maybe," in an amazing reversal, Rick, the conquering sex hero, becomes in song and in his real life (Tanya had left him), the forsaken lover pleading with the love of his life to return. "When did your heart turn to stone . . . why is your silence so loud . . . Maybe we could still be friends," he sings.

On the front cover of *Deeper Still*, a somber, overweight, and discouraged-looking Rick leans against a wall and wears dark glasses, a black jacket, and a white shirt heavily darkened by thick black stripes. On the back cover he is wearing a black shirt with white dots, and black pants. With his head down and his hands hanging at his sides, he walks in profile toward an open door through which bright light is streaming.

Either Rick's voice improved near the end of his life, reviewers had come to appreciate it more, or his death three years before the album was released made them giddy with grief, because *Billboard* called him a "rich-voiced singer." The *Buffalo News* commended the "undiminished resonance" of Rick's voice, calling it "thick, rich, emotive and marked by a grandiose vibrato," and claimed that it "rescued" at least three of the tunes on the CD. No such praise had ever been applied to Rick's previous vocal efforts.

Deeper Still rose to number 19 on the *Billboard* R&B album chart, becoming Rick's highest-charting album on the R&B list since *Wonderful* went to number 12 in 1988. This success was doubly surprising because Rick wasn't alive to promote the product. With *Deeper Still*, Rick's creations had been appearing on the R&B chart for more than twenty-nine years.

In early 2004, after *Deeper Still* was completed, Rick joined Teena Marie in a duet titled "I Got You" on Teena's album *La Doña*. In it, Rick and Teena go over the story of their romance and breakup and pledge their eternal love for each other. With its jazz overtones and interlocking rhythms, it's the most musically complex, and most moving, tune this fiery duo ever recorded.

74

Rick Dies Alone with Drugs in His Veins

After all is said and done, I did all right and had my fun.

—"Before They Make Me Run," Rolling Stones,
written by Keith Richards (1978)

Rick was back on drugs before his death. He'd been in and out of rehab several times but had never really abandoned the source of most of his evils. One of the reasons Tanya gave for leaving him in 1999 was that when she'd go out of the house to buy food, she'd occasionally return home only to find him in the bathroom smoking crack with one of her friends.

The *New York Daily News* reported that an unnamed person walked into an upstairs room at an after-hours club on Valentine's Day in Los Angeles in 2003 and found Rick "with a mound of coke in front of him." The singer "was wearing a bright red suit," the *Daily News* story said. "He pointed to his mound of drugs and said 'Dig in, partner.'"

In mid-2004, Rick's voice sounded greatly damaged when he called Levi Ruffin to arrange for the Stone City Band to begin fall rehearsals for another tour Rick had in the works. "His voice was gone," Ruffin says. "I said, 'Rick, what's wrong with your voice, man?' He said, 'I'm OK,'" Ruffin says, imitating a very raspy voice. "That was the pipe burning his throat. I knew he was smoking that shit again."

It was the same pattern he always followed. He'd stopped several times during his life and had entered rehab programs on several occasions. Each time he left rehab he would exalt the benefits of the drug-free life and forbid those around him to use drugs or alcohol. But then, each and every time, after a shorter or longer interval, he had returned to the drugs.

In the early morning hours of August 6, 2004, Rick James, a man who liked to party endlessly with hundreds of people and who gloried in seemingly endless sexual activity, died alone in his sleep at home—not of a drug overdose but of a heart attack that the nine drugs in his system had helped bring on. He was fifty-six. Rick's apartment in the Hollywood Hills neighborhood was bordered by Dark Canyon Drive and near Forest Lawn Cemetery. Adding to the symbolism, another former Motown superstar, Mary Wells, had rented an apartment in the same complex shortly before her death in 1992.

It was too bad that none of his relatives, friends, or lovers were there, because many of them had learned how to resuscitate him. "I had to revive him myself many times," his brother LeRoi Johnson says. "And I was always afraid of the phone call that no one was there to revive him. I think that happened when he died." Even if they couldn't have resuscitated him from a heart attack, someone could have called for help that might have saved him.

Rick may have had a final female guest in his room earlier that night, however. Ruffin says the woman, who owned a San Jose flower shop, told him she and some others were getting high at Rick's apartment and she was the last one there. "We had been partying all night," Ruffin says she told him. "I was the last one to see him alive and he was getting high. We finished up, and I went home and they found him dead" the next morning.

When the woman told this story, "I wanted to strangle her," Ruffin says. "She was acting like that was her claim to fucking fame."

Rick's housekeeper discovered Rick's body the next morning and notified police. A spokeswoman for the Los Angeles Police Department said officers responding to a radio call about a natural death found Rick's body at about 9:45 AM on August 6. Rick had a habit of using LeRoi's ID throughout his life when he was arrested or otherwise in trouble, and he was carrying it when he died. As a result, the initial Los Angeles coroner's department investigative narrative, case report, autopsy check sheet, and medical report on Rick's death identified Rick as LeRoi Johnson before Johnson was able to convince the appropriate officials they were mistaken. This was "typical Rick, using me as a scapegoat," Johnson says. Rick's three children announced through a publicist that they believed Rick had died of heart failure. There were no signs of foul play.

But because Rick had "a history of chronic stimulant abuse," according to the Los Angeles County coroner, that official ordered that Rick's body be removed from the mortuary to which it had been taken so that an autopsy and toxicological exam could be performed. These tests showed that Rick's children were correct: he had died from a heart attack that killed him within minutes. However, the "effects of multiple drugs," along with focal pneumonia, a localized form of that disease, were listed on his death certificate as "significant conditions contributing" to his death, and "intake of drugs" was listed as the "event which resulted" in the heart problems that killed him.

The drugs in Rick's system were cocaine and methamphetamine, the antianxiety medications Valium and Xanax, the antidepressants Wellbutrin and Celexa, the painkiller Vicodin, the heart drug Digoxin, and the antihistamine Chlorpheniramine. None of them were found to be at levels that were life-threatening in and of themselves.

75

Reactions Run the Gamut

When I die, they'll probably speak well of me.

—Rick James, 1983

Ruffin says his brother called him to tell him that Rick had died and that the conversation "was like two girls crying. It was horrible. He was gone." Interviewed nine years after Rick's death, Ruffin said he still misses his lifelong friend and wishes people would separate Rick's creative life from his drug life. "He was just a fun-loving happy dude who worked his ass off and because nobody gave him shit, he worked hard to get where he was," Ruffin said. "But all they talk about is him getting fucked up [on drugs]."

Ruffin added, "I want everyone to understand, from the depths of my heart and soul, that Rick was a beautiful brother. The drugs got him. . . . But when we didn't have shit and when we first hit, he was the most beautiful thing, the most happy thing you could see in this life." Teena Marie told an interviewer it was "very, very hard" to live with Rick gone. After he died, she stopped working for six months, although her career had been on the rise. Her next album, *Sapphire*, was titled after an unreleased song by Rick and featured "You Blow Me Away," a duet she'd recorded with him. She died six years later.

McDuffie Funderburg called Rick "one of the few interesting people in my life." Robby Takac of the Goo Goo Dolls put his finger on one reason why that was so: Rick "amplified his sounds with a public and private personality that was always larger than life," Takac said. Many singers strive for this, but Rick seemed to do it naturally.

In statements after Rick's death, Berry Gordy called him "a pioneer who took Motown in a whole new direction," and Smokey Robinson honored him as "the original R&B rock star."

Not all responses to Rick's death were as serious or as sympathetic. Shortly after he died, the *New York Daily News* reported that some of Rick's buddies gave him a send-off at a Los Angeles nightclub by ceremoniously blowing marijuana and cocaine smoke at his smiling portrait on the wall.

On one occasion, Rick described himself as "somebody who just stood up for what he believed in, somebody who was down for his race, who wrote some funky songs and made people dance, and who was a pretty good fucking producer." Two years before his death, when asked how he'd like to be remembered, Rick said, "As someone who beat the odds," a defiantly true and profoundly succinct summary of his life and career.

This statement, of course, ignored the crimes Rick had committed and served time for. Artists, however, are often outlaws. While it may seem sacrilegious to lovers of literature to put Rick James in a class with two of his contemporaries, writers Norman Mailer and William Burroughs, all three of these creative personalities were convicted criminals. Those who protest that Rick committed violent acts against women should remember that Mailer, author of *The Naked and the Dead*, stabbed one of his wives in the chest, barely missing her heart, and Burroughs, a drug addict and the author of *Naked Lunch*, killed one of his wives by shooting her in the head. All three fought society's ban on illegal or outrageous conduct not only with their creative works but with their most outrageous weapon, their own flamboyant misbehavior.

All were needed not only for what they created, but so people could see what happened to those who broke society's law and rules. They also were needed so that a surprisingly large number of people could express the rage and frustration they feel at the inhibitions imposed by those same rules, and allow them to imagine doing the forbidden themselves.

76

Two Funerals

Blessed is the man or woman who finds his or her purpose for being.

—Minister Louis Farrakhan

On the evening of August 11, 2004, more than twelve hundred fans attended a public viewing of Rick's body at the mortuary at Forest Lawn Memorial Park in Los Angeles. The next day, at the Hall of Liberty at Forest Lawn, Bishop Noel Jones presided over a public funeral service attended by about the same number of Rick's friends and fans. Bishop Jones was the brother of Grace Jones, who had once joined Rick in his fight against MTV's discriminatory policies.

Rick's sister Camille talked about what drugs had done to Rick. Teena Marie compared herself and Rick to Tammi Terrell and Marvin Gaye. Jan Gaye also spoke, as did actors Darius McCrary, Jamie Foxx, and others. Minister Louis Farrakhan, who had counseled Rick in an effort to keep him off drugs, delivered a speech telling the crowd that pain is the mother of creativity. Yvette "Corvette" Barlowe, formerly Yvette "Corvette" Marine of the Mary Jane Girls—described by one viewer as "scantily clad"—said a few words. Other Mary Jane Girls were in the audience. Rick's daughter, Ty, and his two sons, Rick Jr. and Tazman, also spoke at the service. Stevie Wonder sang "I've Had Some Good Days" and gospel singer Eric Dawkins sang as well, as did

Ali-Ollie Woodson, a former lead singer of the Temptations. Other attendees included Marvin Gaye's daughter Nona Gaye, Berry Gordy, Smokey Robinson, former Motown executive Suzanne de Passe, and singer Jermaine Jackson.

In a tribute of sorts to Rick, to "Mary Jane," one of his most popular songs, and to the marijuana he spent much of his life smoking, someone lit a huge joint that was sitting on one of the speakers onstage. The smoke drifted into the audience. Many of the mourners inhaled. In his coffin, Rick wore his hair in braids and was dressed in a black suit with big black lapels and shiny buttons on the jacket. Two gold pendants hung around his neck and several bracelets covered his left wrist. Charlie Murphy was one of the six pallbearers.

Two days later, a second funeral service for the singer was held in Buffalo. There, six thousand waited for hours to pay their final respects to him as he lay in an open casket in St. John the Baptist Church. The funeral program for the Buffalo service was illustrated with a photo of Rick from his Canada days, wearing his bolero hat and fancy boots but looking somber. Bishop William Henderson officiated at the funeral service, with music provided by seventy gospel singers. In a bow to Rick's Catholic upbringing, Rev. Vincent Cooke, a Jesuit and president of Canisius College, represented the Catholic Church at the funeral.

Rick's pallbearers included Ruffin; his other former Stone City bandmates Oscar Alston, Nate Hughes, and Lanise Hughes; Rick's protégé Mike Militello; Charlie Murphy; Joe Jackson; Zellie Dow; and Aaron Dublin. Former congressman Louis Stokes, Rick's cousin, called Rick "our family's first superstar," and said "he took us all with him on a roller-coaster ride." Rick's body was cremated after the service and his ashes buried in Forest Lawn Cemetery in Buffalo.

That evening, local musicians performed a free tribute concert in Rick's honor at Buffalo's Martin Luther King Jr. Park, saying they hoped it would become an annual event. Known as the Rick James Memorial Funk Fest, it's still being held annually.

Two years after Rick's death, a black granite monument was erected over his grave in Forest Lawn Cemetery in Buffalo. Etched on the stone is a picture of Rick in his thirties wearing a jacket and tight leather pants and carrying a guitar. It's based on the cover of his wildly successful album *Street Songs*.

The two-ton monument is the largest size allowed by the cemetery on a four-plot site. Engraved on it are the words:

> I've had it all
> I've done it all
> I've seen it all
> It's all about love . . .
> God is love.

His daughter, Ty, chose the words and the picture for the monument. The words were taken, with only slight editing, from the final line of Rick's autobiographical song "Taste." Rick's mother is buried in another part of the same cemetery.

77

Rick's Legacy

His legacy continues to inspire new generations of artists
to get their super freak on.

—*Kickin'* CD insert, 2014

Rick left behind the relatively small sum of approximately
$210,000, according to court documents filed the year he died. He
also left an impressive and ongoing musical legacy, combining the funk
of George Clinton, the sound of R&B, and his own bold lyrics into a
unique sound of his own. The number of albums and songs he created,
plus the number of vocalists and groups he sang with, produced, men-
tored, and influenced is overwhelming. The *Philadelphia Inquirer* is not
alone in stating flatly that Rick has influenced virtually everyone doing
R&B and hip-hop today. He is also one of the most sampled musicians
in the history of American popular music.

Rick's influence was obvious even during his lifetime. He claimed
he heard portions of his work utilized in forty songs recorded by others.
MC Hammer's sampling of the bass line from "Super Freak" was the
most obvious example, but Hammer also utilized portions of "Give It
to Me Baby" on his album *Let's Get It Started*. The B-Fats sampled portions of "You and I" in their underground hit "Woppit," and LL Cool J,

Ashanti, the Fresh Prince, and numerous others have cherry-picked and sampled portions of Rick's songs.

Mary J. Blige sampled Rick, among others, on *My Life*, which became 1995's most successful R&B album. Salt-N-Pepa, whose name inadvertently echoed that of one of Rick's early groups, took parts of some of his tunes for their album *Brand New*. The Lo Fidelity Allstars sampled Rick in 1999, as did Jay-Z on his song "I Just Wanna Love U" in 2000. Among the many other artists to sample him were Jennifer Lopez, Busta Rhymes, Dr. Dre, Kriss Kross, EPMD, DJ Jazzy Jeff, Mya, DJ Quik, Keith Murray, and Afrika Bambaataa.

Some musicians just recycled his songs. Shaquille O'Neal lip-synched to "Fire and Desire." And Ol' Dirty Bastard rerecorded "Cold Blooded," although his version of this tune was denounced as "agonized, painfully off-key and misbegotten."

On their album *The Hard Way*, 213 (Snoop Dogg, Warren G, and Nate Dogg) sang "Mary Jane" and a song called "Groupie Luv" in an apparent tribute to Rick. Snoop, on his own, proclaimed himself "the modern day Rick James" on his tune "Pass It Pass It."

Even the groups Rick created begat successor groups, with the Mary Jane Girls inspiring, among others, the Pussycat Dolls and the Spice Girls.

Part of Rick's legacy was the staying power of his song "Super Freak." Although one *Washington Post* writer called it "a paean of praise to a nymphomaniac backstage groupie who is waiting to ingest cocaine and engage in freaky group and oral sex with the singer and his friends," he also noted that grandmothers and great aunts are still dancing to this song at wedding receptions.

What used to be called moral standards have been lowered considerably in the past thirty years, which may account partly for the vast popular acceptance of "Super Freak." But the *Washington Post* speculated that the song's extended popularity is due more to the fact that the music, lyrics, and performance have worked so exquisitely well together that they've burned the song into the global pop consciousness, leaving its naughty intention behind and becoming something else, something permanent. As the *Post* opined, "If you leave this world remembered for one pop song, then you've left it in grand enough style."

Many musicians have gone so far as to record their own memorials to the song "Super Freak" or to the Super Freak himself. On Robyn's self-titled 2005 album, she put Rick and herself in lofty company with the line "She sucker-punched Einstein, outsmarted Ali, and even out-super-freaked Rick James." Then there's the 1998 song "Rick James" by Jude, which starts out with an oral sex scene and includes the oft-repeated line, "Rick James was the original Super Freak." French Stewart, the costar of *3rd Rock from the Sun*, sang the song "Evil Dick" to the tune of "Super Freak."

The power of the "Super Freak" song was such that, like a stone thrown into still waters, it kept expanding the definition of "freak" and "super freak" even while Rick was still alive. And after Rick's death, the term jumped into the literary world.

When Steven D. Levitt and Steven J. Dubner published their bestselling book on rogue economics in 2005, they didn't call it *Rogue Economics*, they called it *Freakonomics*. And when they published their follow-up book in 2009, they titled it *SuperFreakonomics*. Asked by an interviewer if using that title was in any way a homage to Rick, they replied, "The title may show bad taste—on any number of levels—but we just couldn't help ourselves." The *Toronto Globe and Mail* referred to the two authors as "Rick James–riffin' super freaks."

Other book reviewers pointed out that the relationship went deeper still than the title. For instance, when Levitt and Dubner were asked if their book was one "you don't take home to mother," a reference to a line in "Super Freak," they responded, "As for Mom: If she's easily offended, you might ask her to skip Chapter 1." In that chapter, titled "How Is a Street Prostitute like a Department-Store Santa," they argue in part that high-end call girls earn great money and are often treated better than wives. As economists, but surely not as moralists, they then go on to recommend this lifestyle to women who like sex and dislike marriage. Rick would certainly have agreed.

He would also have agreed with the authors' assertion that driving home drunk is many times safer than walking home drunk. If fact, there's nothing in any of Levitt and Dubner's books that Rick would not instantly have agreed with, which, aside from their similar titles, could be why their book and his song will be linked for decades in the public mind.

And Rick had his own literary legacy as well. While in jail he wrote an autobiography titled *The Confessions of Rick James: Memoirs of a Super Freak*. Published in 2007, three years after Rick's death, it ends with his marriage to Tanya in 1997. Noted music author David Ritz, after interviewing Rick on several occasions, rewrote the book as *Glow* in cooperation with Rick's estate. In that 2014 book, writing mostly as Rick, Ritz added material to the narrative, including a discussion of Rick's 1997 album *Urban Rapsody*.

Another part of Rick's musical legacy was the use made of his songs in commercials: "Give It to Me Baby," for instance, was the soundtrack for a Burger King commercial in the late 1990s. And then there's the use of Rick's tunes in church. Yes, you read that right. In 2015, as the drive to legalize marijuana in the US gained momentum, the *New York Times* reported that the First Church of Cannabis had been organized in Indianapolis. According to the paper, the first hymn performed at the church's first service was "Mary Jane." Shocked parishioners at other churches should remember that one of the lines in the song asserts that marijuana "takes you to Paradise."

Even Rick's unreleased tunes are still considered valuable. Sources say that still in the vaults of one record company or another are at least two rock 'n' roll albums by Rick, another unreleased collection called *McBooty's Bump and Grind Revue*, and other musical material.

But all this is nothing compared to the inspiration Rick provided to present-day pop musicians of all stripes and likely will provide to musicians of the future. Most obviously, he inspired numerous people to write songs about his and their struggle with drugs. Many musicians, inspired both by Rick's alleged crimes against women and by *Chappelle's Show*, have written about Rick as a bitch-slap artist. In her song "Rick

James," Keyshia Cole uses the line "Slap the bitch, I'm Rick James." Common's remix of Jadakiss's song "Why" progresses beyond this to ask the interesting question, "Why ain't Rick James remembered for classic hits? / Why do we remember Rick for smackin' a bitch?"

Rick's "I'm Rick James, bitch" statement was referenced in many songs, including Frank Ocean's tune "Bitch I Think I'm Tom Petty" and Madonna's 2014 song "Bitch I'm Madonna" (featuring Nicki Minaj). On the album *Be* by Common, the song "Chi-City" includes the line "What you rappin' for? To get fame? To get rich? I slap a nigga like you, and tell 'em 'Rick James, bitch.'"

Other musicians were inspired by Rick's productivity and musical drive. McDuffie Funderberg of the Mary Jane Girls hit it right on the head when she said the very first thing she would ask Rick if he returned from the grave would be, "What's the next song going to be?"

Rick's pornographic themes and lyrics also have remained influential. Missy Elliott certainly imitated Rick when she named two of her own tunes "One Shot Man" and "Lick Shots." She underlined her musical debt to him when she told one interviewer in 2002 that because records that year were "all about paying bills and relationships . . . we decided to take the sound and the lyrics back to the sexy side, back to the 1980s, when you had records from Rick James."

Beck, in his songs "Sexx Laws" and "Nicotine & Gravy," was also said to evoke the "sex beat of Rick James." The song "Get Up" by 50 Cent includes the line "Rick James would have said she a brick house / Or 50 should go home and see what that bitch 'bout," thus also invoking the title of a song by Rick's fellow Motown superstar Lionel Richie and his fellow Commodores.

Rick's pornographic influence has spread well beyond North America. A *Washington Post* foreign correspondent reported that at Brazil's funk parties, "a frenzied crowd of thousands grind to a female funk singer moaning a song that would make Rick James blush." Rick has also influenced British vocalists Teish O'Day and Omar and many other singers in other countries.

Although Rick himself appeared in only one movie, his look and the attitudes he struck have influenced numerous screenwriters and actors. Characters obviously meant to be him, or resemble him, began popping up in movies before his death and continue to do so. For instance, Eddie Murphy in the movie *Vampire in Brooklyn* dresses like Rick and occasionally wears a Rick James wig. Or, as the *Toronto Star* put it, Murphy "turns into Rick James" in this film.

Even Rick's style of dress has inspired others. A New Zealand newspaper, the *Christchurch Press*, while reviewing a Busta Rhymes performance, noted that Rhymes's outfit included a broad-brimmed bolero hat with little red pom-poms, and wrote, "Rick James, we have located your old outfit."

Rick's hedonistic lifestyle is also still in the news. A bulldog named Rick James won the Instagram contest sponsored by the *Vancouver Courier* in March 2015. According to the newspaper, "just like his namesake, Rick-the-bulldog's life has been a non-stop party of excess and fame and was at the center of a messy love triangle with Hope and Camilla, two neighborhood bitches that love his confident swagger." The paper also noted that Rick finds it hard to leave the house without bumping into his female fans.

Even Rick's criminal career, appropriately intertwined with his musical career, is being imitated. Two men robbed the Indiana Members Credit Union in Indianapolis in September 2015, each of them disguised as different versions of Rick, one of them wearing long hair and the other wearing beaded braids. A *USA Today* network newscaster couldn't resist asking on air if one of the Ricks demanded the money with the phrase "Give It to Me Baby." She also suggested the other Rick was attempting to adopt the flower-power look that the real Rick adopted on the cover of his *Wonderful* album, showing her in-depth knowledge of the real Rick's musical career.

In what may be the ultimate tribute, in October 2015, when Miley Cyrus played the role of Miley Cyrustein at a spoof/charity Bar Mitzvah for actor James Franco, she sang "Super Freak" while wearing a thong leotard. Rick would definitely have approved.

In the future, Rick may live on in different ways. Jeff Jampol, who manages Rick's estate, told an interviewer in 2012 that he was exploring the development of a Rick James hologram, a 3-D character that could walk right up to a viewer, look him in the eye, sing right at him, and then turn around and walk away. Working with Jampol is the organization that developed the Tupac Shakur hologram seen at California's Coachella Valley Music and Arts Festival in 2012, some fifteen years after Shakur's death. Various observers at different levels of sobriety were shocked and amazed by Shakur's lifelike reappearance and his interactions with other performers.

Rick inspired and entertained millions of people, dramatically influenced the lives of his Stone City Band members and his other protégés for the better even while cheating some of them, and definitely hurt a few individuals along the way. The epitaph on Rick's grave doesn't really sound like him. A better epitaph would have quoted a 1979 interview in which he talked about the people who wished they could change places with him, and how they always talked about "the money, the women and the fast cars." He told the interviewer, "I wish they could all have it for one day and see what it really means."

Asked if he'd trade everything he'd ever achieved for some happiness, he responded, "Immediately!! Immediately!! To be content and to wake up happy—that has to be a magical experience."

Sources

Interviews

Rick Abel, Nick Balkou, John Bracken, Dan R. Bruggeman, Dave Burt, Jim Bush, Michael Carr, Bob Doughty, William G. Downey, Stan Endersby, William Gersten, Richard Grand, Les Greenbaum, Camille Hudson, Joe Jackson, Andre Jardine, LeRoi Johnson, Peter Kelly, Daniel LeMelle, Pat Little, Rick Mason, Joanne McDuffie Funderburg, Peter McGraw, Neil Merryweather, Kelly Misener, Syville Morgan, Tony Nolasco, Billy Nunn, Dick Romer, Ed Roth, Levi Ruffin, Mike Rummans, Chris Sarns, George Semkiw, Robert Sheahen, Chuck Stokes, Lori Stokes, Louis Stokes, Shelley Stokes-Hammond, Malcolm Tomlinson, Nick Warburton, Artie Wayne, Harry Weinger, Stanley Weisman, and Richard Wesley.

NEWSPAPERS

Aberdeen American News, 09/21/98, 11/11/98

Amsterdam News, 08/12/04, 08/10/06

Atlantic City Press, 10/26/97

Atlanta Journal-Constitution, 10/31/97, 08/09/04

Austin American-Statesman, 05/18/89

Baton Rouge Morning Advocate, 11/07/83

Bergen Co. (NJ) Record, 04/08/89, 05/18/89

Birmingham (U.K.) Evening Mail, 12/05/00

Boston Globe, 08/30/88, 11/23/90, 10/15/93

Boston Herald, 04/24/83, 06/27/88, 07/22/88, 7/29/88, 08/26/88, 08/23/96

Buffalo News, 10/22/83, 08/20/86, 05/22/90, 05/24/90, 05/25/90, 05/28/90, 06/01/90, 06/26/90, 10/15/90, 11/23/90, 09/22/91, 10/13/91, 07/19/92, 10/10/93, 02/01/94, 05/03/94, 05/21/94, 06/10/94, 06/24/94, 12/12/94, 12/15/94,12/20/94, 06/21/96, 08/22/96, 08/23/96, 08/24/96, 09/15/96, 11/03/96, 01/09/97, 12/05/97, 12/06/97, 01/25/98, 10/27/98, 11/12/98, 11/14/98, 11/22/98, 12/20/98, 10/19/01, 07/02/03, 08/07/04, 08/14/04, 08/15/04, 08/16/04, 08/20/04, 10/24/04, 04/29/05, 05/20/07, 07/10/13

Charlotte Observer, 12/29/86, 07/22/88

Chicago Metro News, 07/11/81, 10/27/84, 10/26/85, 10/18/86, 10/10/87

Chicago Tribune, 08/07/04

Christchurch (NZ) Press, 09/25/98

Cleveland Plain Dealer, 08/15/83, 07/08/88

Colorado Springs Gazette Telegraph, 08/08/89

Columbus (OH) Dispatch, 08/19/13

Daily Variety, 05/23/94

Dallas Morning News, 06/10/79, 08/14/82, 10/22/83, 07/10/88

Dayton Daily News, 09/03/95

Fresno Bee, 03/30/90

Greensboro Daily News, 08/15/81

Greensboro Daily News & Record, 08/01/83

Guardian, 03/22/96, 12/28/98, 08/09/04, 02/10/06, 07/07/07

Hamilton (Ont.) Spectator, 08/07/04

London Daily Telegraph, 08/09/04

London Sunday Times, 08/11/85

London Times, 08/09/04

Los Angeles Daily News, 08/24/93, 09/18/93, 10/09/93, 12/29/95, 08/27/96

Los Angeles Times, 02/25/79, 04/22/79,12/23/79, 11/19/80, 07/05/81, 08/01/81, 08/13/81, 06/20/82, 08/14/82, 08/23/82, 09/28/82, 02/06/83, 02/13/83, 05/15/83, 08/07/83, 08/22/83, 10/16/83, 05/12/85, 06/18/85, 10/20/85, 05/11/86, 07/20/86, 12/13/86, 01/04/87, 02/14/88, 08/20/88, 09/11/88, 12/31/88, 09/17/89, 11/21/90, 02/17/91,

07/21/91, 08/07/91, 08/10/91, 08/22/91, 08/25/91, 08/26/91, 09/12/91, 09/13/91, 09/15/91, 12/12/92, 12/16/92, 12/25/92, 12/26/92, 05/01/93, 08/03/93, 08/07/93, 08/12/93, 08/20/93, 08/22/93, 08/24/93, 08/25/93, 08/28/93, 09/05/93, 09/09/93, 09/14/93, 09/18/93, 09/22/93, 10/08/93, 10/09/93, 01/08/94, 01/15/94, 01/22/94, 02/05/94, 02/10/94, 03/21/94, 05/04/94, 05/19/94, 07/19/94, 07/20/94, 12/10/94, 08/19/95, 03/03/96, 09/07/97, 09/27/97, 10/24/97, 04/11/02, 05/09/02, 08/07/04, 08/10/04, 09/17/04, 12/29/04, 04/13/05, 05/13/05, 12/26/10, 12/28/10, 10/13/11, 11/22/11

Miami Herald, 10/20/83

Michigan Chronicle, 03/08/80

Minneapolis Star Tribune, 08/07/04

Montreal Gazette, 06/02/05

National Post (Canada), 08/15/07

New Orleans Times-Picayune/The States-Item, 08/24/83

New York Daily News, 08/21/97, 11/06/97, 11/24/98, 04/16/99, 08/20/04, 05/13/05

New York Times, 04/21/79, 10/26/79, 09/06/81, 04/06/82, 09/16/83, 09/20/83, 04/30/84, 06/20/90, 08/05/90, 12/20/93, 01/08/94, 01/03/98, 01/06/98, 04/16/99, 08/07/04, 08/09/04, 09/18/04, 10/16/04, 12/26/04, 05/06/05, 06/03/07, 10/02/07, 08/30/14, 12/24/14, 07/02/15

Newsday, 09/12/83, 12/13/85, 08/07/04

Omaha World-Herald, 05/12/85

Orange County Register, 01/21/91, 09/24/97

Ottowa Citizen, 03/22/94

Philadelphia Inquirer, 12/02/83, 09/02/84, 03/09/85, 02/08/87, 06/03/90, 01/23/94,

10/26/97, 05/10/98, 09/06/03, 08/15/04, 05/03/13

Racine (WI) Courier, 07/08/78, 11/19/78

Richmond (VA) Times Dispatch, 07/25/83, 12/08/83

Rockford (IL) Register Star, 09/03/82

San Francisco Chronicle, 10/26/97, 08/07/04

St. Petersburg Times, 12/23/89, 11/28/90, 12/09/94, 11/11/98, 05/19/99, 08/07/99 09/19/99, 10/08/93, 08/09/04, 09/17/04

Toronto Globe and Mail, 07/6/82, 09/17/83, 10/22/83, 06/06/85, 07/23/88, 05/28/94, 11/11/98, 04/16/99, 11/18/02, 10/30/04, 10/26/09

Toronto Star, 07/06/82, 07/23/88, 06/29/89, 08/10/91, 08/15/91, 05/31/92, 11/11/98, 10/26/00, 08/11/04, 12/10/05

Torrance (CA) Daily Breeze, 06/13/88

Trenton (NJ) Times, 08/12/83, 11/11/83,

USA Today, 10/14/88, 08/10/89, 02/21/90, 07/30/90, 10/16/90, 08/07/91, 08/08/91, 08/15/91, 09/13/91, 10/30/91, 05/07/92, 08/25/93, 10/12/93, 01/10/94, 07/20/94, 12/12/94, 02/14/95, 08/29/97, 09/03/97, 10/22/97, 11/24/98, 12/11/98, 12/15/98, 12/21/98, 04/16/99, 09/14/99, 06/18/02, 05/06/04, 08/09/04, 08/17/04, 03/13/07

Washington Post, 11/11/78, 06/22/81, 08/26/81, 10/05/81, 07/11/82, 08/16/82, 02/24/83, 03/18/83, 08/12/83, 10/23/83, 03/16/84, 11/19/85, 12/25/85, 11/20/88, 06/02/91, 08/03/91, 08/10/91, 09/16/91, 01/08/94, 04/09/95, 11/21/96, 10/29/97, 12/31/97, 01/05/98, 01/11/98, 12/02/98, 11/24/99, 10/24/03, 05/31/04, 08/07/04

Washington Times, 08/07/90, 07/29/00

Wire Service Reports

Associated Press, 10/01/78, 04/05/79, 10/27/82, 02/15/89, 09/14/91, 08/07/04

Magazines

Billboard, 03/05/66, 07/22/72, 01/20/78, 03/10/79, 04/28/79, 10/27/79, 12/06/81, 03/27/82, 05/29/82, 02/19/83, 02/25/83, 05/04/85, 12/28/85, 01/11/86, 02/22/86, 04/12/86, 09/02/86, 12/28/89, 10/11/97, 10/25/97, 04/14/98, 07/09/98, 07/16/98, 11/28/98, 04/08/00, 09/23/00, 10/25/03, 02/14/04, 05/22/04, 06/05/04, 07/10/04,

07/17/04, 08/21/04, 05/14/05, 05/13/06, 06/17/06, 12/16/06, 05/19/07, 07/11/09, 06/16/12

Blues & Soul, 09/78

BRE: Black Entertainment's Premier Magazine, 10/17/97

Congressional Record, 10/19/81

Creem, 09/81, 09/82, 08/85

Ebony, 01/84, 02/11

Jet, 07/26/79, 06/26/80, 08/07/80, 02/26/81, 08/27/81, 09/17/81, 10/01/81, 11/12/81, 11/19/81, 08/30/82, 02/14/83, 04/18/83, 07/25/83, 08/15/83, 02/20/84, 04/30/84, 05/07/84, 05/20/85, 06/17/85, 07/04/88, 08/28/89, 08/20/90, 09/17/90, 12/10/90, 09/02/91, 09/09/91, 08/08/94, 12/26/94, 09/09/96, 02/08/97, 02/23/98, 11/30/98, 01/11/99, 04/19/99, 09/13/99, 12/08/03, 08/30/04, 10/30/05

Musician, 11/01/83

New Musical Express, 04/10/82, 08/83, 04/14/84, 06/01/85

New Times, 09/25–10/01/98

Newsweek, 04/19/82, 04/18/83

Onion, 11/28/01, 05/09/02

Oui, 09/82

People, 04/06/98

Right On!, Summer 1982, 03/84

Rolling Stone, 04/14/83, 03/29/84, 03/08/02, 09/17/04

Security Management, 06/01/97

Soul, 10/80

Spin, 10/04

Touch of Classic Soul, 03/08

Variety, 05/08/98, 04/12/99, 09/05/02, 05/30/05

Vibe, 04/94, 11/95, 12/97–01/98, 06–07/00, 11/04, 05/06, 02/07

Online Sources

Langerston, Johnel. Rick James Funeral Video. www.youtube.com/watch?v=DD-Lm9HJQNM

Livingston, Scot, "The Mynah Birds," 05/2002, www.earcandymag.com/rrcase-5.htm.

Paste magazine, 07/2015, www.pastemagazine.com.

Warburton, Nick, "The Mynah Birds Story," 04/2004, updated 07/2005, www.earcandymag.com/rrcase-mynahbirds-part2.htm.

Warburton, Nick, "Rick James's Early Years," 01/08/13, www.nickwarburton.com/wordpress/?cat=7.

Warburton, Nick, "Rick James," 07/01/13, www.nickwarburton.com/wordpress/?cat=21.

Television Shows

Behind the Music: Rick James, VH1, Episode 304, 2013

Unsung: Rick James, TV One, 01/14/15

Liner Notes

I'm Rick James: The Definitive DVD, by Brian Chin, 2009

Court Documents

Motown Record Corporation, Plaintiff, v. Mary Jane Girls, Inc., Defendant, James A. Johnson, Jr., p/k/a/ Rick James et al. Plaintiffs, v. Motown Record Corporation, et al., Defendants. Nos. 86 Civ. 6814 (RWS), 87 Civ. 3438 (RWS), United States District Court for the Southern District of New York.

Gina Perry, Plaintiff, v. James Johnson a/k/a/ Rick James, Defendant, State of New York, Supreme Court, County of Erie, Index No. H-89839, Cal. No 89-569, Hon. Thomas McGowan. Judgment entered July 5, 1990.

The People of the State of California v. Rick James and Tanya Anne Hijazi, Superior Court of the State of California for the County of Los Angeles, 1991.

Mary E. Sauger v Rick James, et al, 08/17/93, Los Angeles Superior Court.

Dissolution of Marriage, 06/16/04, Petitioner James Ambrose Johnson, Respondent Tanya Johnson, Superior Court of California, County of Los Angeles.

Other Official Documents

Autopsy Report, James Johnson, No. 2004-05931, Department of Coroner, County of Los Angeles, 09/22/04

Bankruptcy, James Ambrose Johnson Jr., Case number 1:95-bk-11108-KT, United States Bankruptcy Court, Central District of California, 02/16/95

Certificate of Death, Rick James, State of California, County of Los Angeles, Registrar-Recorder/ County Clerk, State File number 3052004145927, 08/06/04

Will of James Ambrose Johnson Jr., Los Angeles Superior Court, 08/26/04

Press Releases

"Biography of Rick James," Motown Record Corporation, Undated

"'Super' Success Not 'Freaky' for Rick James," Lee Solters Company, Beverly Hills, CA, Undated

"Bio: The Long-Awaited, Much-Anticipated Return of Rick James," Lee Solters Company, Beverly Hills, CA, 10/14/97.

Books

Belfort, Jordan. *Catching the Wolf of Wall Street*. New York: Random House, 2009.

Benjaminson, Peter. *Mary Wells: The Tumultuous Life of Motown's First Superstar*. Chicago Review Press, 2012.

Benjaminson, Peter. *The Lost Supreme: The Life of Dreamgirl Florence Ballard*. Chicago Review Press/ Lawrence Hill Books, 2008.

Benjaminson, Peter. *The Story of Motown*. New York: Grove Press, 1979.

Betts, Graham. *Motown Encyclopedia*. CreateSpace Independent Publishing, 2014.

Bianco, David, *Heat Wave: The Motown Fact Book*. Ann Arbor, MI: Pierian Press, 1988.

Bronson, Fred. *The Billboard Book of number One Hits*, 4th ed. New York: Billboard Books, 1997.

Bronson, Fred. *Billboard's Hottest Hot 100 Hits*, 3rd ed. New York: Billboard Productions, 2003.

Brown, Ashley (ed.). *The Motown Story*. London: Orbis Publishing Ltd., 1985.

Bogdanov, Vladimir (ed.). *The All Music Guide to Soul: The Definitive Guide to R&B*. San Francisco, CA: Backbeat Books, 2003.

Dannen, Fredric, *Hit Men*. New York: Random House, 1990.

Danois, Ericka Blount, *Love, Peace, and Soul: Behind the Scenes of America's Favorite Dance Show Soul Train: Classic Moments,* Backbeat Books, 2013.

Davis, Sharon. *Motown: The History*. Enfield, Middlesex, UK: Guinness Books, 1988.

Denisoff, R. Serge. *Inside MTV.* New Brunswick, NJ: Transaction Publishers, 1988.

Des Barres, Pamela. *Rock Bottom: Dark Moments in Music Babylon*. New York: St. Martin's Press, 1996.

Dimery, Robert and Bruno MacDonald. *Rock & Roll Heaven,* London: Quintet Publishing Limited, 2007.

Einarson, John. *Neil Young, Don't Be Denied—The Canadian Years*. Kingston, Ontario, Quarry Press, 1992.

Evans, Mike. *Neil Young, the Definitive History*. New York, Sterling Publishing, 2012.

Fong-Torres, Ben. *The Motown Album*. New York: St. Martin's Press, 1990.

Gaye, Jan, with David Ritz. *After the Dance: My Life with Marvin Gaye*. New York: Amistad Books, 2015.

George, Nelson. *Where Did Our Love Go? The Rise and Fall of the Motown Sound.* New York: St. Martin's Press, 1985.

Gordy, Berry. *To Be Loved: The Music, the Magic, the Memories of Motown.* New York: Warner Books, 1994.

Green, Thomas H. *Rock Shrines.* East Sussex, UK: The Ilex Press, 2010.

James, Rick, with David Ritz. *Glow: The Autobiography of Rick James.* New York: Atria Books, 2014.

James, Rick. *The Confessions of Rick James: Memoirs of a Super Freak.* Phoenix: Colossus Books, 2007.

Kirby, David. *Crossroad: Artist, Audience, and the Making of American Music.* Milwaukee: New American Press, 2015.

McDonough, Jimmy. *Shakey: Neil Young's Biography.* New York, Anchor Books, 2003.

Murphy, Charlie, with Chris Millis. *The Making of a Stand-up Guy.* New York: Simon Spotlight Entertainment, 2009.

O'Neil, Thomas. *The Grammys: For the Record.* New York: Penguin Books, 1993.

Posner, Gerald. *Motown: Music, Sex, Money and Power.* New York: Random House, 2002.

Reeves, Martha, and Mark Bego. *Dancing in the Street: Confessions of a Motown Diva.* New York: Hyperion, 1994.

Sager, Mike. *Scary Monsters and Super Freaks: Stories of Sex, Drugs, Rock 'n' Roll and Murder.* Cambridge, MA: Da Capo Press, 2003.

Seay, Davin. *Super Freak: The Last Days of Rick James.* A Single Notes Book, 2012.

Singleton, Raynoma Gordy. *Berry, Me, and Motown: The Untold Story.* Chicago: Contemporary Books, 1990.

Smith, RJ. *The One: The Life and Music of James Brown.* New York: Gotham Books, 2012.

Talevski, Nick. *The Unofficial Encyclopedia of the Rock and Roll Hall of Fame.* Westport, CT: Greenwood Press, 1998.

Tyson, Mike. *The Undisputed Truth.* New York: Blue Rider Press, 2013.

Vincent, Ricky. *Funk: The Music, The People and the Rhythm of the One.* New York: St. Martin's Griffin, 1996.

Walker, Michael. *Laurel Canyon: The Inside Story of Rock and Roll's Legendary Neighborhood.* London: Faber & Faber, 2006.

Waller, Don. *The Motown Story.* New York: Charles Scribner's Sons, 1985.

Ward, Ed, Geoggrey Stokes, and Ken Tucker. *Rock of Ages: The Rolling Stone History of Rock & Roll.* New York: Simon & Schuster, 1986.

Warwick, Neil, Jon Kutner, and Tony Brown. *The Complete Book of the British Charts, Singles and Albums.* Omnibus Press, 2004.

Wayne, Artie. *I Did It for a Song.* http://artiewayne.wordpress.com, 2009.

Werner, Craig. *A Change Is Gonna Come: Music, Race and the Soul of America.* Ann Arbor, MI: University of Michigan Press, 2006.

Whitburn, Joel. *Billboard Top 1000 Singles,* 1955–1996. Milwaukee: Hal Leonard Corporation, 1997.

Whitburn, Joel. *Joel Whitburn's Rhythm & Blues, Top R&B Albums, 1965–1998.* Menomonee Falls, WI: Record Research Inc., 1999.

Whitburn, Joel. *Joel Whitburn's Top Pop Albums, 1955–2001.* Menomonee Falls, WI.: Record Research Inc., 2001.

Whitburn, Joel. *Joel Whitburn's Top Pop Singles, 1955–2006.* Menomonee Falls, WI: Record Research, Inc., 2007.

Whitburn, Joel. *Joel Whitburn's Top R&B Singles, 1942–1988.* Menomonee Falls, WI: Record Research Inc., 1985.

Whitburn, Joel. *The Billboard Book of Top 40 Hits, 1955–2009, 9th ed.* New York: Billboard Books, 2010.

Wild, David. *And the Grammy Goes to…The Official Story of Music's Most Coveted Award.* The Recording Academy, 2007.

Young, Neil. *Waging Heavy Peace: A Hippie Dream.* New York, Blue Rider Press, 2012.

Index